Contents

S0-CQR-294

Contents   **vii**

A Note to Teachers About the Course

English For Life is based on the language curriculum philosophy which I have discussed with teachers over many years.

That philosophy originates from the three areas of living in which we all have language needs: the vocational, the social and civic, the personal and cultural. These prescribe the teacher's task to be the development of the powers of enquiry, of judgement and reasoning, and of feeling and experiencing. The day-to-day guidance we give to help students to speak and write the language reveals itself as training them to:

- get information where and when needed;
- give information clearly and completely;
- scrutinize opinions expressed by others;
- express thought-out opinions with sound reasoning;
- derive satisfactions from language used as literature;
- give pleasure and satisfaction to others by using language as literature.

The basic principle of the methodology is the obvious one that the students will not learn what they do not get the chance to practise sufficiently. It is expected, then, that the teacher agrees, for instance, that the only way to teach correctness of grammar in speech and writing is to use ways to help the learners to acquire the required habits through plentiful repetition; that comprehension is developed through discussions, not tests, in which the teacher constantly asks questions like *'What makes you say that? How do you know? What is the evidence for drawing that conclusion? Can you tell where that is said?'*; that the students must get all the support and assistance to read as many novels and other books as possible, and not merely the age-old exhortation to 'love reading'; that only through abundant practice will the students be able to improve their skills in writing letters, stories, arguments, plays, etc.

This last condition requires the teacher to recognize that he or she would not be able to mark or correct everything a student writes since such a policy would deny the students the great amount of practice they need. The students must be set to write a letter, a story, or something else at least once a week and the teacher has to find other ways of 'correcting'. The students have to be guided in judging and correcting their own work, and when the teacher does mark a composition it must not be over-corrected and over-amended and left as a disrespected page of red (or green) scars.

It is with such expectations that English For Life is offered. Each book is targeted to suit the anticipated previous attainments of the students and graded from unit to unit to carry them from one level to the one above. Enough material and exercises are included in each unit to allow the teacher to choose what can be done in class in the given time each week, as well as to allow students to have things to do on their own.

The education of the students is, of course, the purpose of the books, but, without diluting that purpose in any way, the CXC examination has been kept firmly in sight from the very beginning, and students who are taken through the book in the way they should be ought to have no difficulty in passing that examination.

In this new edition of English For Life the opportunity has been taken to improve the overall grading, to put more emphasis on vocabulary building, to broaden the coverage of the CXC syllabus, to give more detailed and specific directions about writing letters, stories, etc., and to increase attention to such literary matters as are well within the perception of the students.

C. G.

1 An Apple For Christmas

Everyday Life

Wisdom in proverbs

When you have a spare moment or two outside of class give some thought to what each of these proverbs or sayings means, and imagine a time when it might be helpful to remember.

Manners maketh man.
Waste not, want not.
As the twig is bent, so is the tree inclined.
A fool and his money are soon parted.

Reading to Enjoy a Story

Getting Ready

When you were quite small did you ever want something so much that you were ready to disobey the rules to get it? Or do you remember getting something that you wanted for yourself alone but decided to share it with others because you loved them?

One Christmas Eve when the six of us girls were ready to go along to Aunt Bless with the basket of cake and ginger beer which Mama made for her every Christmas, Septimus, who must have been six or so at the time, did not want to go. He was in a bad mood.

Mama had not long before come back from town with her bag full of sweets and presents she had bought for us. There were packages of peppermints wrapped in shiny red paper, oranges, a tiny motor-car for Septimus, hair ribbons for us girls in pink
10 and yellow and blue, a big picture book for all of us, and three apples, red and rosy on the top of the bag.

Immediately he saw the apples, Septimus grabbed one of them and ran off. We all ran behind him and caught him under the breadfruit tree at the back of the house before he had time to
15 do more than fondle the rich redness of the apple.

We dragged him back to the house howling and kicking. Mama gave him a lecture: 'No, Septimus,' she scolded, 'there are only three apples, and we must share them among all nine of us.'

We all knew that our father would give Septimus his share, but the principle had to be established that what we had – which was not much – had none the less to be shared among all nine of us.

'I want a whole apple,' Septimus shouted in protest, too young to understand.

'You can't have a whole one,' Mama said, 'and that's that.' When Mama spoke, she spoke.

'And now,' she said, drying his tears with her handkerchief, 'you must stop crying and go with the girls up to Aunt Bless to take her her Christmas.'

Aunt Bless greeted us and hugged all seven of us, one after the other, overpowering us with the scent of Khuskhus root with which she perfumed her clothes, and murmuring 'Bless you, child', with each embrace. She took the basket from Maria, the eldest (very ladylike on these occasions – 'playing Mama') who had a protective arm around Septimus who was still snivelling.

'What's wrong?' Aunt Bless asked, concerned that her darling boy was not happy. 'What's wrong, Septimus? Tomorrow is Christmas!'

Septimus did not answer. He just stood there, fighting back the tears and looking foolish. But his feelings were too much for him and he blurted out between his sobs: 'I want a whole apple and Mama says No!'

Aunt Bless grasped the situation right away. She gathered Septimus to her, her own eyes now swimming with love and feeling, and she hugged him and kissed him and told him not to mind: that Aunt Bless would see that he got a whole apple, because he was her own little Septimus.

At last Septimus stopped crying, and Aunt Bless took him into her bedroom where it seemed to us children that not even the sun went, and then we heard sounds of rummaging and scuffling as if Aunt Bless were turning out all the treasures of her hope chest. And then Septimus' laughter pealed out as clear and silver as a bell.

Septimus came out of the darkness of Aunt Bless's room with his eyes shining bright and as big as saucers and clutching in his hand the biggest and rosiest apple I have ever seen.

All the way home Septimus held his apple to his bosom. He said not a word to any of us. I think we were a little ashamed of him and the scene he made, and we knew that Mama would be angry with us for letting him accept the apple.

When we got home, Septimus ran to the kitchen and we hurried to tell Mama what had happened. All of us tried to talk at the same time, and it was not easy for Mama to get the story. But she did at last, and she was so angry that she did not speak.

She rushed out to the kitchen with all of us trooping behind her. But she was too slow, for Septimus met her at the kitchen-door with a saucer in his hand.

'Bless you, children,' he said, 'Bless you, children.' And he handed Mama the saucer with nine slices of apple on it.

From the story 'Septimus' in *Casuarina Row* By John Wickham,
BARBADOS

Discussion for developing comprehension skills

A Understanding explicit statements:
1 Why did the children go to Aunt Bless?
2 Where did Septimus grab an apple from?
3 What did Mama say about the three apples?
4 Where did the strong scent of Khuskhus root come from?
5 How did Aunt Bless know something was wrong?
6 Who played Mama at times, like the time at Aunt Bless's?

7 What do you understand by '*grasped the situation*' (l. 43)?

8 '*Aunt Bless took him into her bedroom*' (ll. 48–49). What happened then?

9 '*We hurried to tell Mama what had happened*' (ll. 61–62). What did they tell her?

B Using context clues:

1 Suppose you did not know what '*pealed out*' (l. 52) means. What is there in the same sentence to help you to guess what it means?

2 Discuss these in the same way:

'*principle*' (l. 20) '*snivelling*' (l. 35) '*blurted out*' (l. 41) '*grasped*' (l. 43) '*rummaging and scuffling*' (ll. 50–51)

C Seeing implied connections:

1 How are you told what Septimus did with the apple he brought home from Aunt Bless?

2 What was Mama rushing to the kitchen to do?

3 Who made up all '*nine of us*' (ll. 21–22)?

4 What did the storyteller in the story, the narrator, think that Septimus was '*too young to understand*' (ll. 23–24)?

5 Two people clearly treated Septimus in a special way. Why do you think they did?

6 '*I think we were a little ashamed of him*' (ll. 58–59). Why?

7 Why do you suppose Septimus said '*Bless you, children; Bless you, children*' (l. 69)?

8 In everyday life words are often used metaphorically, that is, not with their real meanings but to make a comparison. For instance, Septimus' laughter could not really have '*pealed*' (l. 52). It was not a bell. But the sound of his laughter is compared to the peal of a bell.

How are these words used figuratively in the excerpt?

'*grasped*' (l. 43) '*swimming*' (l. 44) '*silver*' (l. 53)

To Enrich Your Word Bank

Using words you read

In column **A** there are some words from the story about Septimus. In column **B** there are some other words and phrases.

Form teams of six or eight and see if you can fit each word from column **A** with a word or phrase from column **B**.

	A		B
i	immediately	a	safeguarding
ii	fondle	b	pulling and struggling
iii	protest	c	instantly
iv	embrace	d	holding tightly
v	protective	e	hug
vi	snivelling	f	sobbing
vii	blurted	g	touch with love
viii	rummaging	h	searching
ix	scuffling	i	complaint
x	clutching	j	said suddenly and quickly

Opposites

Put your heads together and find a word to fit into each space.

1 *quietly* is to *noisily* as _____ is to *rapidly*
2 *height* is to _____ as *poverty* is to *wealth*
3 *dawn* is to _____ as *depart* is to *arrive*
4 *bold* is to _____ as *guard* is to *expose*
5 *die* is to *live* as *reveal* is to _____
6 _____ is to *lazily* as *recklessly* is to *safely*
7 *joined* is to *divided* as _____ is to *ceased*
8 _____ is to *pursue* as *praise* is to *condemn*
9 *freedom* is to *captivity* as *defeat* is to _____
10 *metaphorically* is to *literally* as _____ is to *entirely*

Grammatical Sentence Patterns

Verb forms and subject words

Words like *gives, knows, knew, went, made, have, writes* and *sang* are called 'doing words' or 'verbs'. They are used to tell something about somebody or something.

What is the verb in this sentence?

A double line of children from the schools passes along the pavement every day.

It is the word *passes* that is the verb that tells something about somebody or something. But what exactly is it telling about in that sentence? Schools? Children? Line? Well, if you ask the question *Who or what passes?* the answer is a *line*. So the word *line* is the exact Subject Word of the verb *passes*. *A line passes*. If the Subject Word had been *schools* or *children* the verb form would have had to be *pass*. Why? Well, study the verb forms in these sentences and see how each is related to its Subject Word.

1 *One* of the children *does* the washing up. (One does)
2 Several other *children* in the place *do* the drying and stacking. (children do)
3 A large *basket* of fruits and vegetables *arrives* every Wednesday. (basket arrives)
4 The heavy *engines* in the factory *make* a great noise. (engines make)

When you have understood why in those sentences *arrives* is used instead of *arrive*, and why *make* is used instead of *makes*, discuss which of the two forms in the bracket after each sentence below must be used in the blank space in the sentence.

1 The calf belonging to the children _____ about in the school. (*runs/run*)
2 The posters carried by the children _____ for a boycott. (*calls/call*)
3 A band of demonstrators _____ often disorderly. (*is/are*)
4 The actions of the teacher _____ an important principle. (*demonstrates/demonstrate*)
5 Behind the demonstrators _____ other children. (*comes/come*)
6 Projects in school _____ to make lessons interesting. (*helps/help*)
7 Parents of schoolchildren _____ not like unruly conduct. (*does/do*)
8 The constable patrolling the areas around the hotels _____ everything carefully. (*observes/observe*)

9   The shouts of the man who _____ the shop were loud and angry. (*owns/own*)

10   The group of interested spectators _____ larger and larger. (*grows/grow*)

Some Idioms We Use

Capture and escape

In English, as in other languages, there are certain phrases that cannot be put into another language. Understanding them is an essential part of learning English.

Put your ideas together and see if you can put each English idiom (a – b) with its meaning (i – vi).

a   to go on the offensive
b   to catch someone red-handed
c   to come at a person
d   to be on guard
e   to show a clean pair of heels
f   to let loose

i   to be ready to defend oneself
ii   to run away
iii to approach someone as if to cause harm
iv   to come upon someone doing something wrong
v   to send out numerous dangerous or harmful things
vi   to begin to attack someone

Writing What You Imagine

Making up a story

Making up stories can be fun if you are not afraid to imagine things happening.

In the story about Septimus what happened had to do with an apple. You yourself could use any object and make up some things that could happen because of it.

Right now, for fun, take an object that someone has in the classroom, anything at all, and pretend it is important to someone or some persons that neither you nor anyone in the class knows.

Place the object where you can all see it while you sit silently for three or four minutes and think of something that could have happened. Ask yourself questions like *To whom did it belong? How did he or she get it? Why was it important? Did anything ever happen to it? How? Why?* and so on.

Then get into small groups of four or five and spend about fifteen minutes asking questions and making up answers. Before going back to your seats try to recall the answers and repeat them.

Then sit in your place and begin to write sentences to tell a story that you think could be told about people and the object.

Stories to Read

A list to get you going

Do you know what is the most important thing you have to do? It is to read books in your spare time. Nothing else is more important.

A short list of novels is given below. They are only suggested ones. You might be able to find others that are just as enjoyable, or more enjoyable. In any case, you must always be reading a book in your spare time. Make it a habit. You will find that you will soon be able to enjoy more than one book a week.

From time to time you might be able to tell your friends in your class about books you read. And sometimes your teacher might ask you to write what you want to say about one of them.

But perhaps your greatest problem is getting books to read. Perhaps it is not known how necessary it is for you to have a good library to get books from. In that case you will have to help yourselves to get books. Here are some ideas to put into practice.

1   Write letters to business firms and persons, asking for help to buy books to make a class library.

2   Make up plays and put them on, charging a very small entrance fee.

3   Make up a class anthology of your own compositions and sell copies for a very low price (your teacher will get your anthology typed and get copies made).

4   Form a book club in your class, asking each person to contribute an amount that will purchase one book with a paperback cover (the amount can be contributed little by little over a whole term). Your teacher will advise you about enjoyable books for people of your age that can be bought in paperback from the bookshops. Once you have got the books, keep them in a safe place for members of your class to borrow one each week.

Now here is a short list for you to begin with. See which ones you are able to borrow, and aim to read at least one every week. (Those written by West Indians and about West Indians have the country that the writer belongs to at the end.)

- *Baba and Mr Big*   C. Everard Palmer,   JAMAICA
- *A Drink of Water*   Samuel Selvon, TRINIDAD
- *Days Gone By*   Harricharan Narine, TRINIDAD
- *Spratt Morrison*   Jean D'Costa, JAMAICA
- *A Cow Called Boy*   C. Everard Palmer,   JAMAICA
- *Humphrey's Ride*   Robert Abrahams, NEVIS
- *The Shark Hunters*   Andrew Salkey, JAMAICA

- *The Bonus of Redonda* Robert Abrahams,   NEVIS
- *Peter of Mount Ephraim*   Vic Reid, JAMAICA
- *Shane*   Jack Schaefer
- *Morassa and Midnight*   Moira Stuart
- *The Family from One End Street* Eve Garnett
- *The Boy Who Was Afraid* Armstrong Perry
- *Emil and the Detectives* Erich Kastner
- *Jim Starling*   E. W. Hildrick
- *Latchkey Children*   Eric Allen

2 Fourth Standard

Everyday Life

Speech sounds to make

In moments of spare time give your attention to this.

When you wish to speak English in a way that most people in the world would accept, i.e. not a dialect of English, you would say *living*, not *livin'*, or *sharing*, not *sharin'*. You would sound the ending, ING, as you would in *ring* and *bring*. Do you? Listen to yourself and see.

If you do not, here are some sentences to say to give yourself some of that practice.

1　They were havING a party because Winston was leavING.

2　When Saphira was lookING at the tear she saw others comING.
3　ReaDING the notice about the meetING was takING him a long time.
4　They were cookING curried goat and makING merry that evenING.

Here are some other words to practise pronouncing correctly in your spare moments, if you now mispronounce any of them:

character　put the stress on the first syllable
definite　say the last syllable like *it*
film　say *fil* and then *m*

Reading to Enjoy a Story

Getting ready

All of us tend to remember certain classes we were in at school and some of our classmates. Don't you?

Think of a class you remember in the primary school you went to and spend three or four minutes sharing your memories with one another. Then read how the narrator of the excerpt below

tells about one of her classes. As you read compare her class with one you remember.

parlour (l. 17) = front room where things like cakes, drinks, buns, etc., were sold
duncey-head (l. 25) = a dunce or very slow learner
ruction (l. 72) = disturbance, quarrelling

> Fourth Standard was a very ordinary class. They came to school for nine o'clock like any other class – or most of them came to school for nine o'clock – for when the bell rang Clem and Harry were usually just pelting across the Savannah.
> 5　Clem had to tie out his grandmother's goat before he came to school and Harry had to deliver bottles of milk. They were

neighbours, and nearly every morning they dashed into the
school-yard together and managed to slide in at the back of the
line just as Mr Greenidge was closing the gate. Anybody who
10   arrived after the gate was shut had to stand outside and wait
until Mr Greenidge was ready to let them in and lead them to
the Headmaster's office.

Fourth Standard was very ordinary. They had as many fights
as anybody else. They fought over the duster because
15   everybody wanted to clean the blackboard; they fought over
who was to be at the head of the line in mornings; they fought
in Miss Aggie's parlour at recess time and at lunch time, fought
and pushed like anybody else to get their dinner-mints or
sweet-biscuits or tamarind-balls. And they didn't fight when it
20   was their turn to clean the latrines; then they just ran and hid
all over the place.

There were twenty-two girls and eighteen boys, so the girls
always won when the class played cricket or tug-o'-war, girls
against boys.

25   Fourth Standard had its Duncey-head and its Bright-spark like
any other class. Joel Price couldn't read further than Page
Nine. He was stuck at Page Nine for so long that he could say

it by heart with his eyes closed, but when Miss turned the page
and he saw Page Ten he would hang his head and his eyes
30 filled up with water. And Emily Joseph was so bright that
everybody said that her mother gave her bulb porridge in the
morning and bulb soup in the night.

Miss was nice sometimes. She didn't beat as much as Mr
Gomes or Miss Davies, and she didn't beat for silly little things
35 like forgetting your pen at home or getting all your sums
wrong.

But she got very angry if somebody talked while she was
talking. Sandra and Shira were always getting into trouble
because they chatted and chatted like a pair of parrots all day
40 long. Miss promised them that when we went on the Zoo outing
she was going to put them in the big cage with the parrots and
leave them there. Miss said the parrots at the Zoo had a nice
big roomy cage big enough for two talkative young ladies to
take up residence, and the parrots would be glad of their
45 company.

Other things she would beat for were not doing your homework, and stealing. When something was stolen, nobody knew how she found out who the thief was, but Miss was always right. As soon as she learned that there had been a
50 theft, she tapped the ruler on the table to call the class to attention. Then she stood and stared at us; she looked at our faces one by one, very slowly, and when she had looked at everybody in turn she started again from the front row, while everybody sat and held their breath; and then her eyes stopped
55 at one face and everybody breathed again and all turned to see who the culprit was. In Fourth Standard you couldn't get away with stealing.

Miss was nice because she took her class outside more often than anybody else. The other children all envied Fourth
60 Standard because whenever the afternoon got really hot we would be seen filing out towards the Savannah. Anybody who talked or made any noise on the way out would be sent back to sit with his book in the empty classroom, but of course nobody was willing to run this risk, so we filed out silently and in the
65 most orderly manner.

Miss said that Fourth Standard was the worst class in the school, but we knew that she'd said the same thing to every Fourth Standard class she'd had, so we didn't believe her. For, all things considered, Fourth Standard was no better or no
70 worse than any other class; they were a very ordinary class.

And then Millicent came. Millicent came and brought pure ruction.

From the short story *Millicent* By Merle Hodge, TRINIDAD and
TOBAGO

Discussion for developing comprehension skills

A Understanding explicit statements:

1 Where were Clem and Harry usually when the morning bell rang? Why?
2 What did Mr Greenidge do on mornings?
3 Why did the pupils fight over the duster?
4 Who was Miss?
5 'She didn't beat for silly little things' (l. 34). What does that mean?
6 Why did Sandra and Shira always get into trouble?

7 What joke did Miss make about Sandra and Shira?
8 What did Miss tap the ruler on the table for?
9 Why did the narrator think that Miss was 'nice'?
10 Who wrote 'Millicent'?

B Using context clues:

1 Find the clue that tells someone the meaning of 'to take up residence' (ll. 43–44).

2 What makes the meaning of 'culprit' (l. 56) clear in the excerpt?

3 Tell what is said in the story that could help someone to guess the meaning of 'envied' (l. 59).

C Seeing implied connections:

1 How many children were in the class?
2 Why did the girls win the tug-o'-war?
3 Why didn't they fight over the cleaning of the latrines?
4 Why did Joel Price's eyes fill with water?
5 Why did they say Emily Joseph was given bulb soup and bulb porridge?
6 Do you think Miss knew who had stolen something by staring at the faces, or what?
7 '... all things considered' (l. 69). Can you put that in other words?
8 Why was nobody 'willing to run this risk' (l. 64)?
9 What impression do you get of Miss?

To Enrich Your Word Bank

Using words you read

Use your knowledge of the words in the excerpt to put each of these into one of the sentences below.

usually deliver arrived managed residence company theft culprit envied risk

1 The rock star was greeted with cheers when he _____ .
2 Being accused of _____ made the girl cry.
3 His family moved to a _____ in a new neighbourhood.
4 Those two girls are in each other's _____ wherever they go.
5 The postman comes every day to _____ letters.

6 The police found the _____ who broke into the office.
7 _____ Clem arrives late but today he was early.
8 Don't take the _____ of crossing until the traffic stops.
9 The losers all _____ the winner of the beauty contest.
10 A little boy _____ to squeeze through the small space.

Words related in meaning

Discuss which word, related in form and meaning to the one in brackets after the sentence, best fits into the blank space in the sentence.

1 A rumour was _____ that the school was to be closed. (*circle*)
2 Our _____ was about the story we read. (*discuss*)
3 A few more lights will _____ the hall. (*bright*)
4 We waited for the _____ bell at the end of the day. (*dismiss*)
5 The saleswoman came to _____ the machine. (*demonstration*)
6 Many sales clerks have a very _____ manner. (*sulk*)
7 We needed a _____ to show the movie. (*project*)
8 You learn to use grammatical phrases by much _____ of them. (*repeat*)
9 The shopkeeper was in a _____ when he saw what was happening. (*furious*)
10 The group of demonstrators was an _____ for a small crowd. (*attract*)

Words of similar meaning

Discuss which one of the four words given with each sentence can best be used to replace the one underlined in the sentence.

1 Josh and his friends <u>tried</u> to get customers to boycott Mr Watson's shop.
planned persuaded attempted jostled

2   The students put a total <u>boycott</u> on the cafeteria.
    ban   poster   strike   picket

3   The demonstration <u>attracted</u> some adults.
    called   drew   delighted   repulsed

4   They thought talking about it would add to the <u>gloom</u>.
    darkness   noise   confusion despondency

5   Mr Watson and Ridley seemed to have <u>similar</u> opinions.
    synonymous   angry   outspoken like

6   The spectators changed their <u>manner</u> when they understood what was happening.
    behaviour   politeness   method techniques

7   Mr Watson made a <u>gesture</u> of washing his hands.
    dance   sign   gesticulation movement

8   The question was whether adults could not <u>discipline</u> children.
    punish   coax   control   deploy

Grammatical Sentence Patterns

Sentences with plural subject words
Compare these sentences:

An honest friend is better than a flattering one because he gives helpful advice.

Honest friends are better than flattering ones because they give helpful advice.

Notice that the second sentence is the plural form of the first sentence.

Change these sentences orally in a similar way.

Take turns around the class for about 30 minutes, starting again with sentence 1 whenever you get to the end of sentence 12.

1   Our teacher does not take her class outside.
2   He pelts across to school when the bell rings.
3   She is a strict teacher who does not like talking in class.
4   That girl talks like a parrot and annoys me.
5   She kneels on the rock and leans over the river.
6   There is a burst of laughter when he shows her his torn trousers.
7   The girl comes forward with some rum she has taken from the men and pours it into a mug.
8   Miss Fan gazes at him with bitter anger and disappointment.
9   Each girl is expected to bring her book to school.
10 He at once busied himself arranging the furniture.
11 There is a good reason why he needs to learn more English.
12 An eagle is a good parent: it takes care of its young.

Spelling

How to learn to spell
Spelling a word correctly depends largely on having a 'picture' of it in your mind. Just as you can close your eyes and remember or try to remember someone's face, so too in learning to spell a word you must try to 'see' the word clearly in your mind, with all the letters in the right places.

Do that now with any words in this list that you cannot spell readily and easily.

recess	empty	tapped	really
bottles	trouble	theft	manner
parrot	porridge	forgetting	neighbours
ordinary	attention	residence	savannah

Now see if you can 'see' the missing letter in each of these words:

drag_ed	lectur_	s_olded	am_ng
hug_ed	cloth_s	gras_ed	so_nds
s_ene	hurri_d	tog_ther	l_ad
becaus_	eno_gh	breath_	beli_ve

Writing Sentences of a Story

The order of telling

When you are telling a story you must narrate the things that happened one after the other in their proper order.

Read the sentences opposite and find which one ought to be first, which second, and so on.

Then write them in their proper order as a paragraph.

a   Then an idea came into his head.
b   He decided to wait for the rain to cease.
c   He wondered if he should take the risk to go out.
d   His mother called out to him, 'Where yuh think yuh goin, young man?'
e   It sounded like the roars of lions.
f   Daniel mumbled, 'Nowhere, Mum.'
g   The drains were overflowing as water rushed into them.
h   He did not even have an umbrella.
i   Daniel looked for a long time at the flooded road.
j   It was a day of heavy rain in July.

When you have some more time, or at home, compose a paragraph of about 10 sentences to begin to tell a story, using this sentence as the first one in the paragraph:

Nattie brought trouble with her when she arrived that morning.

Remember what you learned in Book 1 of *English For Life* and put in full stops, capital letters, commas and quotation marks in all the right places.

Words to Watch

Lead and led

Study the word underlined in each sentence.

Mr Greenidge was ready to <u>lead</u> them in.
He <u>led</u> them to the office.
The bag Harry carried was as heavy as <u>lead</u>.

In the first sentence we pronounce *lead* as 'leed'; in the second we pronounce *led* as led; while in the third sentence we pronounce *lead* as led.

Notice *led*, the past tense of *lead* ('leed') has no *a* in it. Then notice that while *lead* meaning to go first is pronounced 'leed', *lead* meaning a metal is pronounced 'led'.

Now, if you need to, read the sentences aloud a few times.

Worse and worst

Look carefully at the words underlined in this sentence:

Yesterday was <u>worse</u> than the day before, but today is <u>worst</u> of all.

Why are *worse* and *worst* spelt and pronounced differently?

The word *worse* (ending with an *e*) is used if two things are compared but the word *worst* (ending with a *t*) is used when more than two things are compared.

Which one goes into each of these sentences?

a   Maxie behaves _____ than Sheila.
b   In that class the _____ reader was Joel Price.
c   That was the _____ film I ever saw.
d   Your cough is _____ than mine.
e   The boys sing _____ than the girls.
f   I think we got the _____ seats in the stadium.
g   The medicine will keep her from getting _____ .
h   The _____ weather of the year is now on us.

3 This Day And Age

Everyday Life

The world you live in

Here are some matters for you to discuss outside the classroom, or in class if you have the time.

Is it better to live in a big city or in a country village? Why do you think so?

When people speak of 'enjoying nature' in the country, what do they mean?

Cities have many people living in them. What do the people in a city need every day? How do they get what they need?

Factories and vehicles like cars give off poisonous fumes and pollute the air we have to breathe. What do you imagine can be done to lessen pollution of the air?

What problems do people living in the country have?

What problems do people living in a city have?

Reading to Learn Things

Getting ready

What do you know about what goes on in modern cities? Spend a minute or two telling what you know.

Then read the article below and see whether it gives you new information about modern cities, although the numbers in it may be out of date by the time you read it.

liner (l. 9) = a large passenger ship
provincial (l. 11) = belonging to a small area
amenity (l. 11) = anything that makes life pleasant
plants (l. 37) = places with machinery, like factories
voltage (l. 38) = the power or strength of electricity

There are 49 cities in the world with a population of over one million: 49 really big cities. They are scattered throughout the several continents; some stand on the shores of the sea and some rise on the plains. Chicago follows the shores of a lake for
5   34 miles; London has a width of 16 miles, Paris of 12 miles, Rome of about 6 miles. Each of these great cities is a little world in itself.

Skyscrapers – very tall buildings, over 300 feet high, with 30, 40 or more storeys. These buildings are as heavy as a liner and can house over 10,000 people; they have the population of a small provincial town and provide every kind of amenity.

Markets – hundreds of railway trucks and vans come to the wholesale markets of a great city where they unload tons of vegetables, fruit, meat, fish, and poultry. This is where the retail traders come to buy the goods which they sell in their shops.

Department stores – here you can buy anything, from a needle to a motor car. They are very large and sometimes occupy a whole building. They have a very great number of counters for selling goods, and employ hundreds of salesmen and saleswomen. They are always crowded.

The city under ground

Below the streets there is a vast underground city. Many of the comforts we enjoy and the reliability of the city's public services above ground, depend on the smooth running of this subterranean world.

The city under ground

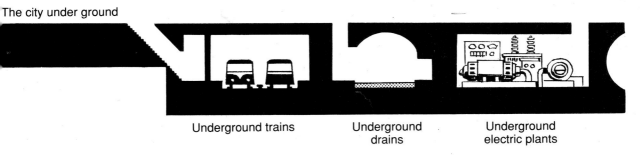

Underground trains   Underground drains   Underground electric plants

Underground trains – trains run through huge tunnels of concrete and iron connecting the various districts of the city. They travel at an average speed far greater than that of traffic above ground.

Drains – in a great city there are thousands of tons of refuse to be disposed of daily. Some is collected by the dustmen; the rest goes into the drains and sewers which form a network several hundred miles long.

Underground electric plants – a large city uses a very great amount of electricity, which may have to be brought from distant power stations. Underground plants regulate the voltage and distribute the current.

Mirror of a metropolis

40 A city with a million inhabitants has about:

1,500 trams, buses and trolleybuses on the roads.

600 miles of road

60,000 motor vehicles

500 miles of drains and sewers

250,000 houses

200,000 telephones

Consumes in one day:

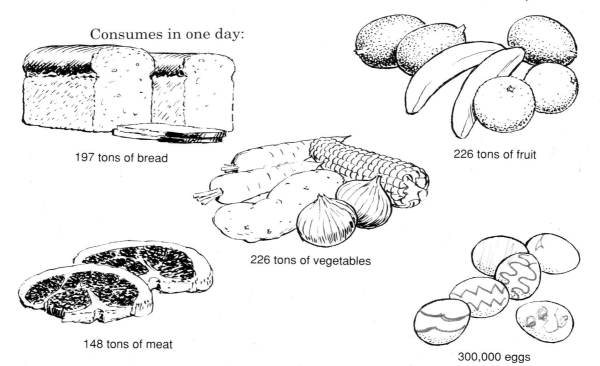

197 tons of bread

226 tons of fruit

226 tons of vegetables

148 tons of meat

300,000 eggs

From *Knowledge, Vol. 1, No. 8*

Discussion for developing comprehension skills

A Understanding explicit statements:

1 What is meant by a '*really big city*'?
2 What is a '*skyscraper*' (l. 8)?
3 What is a '*wholesale market*' (l. 13) for?
4 Who are '*retail traders*' (l. 15)?
5 What are '*large industrial plants*'?
6 In a big city, what means are there for people and goods to move about and for messages and information to travel about?
7 What is a '*terminus*'?
8 How does an underground train get from one place to another?
9 What do you understand by '*refuse*' (l. 31)?
10 How is the refuse of a big city got rid of?
11 Where does the electrical power come from?
12 What are the underground electricity plants for?
13 How do big cities solve the problem of parking cars?
14 What do post offices do to ensure that people can communicate with one another very quickly?
15 Where does the water for a big city come from?
16 What amenities are often placed underground in a big city?

B Using context clues:

1 What word in line 23 is the clue giving the meaning of '*subterranean*' (l. 26)?
2 What is the connection between '*very tall*' (l. 8) and '*storeys*' (l. 9)?
3 If someone did not know what '*disposed of*' (l. 32) means, how does the word '*refuse*' (l. 31) help?

C Seeing implied connections:

1 What does the word *net* have to do with '*network*' (l. 33)?

2 The word *service* is related to the word *serve*. What would you think '*public services*' (l. 24) are?
3 What other name is given in the article for a big modern city?
4 Tell what you think is the reason why so many things are placed underground in big cities.
5 Why do you suppose the writer said a big city is '*a little world in itself* (ll. 6–7)?
6 What skills and knowledge do people need in order to manage a big city?
7 Which amenities mentioned in the article does your country have?

To Enrich Your Word Bank

Using words you read
Discuss together which one of these words fits into each sentence below:

provincial   voltage   various   occupy
provide   amenity   average   distribute

a People work hard to _____ the services in a modern city.
b The Red Cross went to _____ food to the survivors of the disaster.
c There are _____ ways of travelling in a modern city.
d Transformers regulate the _____ of the electricity coming into our homes.
e Parks are an important _____ in cities to provide people with places for relaxation and recreation.
f People who belong to small places are usually quite _____ and narrow in their ideas.
g The _____ speed of the plane in flight is 700 kph.
h There are many families waiting to _____ the unfinished houses.

Words related in meaning

Two different words, related in form and meaning to the one in italics, must be used in the blank spaces in the sentences. Discuss what the two different words are, referring to the article you read if necessary.

1 *occupy*
   a What _____ are you engaged in now?
   b Who is the _____ of that apartment?

2 *terminus*
   a The employers wish to _____ the employment of workers who joined the union.
   b What you do now will _____ what you can do in the future.

3 *press*
   a Put more _____ on the lid to close the can tightly.
   b _____ this lever to open the door.

4 *industry*
   a There are some _____ areas with a few factories on the outskirts of the town.
   b People who are _____ usually reap greater rewards in life.

5 *dispose*
   a What a pleasant _____ your sister has!
   b The workmen must take care of the _____ of the rubble.

6 *transform*
   a A great _____ took place in his character.
   b The _____ giving the house electricity was damaged by lightning.

7 *regulate*
   a There is a _____ in the television set controlling the voltage of the electricity.

   b If you disobey the _____ you will find yourself in trouble.

8 *reserve*
   a All the water was collected in a _____.
   b The refugees were put to live in a special _____ until they could go to other places.

The prefix sub-

Several words begin with the prefix, or first syllable, *sub* which means under or below.

Divide into teams of five or six and see how quickly you can supply the meanings of these words:

subterranean submarine submerge subway subdue subdivide subject subjugate submit subordinate subscribe subsequent

Grammatical Sentence Patterns

Was and were

Why did the writer use *was* and not *were* in this sentence?

a The enslavement of conquered people and prisoners was a common practice.

Well, as you probably know, for the same reason that *was* is used in these sentences:

b The boy *was* a happy boy.
c A large group of pupils *was* on the bus.
d Enslavement *was* a common practice.

In b it is the *boy* that something is said about, and the word *boy* is singular because it means one boy, so *was* has to be used, not *were*. In a and d it is *enslavement* that something is said about, and *enslavement* is a singular word, so it takes *was*, not *were*.

The same is true of *group* in c.

But to help yourself to avoid mistakes in saying sentences like a and c, say these sentences aloud, putting in *was* or *were* in the blank spaces. Whenever you make a mistake say the correct sentence at least three times.

1 A volcanic eruption of gases, mud, and rocks _____ expected any day.
2 That meal of peas and carrots _____ most welcome.
3 Different kinds of food _____ eaten by different tribes.
4 His packet of cigarettes _____ thrown away.
5 A parcel of clothes, toys and decorations _____ posted to you.
6 The clubs in the competition _____ all trying to win.
7 A long line of cars, buses and trucks _____ crawling along the highway.
8 The team of experts _____ staying at this hotel.
9 That heavy load of sand, gravel and stones _____ too much for the truck.
10 The results of the matches played on Saturday _____ very surprising.

Punctuation Signals

Full stops and capital letters
In giving information, you have to be perfectly clear in what you say or write. Putting full stops in the right places is necessary for clear writing, and using your voice to show where a full stop comes is necessary in oral reading.

For practice, read this passage aloud to show where full stops should have been put in. Then write the passage, putting in the full stops and capital letters.

our blood has salt in it when we sweat some of the salt forms on the surface of our skin then we must put back into the blood the salt we have taken from it the more we sweat the more salt we need at the end of a hard race an exhausted runner sometimes needs an injection of salt

Writing to Give Information

The right thing in the right place
Although in everyday life people express opinions and communicate experience most of the time, they often have to give factual information too, without mixing up opinions with it. And they have to do that in such a way that the other person or persons understand clearly.

So, when you are trying to give factual information, you must follow at least three rules:

1 Do not use words or phrases that give opinion. They often cause misunderstandings.
2 Make sure each sentence is in the right place – not too late and not too soon.
3 Make sure each sentence is perfectly clear to someone else, not only to you.

Now read this explanation of a little experiment and point out where those 'rules' are broken:

The God-given water flowing out of the tap will bend towards the cherished comb. It is attracted by the electricity made in the comb and pulls towards it. Turn on the good, old kitchen tap so you get a thin stream of water. Rub your beloved comb so that it gets electricity.

Then hold it near. Take your comb and hold it with one hand.

What sentence should have been put first? Which second? Third? etc. What should be done with the words *God-given, cherished, good, old* and *beloved*? Which word should be replaced by the phrase *is pulled*, to make the meaning clear? At the end of which sentence should the phrase *the jet of water* be put in, to make the meaning of the sentence clear?

If you have seen the faults in the explanation above you can now try to give explanations, directions, instructions and so on of your own.

For practice do one or more of these:

a   Write a list of instructions you would give to a younger person about cleaning a pair of shoes, or cleaning and tidying a room, or making a kite, or using a washing machine, or putting up a tent, or milking a cow, or anything like that.

b   Write the directions you would give to a person to get from your school to a cinema, or from any one place to another.

c   Write the directions for someone to do a little experiment to prove something like how sound travels along a length of cord, or anything like that that you know about.

Words in Literature

Rhyme

What is noticeable about the words at the ends of these six lines taken from a poem?

> The sun's new runway takes a southern track
> to latitudes I hear calling me back
> to heal the sting of winter's sharp attack.
>
> Down a straight line of longitude I trace
> pitch lakes of laughter in each passing face
> and shed my freight to suit the casual pace.

From the poem *Bearings*, Cecil Gray, TRINIDAD

The writer of these lines has used rhyming words to end them. But poets do not always use rhyme. They use it when they wish the repetition of a sound to make a pattern that shapes and holds the poem together in some way.

The pattern of the six lines is aaa bbb, as you learned in Book 1 of *English For Life*.

What is the pattern (or rhyme scheme) of these stanzas taken from another poem?

> You gave a cry that morning you were born
> and then when something nasty caused you pain,
> but later came to learn that most men scorn
> to let such sobs be ever heard again.
>
> You mastered how to hold those feelings in,
> assuming an indifferent, callous stance;
> strut with a careless swagger and a grin
> as if life's damage was not worth a glance.

From the poem *Learning*, Cecil Gray, TRINIDAD

4 Caught Red-Handed

Everyday Life

Private reading
When you have some spare time consider
what this poem is saying and how it is
saying it.

A Sad Song about Greenwich Village

She lives in a garret
Up a haunted stair,
And even when she's frightened
There's nobody to care.

She cooks so small a dinner
She dines on the smell,
And even if she's hungry
There's nobody to tell.

She sweeps her musty lodging
As the dawn steals near,
And even when she's crying
There's nobody to hear.

I haven't seen my neighbor
Since a long time ago,
And even if she's dead
There's nobody to know.

Frances Park, USA

Reading to Enjoy a Story

Getting ready

To be caught red-handed is to be caught in the act of doing something forbidden. Have you ever been caught red-handed? What would you expect if you were caught red-handed stealing fruit from a tree?

Read and see what happened to Beppo under Mrs Belmont's mango tree.

investigation (l. 11) = a careful search
hog-meat string (l. 34) = a twine

Almost everyone in our village has at least one mango tree in his yard. Teppy had one, Mrs Belmont, Mrs Jenkins had two, and we also had one. But among some of the first that started to bring in ripe mangoes was Mrs Belmont's tree. They caught
5 the eyes of many a child but just about as many who saw the fruits resisted the temptation and went his way.

On going back and forth to school I have to pass by this mango tree. It was lunchtime and I was heading back. Someone from the side of the road, where there was a clump of bush, said:
10 'Beppo.' Understand, in a whisper.

My investigation led to my finding Roy squatting in the bush. He signalled and I joined him and was dead quiet about it.

I had no real heart to venture on Belmont property for I had always remembered what Teppy had told me the first morning
15 he had seen me – though he hadn't proved very reliable. Never to venture on that woman's property – for mango or for anything else, he had said. But Roy signalled me and I had joined him.

'What're you doing here?' I whispered.

20 'Bend down, old man,' he said.

I did as he had asked, my heart-beat tripling, and he confided in me that he was waiting for Daphne to head back to school and then we – the guts he had – he and I, could steal into the mango tree and take a few ripe ones.

25 'But she'll catch us, Roy.'

'She doesn't hear too good,' he said.

'Is she deaf or something?'

'I suppose so,' he said.

Just like that, and only that, he supposed so. What a boy! I
30 didn't know which was worse, he or Teppy.

We hunkered down in the bush and I could hear ever so
distinctly my heart beating pit-a-pat-pat. We didn't have to
wait long before Daphne emerged from the house, singing a
ditty and, with a hog-meat string, skipping her way gaily to
35 school. She passed very close to us but we were well hidden
and she wasn't looking for intruders.

'Now,' said Roy. 'But you wait here.'

He must have read my fear of going into the tree. I was mighty
happy to wait. I didn't want to be caught in the branches. On
40 the ground, I thought, I'd stand a chance. I didn't like this
adventure one bit because, if caught, the Old Man would be
sore as hell – Mrs Jenkins, please pardon me again. But Roy, in
his own quiet and mysterious way, had zapped his influence at
me and won.

45 In tree-climbing that boy was like a monkey. Maybe better.
Before I could have said Jack Robinson he had shinnied up
that tree and, swinging from limb to limb, began to fill his
pockets with mangoes. Plummies they were called and no
bigger than plums were they. He could ram no fewer than a
50 dozen of them in his pockets. And was he packing them in.

So absorbed was I in his cunning and agility that I never once
took my eyes off him. Imagine my surprise, then, when
someone tapped me on the shoulder, saying: 'Aha!'

You guessed correctly: Mrs Belmont. She was almost on top of
55 me and terrifyingly tall.

'Stand up!'

I stood up and I trembled.

If what they said of her was true, and if her hate of the Old
Man was genuine and extended to me, then I was going to have
60 it. To the police with me? Court? And then jail?

I wasted no time in pleading my case.

'I didn't mean to, ma'am. It's not me, ma'am. It's the boy in the
tree.'

'Heh!' very cruelly. 'You there in the tree,' she called. 'Come on
65 down here, you little monkey.'

I concluded that this woman could very well be a sadist of some
kind. She was going to do something to us, and she was going
to enjoy herself.

'You little rats,' she went on. 'You bare-faced rats.'

70 Her voice was semi-masculine, rasping a bit but rich and tuneful.

Roy began to climb down. I had never seen anyone as frightened as Roy and to think that he was the gutsy one, the brains behind it. I say he looked the more frightened because,
75 of course, I couldn't see myself to determine the extent of my fright. But he, his eyes were as bulbous as eggs and he shook like anything. He had also wet his pants. Real weak bladder he had.

'Do you know what happens to mango thieves?' Mrs Belmont
80 asked.

'Yes, ma'am,' said Roy, now down on the ground and still trembling. He sought an opportunity to bolt but our captor wasn't taking chances: she held us by our wrists. Yes, sir.

'I was only waiting for him,' I said.

85 'Oh yes? In the bush? Big joke.'
'He asked me to, ma'am. It's you, Roy,' I accused him. 'You're responsible. It was your idea.'

Mrs Belmont wasn't hardly listening. 'What's your name?' she asked.

90 'Beppo, ma'am.'

'Beppo what?'

'Beppo Tate, ma'am.'

'Hah! So you're the one!'

'The one what, ma'am?'

95 She didn't answer. She looked at Roy. 'You,' she said. 'How many years you been stealing my mangoes?'

Roy kept a buttoned mouth.

'Answer me, boy!'

'I won't do it again, ma'am.'

100 'Unload your pockets.'

He did it and with so much speed.

'Wet your pants, eh?' she observed. 'Well that's punishment enough, my man.'

'Yes, ma'am.'

105　'Run along.'

He scooted. Boy did he scoot! The path was a beaten one and his bare feet flagged it with a sound akin to a whip's lash. He didn't look back once. As far as he was concerned we weren't friends, he hadn't got us into this, and I hadn't been left behind
110　holding the bag, so to speak. From now on, I thought, I'd have to watch that boy. He had got me in deep waters with Teppy. And now this. I'd have to be careful of keeping company with him. He had made me accessory to this theft and had – lucky brat – left me in the mess.

From *The Wooing of Beppo Tate* By C. Everard Palmer, JAMAICA

Discussion for developing comprehension skills

A Understanding explicit statements:

1 To tempt is to draw someone to do something wrong. What do you think '*resisted the temptation*' (l. 6) means?
2 Give a phrase that could be used instead of '*confided in me*' (ll. 21–22).
3 *Sought* is the past tense of *seek* or look for. An opportunity is a chance. Put the phrase '*sought an opportunity*' (l. 82) into your own words.
4 What had Teppy told Beppo?
5 Why didn't Daphne see Beppo and Roy?
6 Why did Beppo not climb the tree?
7 '*Someone tapped me on the shoulder*' (l. 53). Who?
8 What happened to Roy before he came down from the tree?
9 Who was holding whom by the wrists?
10 What did Roy do when Mrs Belmont said '*Run along*' (l. 105)?

B Using context clues:

1 How can you tell what the writer means by '*hunkered*' (l. 31)?
2 When you read the sentence after the one in which '*sadist*' (l. 66) is used, what does that sentence tell you about the meaning of '*sadist*'?
3 What remark made just after '*captor*' (l. 82) can you use to guess the meaning of '*captor*'?

4 Look for clues in the same way that suggest the meaning of each of these:

'*venture*' (l. 13)　'*ditty*' (l. 34)
'*akin*' (l. 107)　'*accessory*' (l. 113)

C Seeing implied connections:

1 What shows that Roy had influence over Beppo?
2 Why did Beppo hear his heart beating '*pit-a-pat-pat*' (l. 32)?
3 Why did Beppo think they were intruders?
4 What did Roy's skill as a climber seem to tell?
5 Why didn't Beppo hear Mrs Belmont coming?
6 When they were caught, what did Beppo think Mrs Belmont would do to them?
7 '*So you're the one!*' (l. 93). What does that tell you about Mrs Belmont?
8 What do you suppose '*left behind holding the bag*' (ll. 109–110) means?
9 In what ways did Beppo change his opinion of Roy?
10 '*And now this*' (l. 112). Why did Beppo think that?

To Enrich Your Word Bank

Using words you read
In groups of two or three sit together and help one another to fit these words into the sentences below.

resisted   investigation   venture
reliable   confided   emerged   intruder
genuine

a   At the end of the play a crowd _____ from the theatre.
b   The teacher carried out an _____ to find the culprit.
c   She was only pretending she felt _____ regret.
d   He urged me to do it but I _____ to the end.
e   I made a mistake when I _____ all my secrets to her.
f   How _____ is the promise of a liar?
g   Into the man's house an odd _____ entered.
h   Why shouldn't we _____ into forbidden places?

Choosing the right word
Discuss which of the four words given with each of these sentences fits into the blank space in the sentence.

a   The dress she wore had a pretty _____ on the hem.
fashion   embroidery   model   fringe

b   Ignorant people in some other countries believe that West Indians live in huts with _____ roofs.
coconut   aboriginal   thatched universal

c   The workers _____ only the best oranges from the trees.
plucked   pared   reaped   deployed

d   The tape had _____ itself between the cogs of the machine.
selected   woven   originated bandaged

e   With the increase in the price of oil, countries tried to use _____ energy.
principle   scientific   solar   delivery

f   Every sun in the universe is the hub of a _____ of planets.
galaxy   system   law   gravity

Words with similar meanings
Discuss which one of the four words or phrases given with each sentence can best be used in place of the underlined word or phrase in the sentence, without changing the meaning of the sentence.

1   I was trying to <u>take in</u> the meaning of the poem.
admit   allow   absorb   swallow

2   The thieves ran down <u>a narrow lane</u> and got away.
a boulevard   an avenue
a driveway   an alley

3   The audience was <u>amused</u> by the antics of the clown.
thrilled   entertained   bemused bored

4   When the door was opened the prisoners <u>emerged</u> from the darkness.
appeared   escaped   exhumed emitted

5   We walked through the garden in a world of <u>enchantment</u>.
obeah   fascination   hypnosis   love

6   She waited <u>expectantly</u> to see what would happen.
patiently   confidently   irritatedly anxiously

7   He approached the people in a <u>nervous and diffident manner</u>.
panicky   terrified   timid   hysterical

8 The palace was a place of <u>splendour</u> and luxury.
   radiance   ceremony   immensity authority

9 He could not hide his <u>strong feelings of dislike</u> to see such behaviour.
   disgrace   disgust   distortion dissent

10 They were in such strange <u>garb</u> the people did not like them.
   company   garments   places armour

6 The parts of the back he can see _____ a black-brindled colouring.

7 The Comprehensive School with two thousand pupils _____ several tennis courts and swimming pools.

8 Earl Campbell, having to go away, _____ to get someone to take his dog.

9 Did you notice all the things she _____ not done?

10 This is one of the dogs that _____ to run in the race.

Grammatical Sentence Patterns

Has and have

In a certain story the writer makes his characters – the members of the Reynolds family – speak as he thinks they would probably speak in real life. For instance, Mrs Reynolds says *I tell you what he haven't got*. As a different person she might have said *hasn't* instead of *haven't*. In correct English *has* and *have* are used in the same way as *was* and *were*, which you dealt with in the last unit.

Say these sentences aloud, putting in *has* or *have* in the blank spaces. If you make a mistake you should repeat the correct sentence at least six times.

1 One of the dogs _____ a sore paw.
2 Greyhound racing on certain days _____ been stopped.
3 The running of races _____ been postponed.
4 The ears of our dog _____ to be treated with powder.
5 A coal shed in such places _____ a vital use in winter.

Some Idioms We Use

Getting them right

Remember every language has certain groups of words that have a special meaning in that language. An example of that in English is the phrase *cut and dried* meaning *with everything exactly arranged and ready beforehand*. Groups of words like that are called idioms. You cannot, as a rule, get their meanings by looking at the meaning of each word, and you cannot translate the words into another language and keep the meaning. The idioms of a language must be learnt by anyone learning that language.

Here are some English idioms to learn:

Idiom
a   dead silence
b   in black and white
c   hit below the belt
d   took to his heels
e   did not turn a hair
f   into the bargain
g   has the subject at his fingertips
h   a willing horse

Meaning
complete silence
in writing

fight unfairly
ran away very quickly
remained completely calm
in addition
knows the subject thoroughly
someone who works willingly – too
willingly

Which of the above idioms fits into the
blank space in each of these sentences?

1 When the teacher asked the question
   there was _____ .
2 Because she is _____ everybody
   leaves her to do everything.

3 As soon as he saw me approaching he
   _____ .
4 I knew she said it because I have it
   _____ in a letter.
5 Although everybody threw curses at
   him he _____ .
6 I will ask Jim what the answer is
   because he _____ .
7 In any dispute she will _____ to try
   to put down someone else.
8 We got wet _____ apart from
   having to walk all the way.

Writing A Letter

Telling a friend what happened

In Book 1 of *English For Life* you learnt
how to set out a letter to a friend. Now say
what goes into these numbered blocks.

In everyday life you will want to write
letters to friends at times. Now is the time,
not later, to get all the practice you can.

Quite often you will want to write to a
friend telling him or her about something
that happened, just as Beppo told about
how he and Roy were caught. This week
use some of your time to practise doing
that.

```
                                    1
```

```
          2
```

```
                    3
```

```
                    4
```

First, get into small groups of five or six and share your memories of times when you were caught doing something forbidden. Tell one another as much as possible about where you were, how you came to be there, what you tried to do, how you were caught, what happened then, and what happened afterwards.

Ask one another questions like *What did you see? What did you hear? What did ... say? How did it feel? How did it taste? How did it smell?* and so on.

When you have done that to fill your mind with what you can put into a letter, arrange for each member in the group to get a letter from another member. Then take some time in class or at home and write the letter to the person you have to write to, giving the details of the story of how you were caught red-handed.

Don't forget to use full stops to prevent your sentences from getting mixed up.

About the Language

Nouns and verbs

In these two sentences the word promise is used in two different ways. What are the two different ways?

Miss made a *promise* that she would put them in a cage.
Miss *promised* them she would put them in a cage.

You will notice that in the first sentence the word *promise* is used as a name of something – as a noun – while in the second sentence *promise* is used as a doing word or verb.

Now consider the underlined word in each of these sentences and discuss whether it is used as a noun or as a verb.

1 We want to take part in the <u>contest</u>.
2 All of us will <u>contest</u> against one another.
3 If you <u>practise</u> very hard you are likely to succeed.
4 Report for <u>practice</u> at five o'clock.
5 The angry man shouted out in <u>protest</u> against the discourtesy of the attendants.
6 The people of a small place <u>protest</u> against any new idea.

See if you can also use the following words in two sentences each to show how each can be used as a noun and then as a verb:

love   lead   race   run   touch

5 Saying Yes To Falsehoods

Everyday Life

Opinions you hear

Use some spare time at home or in school to consider this matter very carefully.

When you are talking with your friends do you ever say things like *That miserable teacher kept us back* or *Those rowdy, stupid boys are standing by the gate* or *She had a great birthday party with terrific music* or *The film was so fantastic I couldn't miss it?* Whenever you use words like *miserable, rowdy, stupid, great, terrific* or *fantastic*, you are giving your opinion about something. You can't prove any of them to be true or false as a fact. They can be called *opinion words*.

The words *miserable, rowdy* and *stupid* say that you do *not* like something: you disapprove. But the words *great, terrific* and *fantastic* say that you like whatever it is you mentioned: you approve of it. So words like *miserable, rowdy* and *stupid*

we might call *disapproval words*, and words like *great, terrific* and *fantastic* we might call *approval words*.

Now test yourself. Discuss which are the *opinion words* in the following sentences, and which of them are *approval words*, and which are *disapproval words*.

a   The lesson was boring and the foolish teacher went on and on.
b   Those pretty girls look beautiful in their stunning fashions.
c   She is a dunce.
d   The book must have been written by a good writer because it was very exciting.
e   An ugly old man passed by with a lazy boy at his side.
f   He is an amusing entertainer with a thrilling voice.
g   She stuck to her stubborn opinion, although I told her she was wrong.

Reading to Enjoy a Play

Getting ready

A custom is something people do because others did it for many, many years before. Do you think people should follow a custom just because their grandparents did? See whether the playwright who wrote the play below, *He Who Says No*, agrees with your opinion.

You may need a double period to read the

play. Take turns being The Teacher, The Boy, The Mother and The Three Students. The rest of the class could be The Great Chorus.

megaphone (l. 140) = something shaped like an ice-cream cone that you hold to your mouth to make your words louder
to introduce (l. 193) = to begin to do
valid (l. 204) = having good reasons

Scene
Japan, many years ago

1
GREAT CHORUS: Above all learn when to say Yes.
Many say Yes without understanding.
Many are not asked, and many
Say Yes to falsehoods. Therefore
5   Above all learn when to say Yes.
(The TEACHER *is in Room 1, the* MOTHER *and the* BOY *in Room 2.)*
TEACHER: I am the teacher. I teach school in the city and I have
a student whose father is dead. He has only his mother to take
care of him. I've come to say goodbye to them now because I am
10   about to start a trip over the mountains. *(He knocks at the*
door.) May I come in?
BOY: *(stepping from Room 2 into Room 1)* Who is it? Oh, the
teacher; the teacher's come to visit us!
TEACHER: Why haven't you been to school for so long?
15   BOY: I couldn't come because Mother was sick.
TEACHER: I didn't know that. Please tell her I am here.
BOY: *(calling into Room 2)* Mother, teacher is here.
MOTHER: *(sitting in Room 2)* Ask him to come in, please.
BOY: Please come in.
20   *(They enter Room 2.)*
TEACHER: I haven't been here for a long time. Your son tells me
you've been sick. Are you feeling any better now?
MOTHER: No need to worry about my illness. It left no bad
effects.
25   TEACHER: Glad to hear it. I came to say goodbye to you because
I'm going on a research trip over the mountains soon. For in
the city beyond the mountains live the famous teachers.
MOTHER: A research trip over the mountains! Yes, indeed, I've
heard that the famous teachers live there, but I've also heard
30   that the trip is dangerous. Were you thinking of taking my boy
with you?
TEACHER: That's no trip for a child!
MOTHER: I agree. I hope you will return safely.
TEACHER: I have to go now. Goodbye. Get well. (TEACHER *goes to*
35   *Room 1)*
BOY: *(follows the* TEACHER *into Room 1.)* I want to say
something.
(MOTHER *listens at the door.)*
TEACHER: What do you want to say?
40   BOY: I want to go over the mountains with you.
TEACHER: As I've already told your mother
The trip is hard and dangerous.
You won't be able to come along. Besides: How can you want to

leave your mother
45   When she is ill?
Stay here. It's really impossible
For you to come along.
BOY: Just because Mother is sick, I want
To come with you;
50   I must get her
Medicine and advice
From the famous doctors in the city beyond the mountains.
TEACHER: But would you agree to everything that might happen
to you on the trip?
55   BOY: Yes.
TEACHER: I must talk this over with your mother. (*He returns to
Room 2. The* BOY *listens at the door*.) As you see, I've come
back. Your son has asked to come with us. I told him he
couldn't leave you while you are still ill; and also that it is a
60   hard and dangerous trip. It was out of the question for him to
come along, I said. But he said he had to come with us to the
city beyond the mountains to get medicine and advice for you.
MOTHER: I heard what he said. I know the boy means well and
would like to make the dangerous trip. Come in, Son. (*The* BOY
65   *enters Room 2*.)
Ever since
Your father left us
I've had no one
But you at my side.
70   You were never longer
Out of my mind and out of my sight
Than it took
To prepare your meals,
To fix your clothes and
75   To earn a living.
BOY: What you say is true. But still you can't get me to change
my mind.
BOY, MOTHER, TEACHER: I am (He is) going ... to make the
dangerous trip
80   To get for your (my, her) illness
Medicine and advice
In the city beyond the mountains.
GREAT CHORUS: You saw that no argument
Could move him.
85   Then the teacher and the mother said
In one voice:
TEACHER AND MOTHER: Many say Yes to falsehoods
But he says Yes not to illness
But that illness be healed.
90   GREAT CHORUS: Now the mother said:

MOTHER: I have no more strength.
If it has to be
Go with the teacher.
But hurry, hurry
95 Return to me soon.

2
GREAT CHORUS: The people have started
On the trip over the mountains
Among them the teacher
And the boy.
100 The boy was not equal to the strain:
He overworked his heart
In the hurry to return.
At dawn at the foot of the mountains
He could hardly
105 Drag himself on.
(*Into Room 1 enter the* TEACHER, THREE STUDENTS *and finally the*
BOY *with a jug.*)
TEACHER: We climbed rapidly. There is the first hut. Let's rest
there a while.
110 THREE STUDENTS: We'll do that.
(*They step on the raised platform in Room 2. The* BOY *holds the*
TEACHER *back.*)
BOY: I want to say something.

TEACHER: What do you want to say?

115 BOY: I don't feel well.

TEACHER: Not another word. Whoever undertakes a trip such as this must not say such things. Perhaps you're just tired, not being used to climbing. Stop and rest a while.
(*He steps on the platform.*)

120 THREE STUDENTS: It seems that the boy is tired from climbing. Let's ask the teacher.

GREAT CHORUS: Yes, do.

THREE STUDENTS (*to the* TEACHER): We hear that the boy is tired from climbing. What's the matter with him? Are you worried
125 about him?

TEACHER: He said he didn't feel well, but he really is all right. He is tired from climbing.

THREE STUDENTS: Then you aren't worried about him? (*Long pause, then the* STUDENTS *among one another*):
130 Do you hear? The teacher said
The boy is only tired from climbing.
But doesn't he look strange?
Right after the hut comes the narrow pass.
Only clutching the cliff
135 With both hands
Can you pass.
We can't carry anyone.
Should we follow the great custom
And hurl him into the valley?
140 (*They call down to Room 1, forming a megaphone with their hands*):
Are you sick from climbing?

BOY: No!
See, I'm still standing up.
145 Wouldn't I sit down
If I were sick? (*Pause. The* BOY *sits down.*)

THREE STUDENTS: We'll tell the teacher. Sir, when we asked you before about the boy you said he was only tired from climbing, but now he looks so strange. He even sat down. We say it with
150 dread, but since ancient times a great custom has ruled here: he who can go no further is hurled into the valley!

TEACHER: What? You want to throw this child into the valley?

THREE STUDENTS: Yes!

TEACHER: As you say. This is a great custom existing since
155 ancient times. How can I oppose it? But doesn't the great custom also demand that we should ask the sick one if we should turn around for his sake? I feel a deep sorrow for this human being. I'll go and gently tell him of the great custom.

THREE STUDENTS: Please do. (*They face each other.*)

160 THREE STUDENTS AND GREAT CHORUS: We'll ask him (They asked

him) whether he demands (demanded)
That we (they) turn around now for his sake.
But even if he demands (demanded) it,
We will (They would) not turn back
165 But hurl him into the valley.
TEACHER: (*has gone down to the* BOY *in Room 1*) Listen closely.
Since ancient times a law has ruled that he who falls ill on
such a trip must be hurled into the valley. Death is instant. But
the custom also demands that we should ask the sick one if we
170 should turn back for his sake. And the custom demands that
the sick person answer: You shall not turn back. If I could take
your place, how gladly I would die.
BOY: I understand.
TEACHER: Do you ask that we turn back for your sake? Or do
175 you agree that we throw you into the valley as the great
custom demands?
BOY: No! I do not agree.
TEACHER: (*calling from Room 1 to Room 2*) Come down here! He
did not answer as the custom demands. He who says A, must
180 also say B. When you were asked before whether you would
agree to everything that might happen on this trip, you said
yes.
BOY: The answer that I gave was false. But your question was
even falser. He who says A, does not have to say B. He can also
185 realise that A was false. I wanted to get medicine for my
mother. But now that I am sick myself, it's no longer possible.
And I want to turn back immediately now that things have
changed. So I ask you to turn back and to bring me home.
Surely, your research can wait. If there's something to learn
190 over there, as I hope there is, then it can only be that in a
situation such as ours now, we should turn around. And as for
the great ancient custom, I see no sense to it. Rather, I need a
great new custom, one we must introduce here and now: the
custom to give each new situation new thought.
195 THREE STUDENTS: (*to the* TEACHER) What are we to do? What the
boy says is sensible even if it is not heroic.
TEACHER: I leave it up to you to decide what to do now. But I
must tell you: people will hurl laughter and disgrace at you if
you turn back.
200 THREE STUDENTS: Isn't it a disgrace that he speaks for himself?
TEACHER: No, I see no disgrace in that.
THREE STUDENTS: Then we'll turn back and no laughter and no
abuse shall keep us from doing the sensible thing: and no
ancient custom shall keep us from agreeing to a valid thought.
205 Lean your head on our arms.
Don't strain yourself
We'll carry you carefully.

GREAT CHORUS: So the friends took the friend
And established a new custom
210 And a new law
And they brought the boy back.
Side by side they walked pressed together
Against the abuse,
Against the laughter, with open eyes,
215 No one more cowardly than his neighbour.

The End

He Who Says No By Bertold Brecht (translated by Berhard Nellhaus), GERMANY

Discussion for developing comprehension skills

A Understanding explicit statements:

1 In which country, and when, were the events of the play supposed to have taken place?
2 Why was The Teacher going over the mountains?
3 Why did he say *'You won't be able to come along'* (l. 43)?
4 What happened to The Boy *'at dawn at the foot of the mountains'* (l. 103)?
5 *'... since ancient times a great custom has ruled here'* (l. 150). Which custom was that?
6 What would have happened if the great custom had been followed?
7 *'I need a great new custom'* (ll. 192–193). What new custom did The Boy propose?
8 What did The Three Students think was *'a disgrace'* (l. 200)?

B Seeing implied connections:

1 Why are *'He is'* and *'my, her'* put in brackets in lines 78 and 80?
2 *'... a disgrace that he speaks for himself'* (l. 200). According to that remark, how was a person expected to behave?
3 In what way was turning back a bad thing to do?
4 *'... doing the sensible thing'* (l. 203). What does that have to do with great customs?
5 *'Against the abuse, Against the laughter'* (l. 213 and 214). Who would abuse and laugh at them?
6 Which one of these is the play about?

a a boy's love for his mother
b how teachers and students behave
c the need for us to question customs we follow
d going on a trip in a difficult situation
e trying to do more than you are able to.

To Enrich Your Word Bank

Words about plays
Put your ideas together and try to fit each of these words where it belongs:

playwright dialogue comedy tragedy character scene act audience

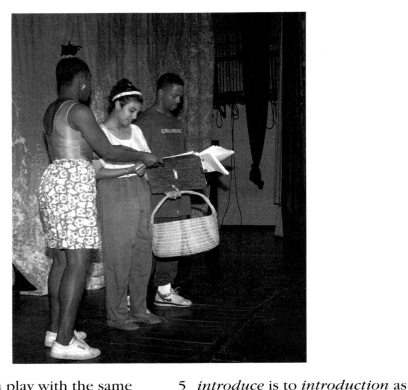

a   part of an act of a play with the same people on the stage

b   the words spoken by the people in a play

c   the people who go to a theatre to see a play

d   the writer of a play

e   a part of a play, often with different scenes in it

f   a play with a happy ending

g   a person that an actor has to pretend to be in a play

h   a play that ends sadly

Words related in meaning

Put on your thinking caps and deduce the word for each blank space:

1   *false* is to *falsehood* as *hero* is to _____

2   *sense* is to *sensible* as *reason* is to _____

3   *custom* is to *customary* as *use* is to _____

4   *fame* is to *famous* as _____ is to *triumphant*

5   *introduce* is to *introduction* as _____ is to *obedience*

6   *disgrace* is to *disgraceful* as *horror* is to _____

7   *decide* is to *decision* as _____ is to *relief*

8   *establish* is to *establishment* as _____ is to *circle*

9   *danger* is to *dangerous* as *speech* is to _____

10   _____ is to *conclude* as *argument* is to *argue*

11   _____ is to *long* as *equal* is to *equality*

12   *admire* is to _____ as *advise* is to *advisable*

13   _____ is to *explanation* as *exist* is to *existence*

14   _____ is to *satisfactory* as *danger* is to *dangerous*

15   _____ is to *description* as *prepare* is to *preparation*

16   *proof* is to _____ as *death* is to *die*

Choosing the right word

Discuss which of the four words given with each sentence best fits into the blank space in the sentence.

1 I wanted to hear your _____ of why such a thing happened.
   tone explanation resolve approval

2 We did what was _____ done on Saturdays.
   hastily uncertainly usually inadequately

3 She made a _____ promise to wait for us.
   definite delicate sensitive impatient

4 You must not _____ to speak the truth.
   enlist conspire announce hesitate

5 It was her firm _____ to send the dog away.
   tone explanation resolve approval

6 He stepped _____ into the room, hesitating when he entered.
   hastily uncertainly usually inadequately

7 The _____ expression on her face showed that she had strong feelings.
   definite delicate sensitive impatient

8 I will try to _____ the courage to ask the question.
   enlist conspire announce hesitate

Grammatical Sentence Patterns

How to ask questions

In the play you read The Teacher asked *'Why haven't you been to school for so long?'* (l. 14) and The Boy stated *'I couldn't come because Mother was sick'*.

Here is another statement:

I didn't know that.

Changed into a question pattern, that statement would be:

Didn't I know that?

One of the speech habits you might have is saying a statement when you mean to ask a question, or sometimes using the wrong form of the verb in a question. If so, it would be helpful for you to practise framing questions properly.

Take these statements and change each one *orally* into a question. If you make a mistake repeat the proper question a few times.

a The teacher came to the house.
b He spoke to the boy.
c The boy's mother had been sick.
d She prepared his meals.
e I feel a deep sorrow.
f He looks strange.
g They climbed the mountain.
h He overworked his heart.
i He demands it.
j I have no more strength.
k He speaks for himself.
l The students wanted to follow the custom.
m I am going to make the trip.
n I think we need a new custom.
o He said he didn't feel well.

Using a Dictionary

Finding a word

In a dictionary words are arranged in alphabetical order; that is, words beginning with *a* come before words beginning with *b*, and, in the *a* words, words beginning with *ab* come before words beginning with *ac*.

See how long it would take you to arrange these words in the order in which you could find them in a dictionary.

custom   ancient   hurl   exist   student instant   introduce   valid   effect   advice clutch   establish   chorus   situation research   earn

When you have done that, use a dictionary and find the meanings of any of the words that you do not know the meaning of.

Writing What Characters Say

Dialogue for a scene

When you read a play you see that what the actors and actresses have to say, in pretending to be the characters they are playing, is set down like this:

BOY: (*stepping from Room 2 into Room 1*) Who is it? Oh, the teacher; the teacher's come to visit us!
TEACHER: Why haven't you been to school for so long?
BOY: I couldn't come because Mother was sick.
TEACHER: I didn't know that. Please tell her I am here.

BOY: (*calling into Room 2*) Mother, teacher is here.
MOTHER: (*sitting in Room 2*) Ask him to come in, please.
BOY: Please come in.
(*They enter Room 2.*)
TEACHER: I haven't been here for a long time. Your son tells me you've been sick. Are you feeling any better now?
MOTHER: No need to worry about my illness. It left no bad effects.

Near the margin the name of the character is written (usually in capital letters, sometimes in italics, and sometimes just underlined). Then a colon (:) follows, but sometimes a full stop follows. Then the words to be spoken by that character at that time are written and any directions telling the actor what to do or how to speak are put in brackets.

It is not at all difficult to practise writing your own dialogue for a play. Just get into groups of about four or five and choose a situation you are familiar with, such as a conversation between a teacher, two parents and two students.

One of the group must be the teacher and the others would be the other characters. Now you are going to improvise or make up for yourselves what went on. Each one must pretend to be a character and just say things that character might say as if the conversation or scene is happening right now.

When each character has had at least two chances to speak, stop and try to remember exactly what was said and repeat the dialogue.

Then go back to your desks and begin writing the scene your group just made up, setting it down as a playwright would do in writing a play.

Drama for Fun

Speaking and doing

Pretending to be another person and in another situation can be fun if you do it seriously. The challenge is to communicate to the audience the right feelings.

Practise saying these sentences as you imagine the persons who said them would have spoken:

a 'Call the police.'
b 'Go and call them yourself.'
c 'You need the fire brigade and the army.'
d 'What's all this? What's all the fuss?'
e 'Why don't you get your animal out of the way?'
f 'The man's a fool, knows nothing about animals, or people.'
g 'Now, Sprat, I am going to clean the wound and dress it.'
h 'Don't argue or you will be bitten both by the mule and me.'

Now practise doing the following scenes without speaking at all. You may have to go to the school auditorium or the schoolyard if you cannot clear a space in your classroom.

a the boy, the teacher and the students climbing the mountain
b the boy feeling ill from the strain
c the boy creeping to the door to listen
d the mother listening at the door
e the students and the teacher carrying the boy back

f some people pulling a heavy cart (just imagine the cart, do not use a desk)
g a crowd moving away in silence as the police ask them to move (the police must say nothing)
h moving through a thick crowd to get to the front (do this individually with no crowd there)
i pushing yourselves through the strong current of a river
j a group of people carrying a heavy trunk of a tree.

6 Strange Sounds At Night

Everyday life

Grounds for beliefs

In your spare time or in class if there is time, have a discussion with your classmates about these questions.

1 When someone expresses an opinion to you do you recognise it as an opinion and not a fact?
2 Can you think of any occasion when what someone believed made him or her do certain things?
3 Think of some beliefs or opinions you know some people have and try to figure out how they might have come to believe them.
4 Do people always have good reasons for the beliefs that make them do things?
5 How often do you ask yourself what reasons or grounds you have for believing something?

Reading to Enjoy a Story

Getting ready

How do you feel when you hear strange sounds in the night? What do you think makes strange sounds at night?

The Grenadian girl, Nellie, in this part of a story tells about an occasion when she heard a sound in the bedroom in the middle of the night. Find out what terrified her and her sister.

consoled (l. 7) = comforted, made someone feel better
all and sundry (l. 17) = everybody
literally (l. 32) = actually, really
jumbies (l. 41) = ghosts, *duppies* in Jamaica

Mr David Lang who also worked in the Department of Agriculture with Daddy, but in the country, had come into town for meetings and was asked to stay with us.

Vince and Selby were moved in Jessie's room, May went into
5 the dressing-room and Jessie moved in with me. Mr Lang would have the boys' room. We were banished from the dining room quite early that evening and consoled ourselves cutting out pictures from magazines and sticking them in our scrap books. We got sleepy so got into bed without tidying up our
10 mess.

It was a lovely, cool night and Jessie and I snuggled under our blankets and fell fast asleep.

I awoke and could feel Jessie gripping me with fear. Alert, I could hear slippered feet dragging themselves towards our bed.

15 Now if anything bothered me, I would keep quiet and seek the best way out. Jessie was entirely different; she would let it be heard by all and sundry that things did not suit or please her and someone *must* come to her aid.

The footsteps approached the bed and Jessie yelled, 'Oh Gawd,
20 help, *help*!'

Vince in the adjoining room did not wait for anything more and shot out of bed making for the safety of his own room, where he was grabbed by Mr Lang and sent back to his bed.

The footsteps started again, sweeping towards us, nearer,
25 nearer and Jessie yelled, '*Oh, Gawd, Oh Gawd, Oh Gawd*!'

We both knew it was an evil ghost. I begged her to keep quiet as Mother and Daddy would be ashamed of us, what with a guest in the house and all that! Jessie cuffed me and bawled, '*I don't care*!' And the footsteps scraping the floor came yet
30 nearer.

'*Murder, police, help*!' shouted Jessie, and Vince again took off to Mr Lang, who was thoroughly annoyed and literally chased him back.

So far, Selby had slept through everything.

35 'Hush Jessie, no one can hear us. Let's pretend we're asleep,' I
whispered.

'*Pretend*!' bellowed Jessie, '*this is no time to pretend*!' and, as
the steps swished across the floor, the scream she emitted sent
Vince *and* Selby scuttling. Selby made a beeline for Mother's
40 bed where the jump he made awoke both parents.

'Jumbies,' he said, 'jumbies all about.'

Jessie's bellows were like angry waves. They pounded
relentlessly one after the other and Mother and Daddy arrived
bearing lamps. Sitting on the side of our bed, we hugged them,
45 trying to tell our tale of the slippered ghost; just then, the feet
began approaching again. We buried our heads in their laps,
utterly terrified.

Daddy made us sit up and very sternly told us that our fright
had been caused by ourselves. Pointing to the many pieces of
50 paper we had cut from magazines and had left on the floor, he
told us, 'Keep looking.'

We did. The breeze blew, scraping the crumpled paper along
the floor. We felt awfully silly and were tucked into bed with a
reassuring, 'Good night.'

55 In the morning at breakfast, Mr Lang, on hearing our side of
the story, gave his, saying how he'd nearly taken a pot shot at
Vince, mistaking him for a burglar.

We laughed so much in the beautiful daylight that Selby was
made to leave the table. He had popped a piece of toast into his
60 mouth. Then, because he was overcome with laughter, the food
had shot out, sprayed across the table and landed in the butter
dish.

From the story *A Grenadian Childhood* By Nellie Payne, GRENADA

Discussion for developing comprehension skills

A Understanding explicit statements:

1 Who was invited to stay with the
family that night?
2 What did the children do when they
left the dining room?
3 Why did Nellie wake up?
4 What did she hear?
5 How did Jessie behave hearing the
sound?
6 Where did Vince go?
7 Why did Nellie tell Jessie to keep
quiet?

8 What had Mr Lang '*thoroughly
annoyed*' (l. 32)?
9 Where did Selby go?
10 Who brought lamps into their room?

B Seeing implied connections:

1 '*Vince and Selby were moved into
Jessie's room*' (l. 4). Why?
2 '*... without tidying up our mess*'
(ll. 9–10). What mess?
3 '*We both knew it was an evil ghost*'
(l. 26). How did they know?

4 'They pounded relentlessly'
(ll. 42–43). Who pounded?
5 What did their father show them when he came to the room?
6 'The breeze blew, scraping the crumpled paper along the floor' (ll. 52–53). How was that connected with what happened?
7 'We felt awfully silly' (l. 53). Why?
8 Why was Selby 'overcome with laughter' (l. 60)?

C Using context clues:

1 Say what the clue is that tells the meaning of 'emitted' (l. 38).
2 How is the meaning of 'adjoining' (l. 21) easy to guess?
3 What suggests the meaning of 'bellows' (l. 42) to someone?
4 Name the clue – word or phrase – that helps to tell the meaning of each of these words:
'banished' (l. 6)   'snuggled' (l. 11)
'scuttling' (l. 39)   'relentlessly' (l. 43)

To Enrich Your Word Bank

Using words you read
Into which sentence does each of these words fit?

banish console snuggled alert emit relentlessly

1 We have to be _____ to catch those who try to fool us.
2 The pups _____ up under their mother for warmth.
3 Vehicles on the road _____ dangerous fumes.
4 You should _____ from your mind all thoughts of ghosts.
5 The rain poured _____, washing away the soil.

6 Do you think empty promises will _____ me for my loss?

Words related in meaning
After each of these sentences there is a word in brackets. Discuss what word, related in meaning to the word in brackets, fits into the blank space in the sentence.

a The fumes from the exhaust of a car are _____. (*poison*)
b Each patient was given an _____ of the vaccine. (*inject*)
c Our knowledge depends on _____ tests. (*science*)
d He was taking his _____ stroll around the park. (*habit*)
e It is _____ to have to change a tyre. (*trouble*)
f We should all have _____ feelings towards one another. (*brother*)
g Living in _____ with one another destroys people. (*enemy*)
h Your behaviour is all _____ since you do not honestly feel sorry. (*pretend*)

Choosing the right word
Discuss which of the following words fits into each of the blank spaces in the sentences below.

hesitated reluctant urge envious coax manage control contented incident smear

1 Because she was _____ to leave she was not willing to get up.
2 He was reluctant to dive into the water so he _____ on the diving-board.
3 Jograj used the whip to _____ the horse to go faster.
4 Her friend was _____ of the chance she got to go to Paris.
5 How did you _____ to do all of that so quickly.

6 As you grow older you should learn to _____ yourself better.

7 The buffalo was _____ to lie and wallow in the mud.

8 An unpleasant _____ took place when the match was being played.

9 I used some sweet words to _____ Stella into lending me her bicycle.

10 The mischievous girl took some ink to _____ it on the clean page.

Grammatical Sentence Patterns

Asking questions

Many questions that we ask must begin with *do, does, was, were, has* and *have*. But mistakes are often made with the framing of such questions.

You should spend a little time using the tables below repeating the correct patterns to make them into habits.

Say as many sentences as you can from each table as loudly and as quickly as you can.

Do	I	want to go?
	you	like the book?
	we	come to school?
	they	do the work?
	the children	practise enough?

Does	he	walk to school?
	she	like to sing?
	the girl	do it well?
	your friend	jog every day?
	everybody	pass my way?

Have	you	finished the job?
	they	taken the advice?
	we	received the letter?
	the tenants	called the police?
	Ray and Sam	been there?

Has	he	sent the message?
	she	gone home?
	the old man	seen it?
	the driver	sat down?
	your brother	come as yet?

Were	you	being attended to?
	they	having a good time?
	we	sitting in the room?
	the students	told what to do?
	Mike and Pat	asked any questions?

Was	she	being funny?
	he	annoyed with you?
	the guest	sleeping soundly?
	your father	doing anything?
	the visitor	given the message?

Spelling

'Seeing' the letters

Practise seeing in your mind's eye the missing letter in each of these words used in the excerpt.

maga_ines   slip_ered   grip_ing   he_rd
appro_ched   saf_ty   grab_ed   yel_ed
gu_st   an_oyed   thoro_ghly   emit_ed
scre_m   ter_ified   burgl_r   to_st

Words in ghost stories

Choose some of these words which you think you might want to use in telling a ghost story and try to 'see' each one without looking at it.

fear   panic   afraid   dread   evil   terror
frightened   tremble   phantom   hideous
chilling   weird   eerie   horrible
gruesome   quake   startle   chatter
scared   uncanny

Writing a Story

Being frightened

All of us can remember an occasion when something got us frightened. Take a minute or two to recall a day or a night when something made you afraid.

When you are ready with something you remember, take turns telling the rest of the class about it, trying to use some of the words from the ghost stories' list.

Those listening must help the storyteller by interrupting with questions to make him or her give more details and say things in the right order. Ask questions like *When did that happen? What happened next? What was heard? What was seen? How did you feel? What was said? What did you do?* and so on.

Later on, at home or in class, begin writing your own story by first making a sentence to start it going, like *I was sitting alone at home reading a book*, or *That*

night it was very quiet but I couldn't sleep, or something like that. Then add another sentence, then another, and another, going on until you have told everything.

While you are writing do not forget to mention things heard, seen, felt, smelled, and, perhaps, tasted. Remember, too, to say things that happened in the right order, separating your sentences with full stops.

When you have finished get together with three or four of your classmates and correct one another's stories, checking on grammar, punctuation and spelling. (You may use your dialect for what people in the story say.) Then collect all stories written by members of the class and bind them together in some way to make a collection or anthology. Make a cover for it, like a book, and give it a title.

Words in Literature

Alliteration

You are familiar with how poets sometimes use words to end lines of their poems with rhymes. But there are other ways that poets use words for their sounds.

Read these lines aloud and see whether you notice the sound the poet has chosen certain words for:

a   In a summer season when soft was the sun

b   Many a morning on the moorland did we hear

Did you notice that, while in some poems the same sound is repeated to make rhyme at the *end* of words (e.g. *turn* and *burn*), in the lines above certain words have the same sound at the *beginning*, i.e. in (a) *summer, season, soft* and *sun*, and in (b) *many, morning* and *moorland*.

Repetition (repeating) of a sound at the *beginnings* of words is called *alliteration*,

and it is used for the words to have an effect on the reader's ear and make the words more memorable – easy to keep in mind.

Look for it in these phrases:

i   first and foremost
ii dead as a doornail
iii do or die
iv with might and main
v   wild and woolly
vi sink or swim

Now find it in these lines:

1 The blazing brightness of the beauties beam.
2 When to the sessions of sweet silent thought.
3 And wild with old woes new wail my dear time's waste.

7 That Cricket Bat

Everyday Life

Politeness in daily living

How people speak to one another in their daily living helps to make life pleasant or unpleasant for all; it affects the quality of their lives.

In your spare time give these matters some thought.

Try to think of as many occasions as you can when people should say *Thank you*.

For instance, when a shop assistant (or store clerk) is handing a customer what was purchased, or when someone holds a door open for another.

Think of as many occasions as you can when you should say *Sorry* or *Excuse me*. For instance, if you find yourself standing in someone's way; if you kept someone waiting; if you made a noise; and so on.

Reading to Learn Things

Getting ready

When children cannot afford a real cricket bat, what do they use? Is it as good as a real bat? If not, why not? Is there any special way to make a cricket bat? How is it made?

Perhaps the following article will tell you something you did not know before.

Did you know that all the best cricket bats in the world are made from only one kind of tree, the English willow? The Test cricketers of all the great cricketing countries – Australia, England, India, New Zealand, Pakistan, South Africa, the West
5 Indies – use bats made from English willow.

Did you know, too, that there actually is a tree called the cricket-bat willow? 'Cricket-bat' is not just a nickname. It is the tree's proper name. If you look in any good tree book you will find it mentioned as the tallest, straightest member of the
10 large willow family. It was called 'cricket-bat' because its white, straight-grained wood was found to be better for cricket bats than the wood of any other willow.

It is a very fast-growing tree. In fact it is ready to be cut into cricket bats when it is only 15 years old. During the last
15 century 1000 bats came from one huge willow. But today the usual number is about 40.

The early cricket-bat makers – some of whom were also famous cricketers – tried many different woods. They tried oak and beech and even mahogany. But these hardwoods were too heavy. They split too easily and they were not springy enough.

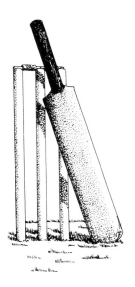

Willow is the perfect wood for cricket bats because, although it is a softwood, it is tough, light and 'elastic'.

Have you ever watched Gary Sobers, Viv Richards, or Gordon Greenidge batting? Perhaps you have seen them on television. These great batsmen hit a cricket ball as hard as anyone else in the world. Just think of the hammering their bats must get! Yet they hardly ever break or splinter.

Good batsmen take a great deal of trouble in choosing their bats. First they pick out a bat with a beautiful grain in the wood. A bat drives more sweetly if its grain is straight and narrow. Then they feel its weight, swing it, twiddle it. For above all they want a bat which has perfect balance.

Have a look at a good cricket bat. You will see how perfectly shaped it is. If a cricket bat were not perfectly shaped it would not have perfect balance. And if it did not have perfect balance, a batsman would not be able to make his strokes properly.

First the beams of willow are 'seasoned' for at least two years in sheds – and sometimes for four. Then the craftsmen shape the wood very carefully. Finally the handle has to be fitted. The handle is made from cane, cut in the jungles of Borneo. The joint has to be very strong.

So the making of a cricket bat is a very skilled job indeed. It is the job of a craftsman. It takes months, sometimes years, to turn a slice of cricket-bat willow into its final form as a cricket bat.

Is it surprising that cricket is sometimes called King Willow?

From *Finding Out, No. 34*

Discussion for developing comprehension skills

A Understanding explicit statements:

1 What tree is used to make the best cricket bats?
2 Why is willow the perfect wood for cricket bats?
3 What makes the cricket-bat willow tree the best willow for cricket bats?
4 Why is mahogany not a good wood for cricket bats?
5 What does a cricketer test for in a cricket bat?
6 Why is the grain of the wood important to a batsman?
7 How many bats are usually made from a tree?
8 How soon is a cricket-bat willow tree ready to be used to make bats?
9 How long does it take to make a bat?

B Seeing implied connections:

1 What is meant by the 'willow family' (l. 10)?
2 In what country does the English willow grow most?
3 What is meant by 'strokes' (l. 41)?
4 'A bat drives more sweetly' (l. 35). What does that mean?
5 What is an unseasoned bat?
6 Why do you suppose the handle has to be of cane?
7 How is a craftsman different from other people who make things?
8 What title would you give to paragraph 9 (ll. 42–47)?
9 How are enough willow trees found to make bats?

To Enrich Your Word Bank

Words related in meaning

Discuss which word, related in form and meaning to the one in brackets after the sentence, best fits into the blank space in the sentence.

1 Those were the _____ runs made by Sobers. (*actually*)
2 There must be a certain amount of _____ in a cricket bat. (*elastic*)
3 A craftsman always tries to achieve _____. (*perfect*)
4 The most _____ cricketers in the world are West Indians. (*skill*)
5 A slow bowler has to be very _____ to fool the batsman. (*craft*)
6 Some girls are quite _____ with the game of cricket. (*family*)
7 If a bat is too _____ for you, you should not use it. (*weight*)
8 Clive Lloyd was a very _____ fieldsman. (*willow*)

Words about games

1 Here are some words used in talking about the game of cricket:
innings overs fieldsmen delivery appeal crease

Between you, collect as many other words as you can related to playing cricket.

2 Get into small groups and collect lists of words related to any two or more games that you know about, e.g. netball, football.

Words for phrases

Discuss which of the four words given with each sentence could be used to replace the underlined phrase in the sentence.

1   It is not everything you eat that gives you <u>what your body needs for energy and tissues</u>.
alimentary   digestion   nourishment   deficiency

2   I saw the <u>ones who were captured</u> being taken to the prison.
captors   slaves   criminals   captives

3   We should always question the <u>practices we commonly follow</u> in our country.
habits   customs   regulations   laws

4   It is interesting to look at the <u>things that happen one after another</u> in the digestion of food.
process   procedure   programme   protraction

5   What <u>kind of matter</u> is that helmet made of?
quality   degree   fabrication   substance

6   Those articles are all <u>of the home</u>, as you can see.
homely   domestic   private   domiciled

7   In this country there are <u>different levels</u> of freedom for different people.
elevators   plaques   degrees   attitudes

Grammatical Sentence Patterns

Telling about past happenings

In excerpts from stories that you have read you met words like *fell, awoke, made, started, resisted, caught* and *joined*.

They are all past tense forms of verbs but many young people growing up in your country do not have the speech habit of using them when they have to be used.

Do you find yourself ever saying something like *run* for *ran*, or *walk* for *walked* when you wish to speak or write English? If so, you need a lot of practice to get the habit of using past tense forms when necessary. You can use the drills below in team games to get a little practice now. Remember to speak loudly and as quickly as you can.

Take this sentence:

The clouds lazily drifted out of sight.

If you change *clouds* to *boys* and make other changes, you might make a sentence like *The boys quickly scampered out of sight*, or *The boys slowly sauntered down the road*, or something like that. But you can make only one change at a time if you wish, as long as your sentence makes sense.

Try doing that, using these for practice. Do it as a game, with teams competing.

The crowd The voices The smoke	slowly gradually lazily leisurely drowsily	drifted moved wandered faded melted	out of sight. away. into the distance.

Now do the same with this sentence:

An old red car rattled and groaned as it moved along.

Use these substitutions:

| A rickety cart
An ancient van
A dilapidated bus
An overloaded truck
An erratic jitney | shook and shivered
rumbled and rattled
tottered and trembled | as it moved along.
on its weary way.
as it lumbered on.
creaking with pain. |

Punctuation Signals

Question marks
What is the punctuation mark at the end of each of these sentences? Why is it used instead of a full stop?

1 What's all this?
2 What's all the fuss?
3 Why don't you get your animal out of the way?

It is easy to forget to put the question mark at the end of a question if you don't give yourself enough practice doing it.

Take the following sets of words and rearrange each set into a question. Write the question and put the question mark at the end.

1 job sir this is your
2 mule get up can that we help
3 right you all are
4 wound clean going you are to the
5 heard thought did humming say he he he a
6 Dad mules are whose all those
7 why you called do Duppy Bay know it's
8 it it haunted really is isn't

Writing a Letter to a Friend

Giving information
Imagine that a pen-pal from another part of the world has written to you asking about a game played in your part of the world. He or she wants information with respect to these questions:

Who judges when a rule has been broken?
Are there penalties for when a rule is broken?
How does the person or team win the game?
What equipment is needed to play the game?
Where is it played?
How are points or runs or goals won?
How many people can play the game at once?
How is the score counted?
Is the game divided into parts?

First, arrange the questions in the order in which they should be answered, putting the first question to be answered first, and so on.

Then write your address and today's date where they have to be written, and *Dear* ... where that must be put. (See Unit 4 if you need to be reminded.)

Write a sentence, or more than one sentence, to answer the question you put first in the list. Remember the full stop or full stops.

Continue with other sentences to answer the other questions in the order you decided on, and end your letter in the usual way as you learnt in Book 1 of *English For Life*.

Words In Literature

Accent, beat and rhythm

If you were saying these sentences your voice would place more stress or weight on the parts in capitals:

WHERE are you GOing NOW?
or
Where are YOU going NOW?

In speaking English people put more stress or emphasis on certain words in a sentence and on certain syllables or parts of words.

When poets write poems they choose words to give their lines a certain set of beats or stresses to make a rhythm.

Here is a line that goes ti TUM ti TUM ti TUM ti TUM ti TUM:
Two kínd old ládies gáve him thŕee or fóur

Here is one that goes ti ti TUM ti ti TUM ti ti TUM ti ti TUM:
At the báck of the ínn on the wáy to the brídge

Those are just two kinds of rhythm. Several kinds are used.

Read these aloud to find out on which words or syllables the stress falls and to hear the rhythm.

i   I put my eye upon this page.
ii   Slowly and solemnly after the parade.
iii While flowers spread their colours for the passing world.
iv   Not a drum was heard, not a funeral note.
v   I journey through graveyards where stanzas are terse.

8 Through A Stranger's Eyes

Everyday Life

The wisdom in proverbs

In your spare time, together with a friend or friends, discuss which of the following proverbs match the meaning given below them. For example, 4 and i go together.

1 Every cloud has a silver lining.
2 It never rains but it pours.
3 A bird in the hand is worth two in the bush.
4 Look before you leap.
5 Once bitten, twice shy.
6 Nothing ventured, nothing gained.
7 Too many cooks spoil the broth.
8 Many hands make light work.
9 Opportunity knocks but once.
10 Empty vessels make most noise.

Meanings:

a Confusion is caused when too many people are responsible for doing something.

b The more helpers there are, the easier the work will be.
c A good chance comes once only.
d If you do not take risks, you will not make a profit.
e Something good comes from every trouble or problem.
f Usually trouble or problems come several at a time.
g Something which you already have is better than a promise of something which is not yet yours.
h Foolish persons talk most.
i Think carefully before taking any action.
j Once caught or hurt, a person avoids being caught or hurt again.

Reading to Enjoy a Poem

Getting ready

Here is a poem written by someone who visited Jamaica at some time in the 1950s and took a ride on a bus. Think of a bus ride you yourself have taken when you read it and see what his eyes and nose took in.

gloomy (l. 3) = sad
resigned (l. 3) = making no complaint
quadroon (l. 8) = of mixed race
dandies (l. 8) = stylishly dressed men

Jamaican Bus Ride

The live fowl squatting on the grapefruit and bananas
in the basket of the copper-coloured lady
is gloomy but resigned.

The four very large baskets on the floor
5   are in everybody's way,
as the conductor points out
loudly, often, but in vain.

Two quadroon dandies are disputing
who is standing on whose feet.

10 When we stop,
a boy vanishes through the door marked ENTRANCE;
but those entering through the door marked EXIT
are greatly hindered by the fact that when we started
there were twenty standing,
15 and another ten have somehow inserted themselves
into invisible crannies
between dark sweating body and body.

With an odour of petrol
both excessive and alarming
20 we hurtle hell-for-leather
between crimson bougainvillaea blossom
and scarlet poinsettia
and miraculously do not run over
three goats, seven hens and a donkey
25 as we pray
that the driver has not fortified himself
at Daisy's Drinking Saloon
with more than four rums:
or by the gods of Jamaica
30 this day is our last!

By A.S.J. Tessimond, ENGLAND

Discussion for developing comprehension skills

A Understanding explicit statements:

1 Finish these sentences:
   a The '*copper-coloured lady*' (l. 2) carried _____.
   b The conductor pointed out that _____.
   c The dandies argued about _____.
   d Those '*greatly hindered*' (l. 13) were those who _____.

2 Who or what was '*gloomy but resigned*' (l. 3)?

3 Which phrase tells you the passengers did not do what the conductor asked?

4 How did people disobey the signs on the bus?

5 How many more people found space to stand up after the bus started?

6 In which line of the poem does the writer say the bus was going too fast?

7 '*Petrol*' (l. 18) is gas for a vehicle. Why did the traveller mention petrol?

B Using context clues:

1 Which line tells the reader what '*disputing*' (l. 8) means?

2 What fact would help someone to guess the meaning of '*hindered*' (l. 13)?

3 Is there a clue – a word or a phrase – that can help a reader to guess the meaning of any of these words? '*inserted*' (l. 15) '*crannies*' (l. 16) '*odour*' (l. 18) '*hurtle*' (l. 20)

C Seeing implied connections:

1 Finish these sentences:
   a Some passengers carried baskets because _____.
   b The writer smelled _____.
   c At Daisy's Drinking Saloon the driver _____.
   d The phrase '*fortified himself*' (l. 26) means _____.

2 Why did the writer use the word '*gloomy*' (l. 3)?

3 What did he notice outside as the bus went along?

4 Why did he say '*miraculously*' (l. 23)?

5 '*... this day is our last*' (l. 30). What made the writer think that?

6 Name five things the writer found unusual and unexpected.

To Enrich Your Word Power

Using words you read

In which sentence below would you use each of these words?

squatting   disputing   hindered inserted   odour   excessive   hurtle fortified

1 The key was _____ into the lock but would not turn.

2 There was a strong _____ of perspiration in the bus.

3 Some small boys were _____ on the steps waiting for the bell.

4 The bulldozer made an _____ amount of noise.

5 When I tried to enter the yard some potholes _____ me.

6 There is no point _____ who is right and who is wrong.

7 The whole place was _____ against burglars.

8 The planets of our solar system _____ through space.

Words about a bus ride

Here are some words people use in telling about a bus ride. See how many of them you can use in oral sentences of your own.

station   fare   aboard   trip   distance
conductor   passengers   traffic
pedestrians   destination   squeeze

scramble jostle clamber congestion possessions belongings load jammed obstruct route jerk accelerate swerve rattle sweat scent perspiration shatter gossip squabble bicker junction avenue swerve scenery pleasant humour departure transfer

Words with similar meanings

Discuss which one of the four words given with each sentence can best be used to replace the word or phrase underlined in the sentence, without changing the meaning of the sentence.

1 What a great <u>clackity, clanking noise</u> you are making!
   explosion   report   din   eruption

2 The house looked <u>dull and gloomy</u> in the dim light.
   staid   boring   annoying   dreary

3 I <u>put away</u> all those thoughts from my mind.
   cherished   banished   perished vanished

4 I had a <u>gnawing</u> pain in my stomach.
   distressing   squatting   trivial excessive

5 We gave up in <u>despair</u> when we failed again.
   impatience   hopelessness   sulkiness anger

6 He saw the bird <u>grasp</u> the mouse.
   cram   coerce   clutch   coax

7 She felt she had been <u>looted</u> of a precious possession.
   robbed   informed   detained retrieved

8 You have a <u>gloomy</u> look on your face, as if you have seen something horrible.
   wretched   angry   hanging   puzzled

A puzzle to solve

What are the missing letters for the spaces of this crossword puzzle? Use the given clues to solve it.

Across
1   Like
5   Gleam or twinkle
8   Did sit
9   An exclamation
10 Whether
11 Secure with a knot
13 Finish
14 Prefix meaning 'out of'

Down
1   Let itself down
2   Spanish for 'yes'
3   I – thinking
4   Goes with 'either'
6   Covered or hidden
7   Whole
12 Not out

Grammatical Sentence Patterns

Past tense with past tense

Look at the verbs in italic letters in these sentences:

They *entered* and *placed* their baskets in the way.
Thirty of them *stood* and *squeezed* together.

It is fairly common to hear someone say something like:

They *came* and *leave* baskets in the way.
or

They *ran* and *hide* in the bushes.

Can you spot the errors?

If you sometimes make mistakes like that you should spend some time practising to say the right thing to try to get the habit you need. You can use the table below to get a little practice.

Say 40 or more sentences aloud as quickly as you can, using something from box 1, something from box 2 and an ending of your own.

1	2	3
Clem and Harry The new pupil, Millicent, A few of us The audience Our old teacher The clever thief Emily The disorderly group of commuters	stood and clapped sat and cried wrote and told ran and held jumped and caught turned and saw lifted and carried went and took entered and stole pushed and fought	

Some Idioms We Use

To do with cats and dogs

Discuss what the underlined English idioms in these sentences could mean.

1 The mangoes were rotting on the ground but like <u>a dog in the manger</u> he refused to let us take some.

2 After doing all that work I was <u>dog-tired</u>.

3 Everything <u>goes to the dogs</u> in this country because nobody takes care of anything.

4 Instead of starting up the quarrel again, you should <u>let sleeping dogs lie</u>.

5 He and his wife led <u>a cat and dog life</u>.
6 When people do not help one another, <u>dog eats dog</u>.
7 It's a <u>dog's life</u> trying to please everybody.

8 I couldn't come out because it began <u>to rain cats and dogs</u>.
9 We didn't want Pat to know but Ralph <u>let the cat out of the bag</u>.

Writing a Story

A ride on a bus

Most of us have ridden on a bus. Some of us do it often. So it is not difficult to remember things that we saw, heard, smelled and felt while travelling. You can use your memory of those things to make up a story of a ride on a bus.

To get a lot of memories to use, divide yourselves into groups of about six or eight and form small circles. In each group begin by deciding who the person is on the bus – a visitor, a vendor, a

schoolgirl, or somebody else – and imagine the bus is just about to start off. Let your imaginations bring whatever images they can to you and say just what you 'see' in your mind's eye, like *The conductor is shouting to a passenger*.

When you have done enough of that – perhaps for 10 minutes – go back to your desks and begin to write a story telling what you yourself imagine happening on the bus. Put down things as if they are happening now, as you write, that is in the

present tense (e.g. *The woman puts the heavy bag on her lap*).

You will notice that the writer of the poem *Jamaican Bus Ride* tells his story in the present tense and says '*is*, '*are*', '*points out*', '*are disputing*', '*a boy vanishes*' and so on.

You may use this sentence as the first sentence of your story:

The bus is already getting crowded.

Drama for Fun

A scenario to work on
Here is a small bit of a scenario. Form small groups and improvise the dialogue and the action:

Some vendors are behind their stalls calling out things they are selling and exchanging remarks about the news in the newspapers and on the television. Mike, who was strolling slowly to school, stands and stares at the things on sale. He thinks about how delicious they must taste. A vendor asks him what he wants and tries to encourage him to buy this, then that, then something else, and so on. Mike in turn asks how much for this, for that, and so on. Then he asks for something in particular. The vendor begins to hand it to him. Mike takes out his money, but it is not enough. He stammers in embarrassment. Some of the vendors laugh and make unkind remarks. But the vendor says he has a son just like Mike and he doesn't think the others should make fun of Mike. He gives Mike what he wants and tells him to keep his money. Mike takes it shyly and reluctantly and then expresses his thanks as he slowly walks away. All the vendors look at him with kindness on their faces and make kind remarks.

9 No Meal For Hungry-Belly

Everyday Life

Labels people put on people
Discuss this in your spare time.

Just like the labels on goods in supermarkets, a label (or stereotype) is often put on a person because he or she is of a certain race or from a certain place.

For instance, people often put a label on a Chinese person by saying that Chinese people are inscrutable (mysterious). They say that is typical of Chinese people. And there are other labels put on other people.

Can you remember hearing any of them?

What labels have you heard applied to

teenagers, women, teachers, people from a particular Caribbean country, Americans?

Would you say that every person or individual of a group is exactly like every other one of the group?

What should you do when you hear somebody label a person with a popular stereotype?

Should people try to persuade others and get them to follow their opinions by using such labels or stereotypes?

How do you think that your education can help you to refuse to accept stereotypes?

Reading to Enjoy a Story

Getting ready
Do you remember a time when something people needed was scarce in the shops or supermarkets? What did people do to get some of what was still in the shop? Did some people get it while others did not? Or was it equally shared out? Did everybody behave in a fair and just way?

In the short story from which the excerpt is taken there is a shortage of something people need and they crowd into the supermarket to try to get some. But not

everybody believes in equal sharing, or even that poor people are more important than dogs. When you read the excerpt look closely at the behaviour of Mrs Gregory.

incredulously (l. 10) = hardly believing
elevated (l. 41) = raised higher
a second-generation Jamaican (ll. 40–41) = someone who was born in Jamaica but whose parents came from elsewhere
typical (l. 42) = usual or normal for that type
inscrutability (l. 43) = mysteriousness

A small security guard with a huge German Shepherd on a leash barred my way into the supermarket.

'I just need a bag of corn meal,' I told him.

'Yu can't go een.'

5 'For the dogs,' I said. I put out my hand to pat his animal.

'Hey!' He dragged the dog away. 'Him wi' bite yu.'

'Not me,' I said. 'He'll bite if you order him to; or if he smells fear. But I'm not afraid of dogs.'

I patted the dog's head and its tail twitched, a mere suggestion
10 of a wag. The guard looked at me incredulously. I smiled down at him.

'Please let me pass.'

He glanced behind him into the supermarket, then back at me. 'A riot goin' on in dere, yu know.'

15 'I'm not afraid.'

He scratched his head. 'Ah don't even tink dem have any corn meal.'

'Allow me to go and find out for myself, officer. The manager knows me and usually keeps back a few scarce items in the
20 storeroom for me. I'm Mrs Gregory.'

'Mrs Gregory?' he echoed. Clearly didn't know me. Probably didn't read the newspapers.

I told him who I was, or rather who my husband was. Reluctantly he stepped aside.

25 'Well, try yu luck, Mrs Gregory. But ah don't tink yu can get pass dem women inside just now. Maybe when de police come.'

'The police have been sent for?'

The little man nodded. 'Is only police can control dem women when dem start gwaan like – like – animals.'

30 'What's the problem?' I asked.

He shrugged. 'Dem tink de manager hoarding scarce goods in de storeroom, flour, an rice, an soap. Se dem trying to bruk down de door.'

'I'm sure the manager bought whatever goods he has with
35 hard-earned cash,' I said. 'They're his, and he's entitled to do whatever he wants with them. I'll bet if their neighbours tried to break down their walls to get their goods they'd be extremely annoyed.'

I went inside and walked over to the manager, a pleasant, well-
40 dressed Chinese gentleman of about forty – a second-generation Jamaican. From the little elevated cubicle that

served as his office, he was watching – with typical Chinese
inscrutability – the dozen or so women who were yelling at the
top of their voices while they beat against the storeroom's
45 drawn steel shutter.

'Good morning, Mr Lowe,' I said. 'I'm sorry about this little
trouble you're having.'

'Lue,' he said. 'Good morning, Mrs Gregory.'

'You know, Mr Lue,' I continued, 'the one thing that's wrong
50 with this country is that it's overpopulated.'

He glanced at me briefly, then back at the howling pack of
women. They weren't harming the shutter, but I suspected he
was worried about them turning to the goods on the shelves.

'Really, Mrs Gregory?' he said.

55 'Sure. You have a big supermarket here. If you didn't have so
many hungry-belly creatures to cater to –' I indicated the mob
'– and their hungry-belly offspring, the goods you store here
would be quite adequate.'

He glanced at me again. Inscrutably. I wondered if he hadn't
60 understood my point.

'In other words,' I explained, 'your goods are only scarce
because so many people want them.'

He smiled. 'You may be right. And how can I help you today?'

'I need about ten pounds of corn meal,' I said. 'For the dogs.'

65 He looked grave. 'We have only a little corn meal left, you know, and they want it.' He glanced at the women and hesitated. 'Couldn't you buy some of the tinned dog food for today?'

'Oh, I have lots of the tinned stuff. But I need the meal to mix
70 with it. At three dollars a tin, it's too expensive to feed my four dogs with tinned meat alone.'

'I see. Well, could you wait awhile? As soon as the police get those women out of the store, I'll be able to get to the corn meal.'

75 'They won't be long, will they?'

'I hope not,' he said, eyeing the women.

I frowned. 'You can never tell with the police though, can you? They might be in the middle of a domino game or something. Tell me, is anyone in the storeroom?'

80 'A couple of packers. Why?'

'I wonder if I could persuade them to pass me the corn meal?'

He shook his head. 'You'd never get past those viragos. I think you should wait.'

Smiling at him, I said, 'My husband's favourite adage is:
85 "Nothing tried, nothing done".'

From the short story *Dog Food* By Michael Reckord, JAMAICA

Discussion for developing comprehension skills

A Understanding explicit statements:

1 How was Mrs Gregory barred at the door of the supermarket?
2 Why did she want a bag of corn meal?
3 How did the dog behave towards her?
4 What did the women inside believe about the manager?
5 What were they doing?
6 Where was the manager?
7 How did Mrs Gregory explain why goods became scarce?
8 What did the manager tell Mrs Gregory she should use instead of corn meal?

9 Why did he ask her to '*wait awhile*' (l. 72)?
10 '*You can never tell with the police though*' (l. 77). What did Mrs Gregory mean by that?

B Using context clues:

1 How does '*didn't know me*' (l. 21) give a clue to the meaning of '*reluctantly*' (l. 24)?
2 In what way is the phrase '*scarce goods*' (l. 31) linked to the meaning of '*hoarding*' (l. 31)?

3 What is the clue that tells the meaning of '*cubicle*' (l. 41)?

4 Tell which word or phrase is a clue to the meaning of each of these words: '*indicated*' (l. 56)   '*adequate*' (l. 58) '*viragos*' (l. 82)   '*adage*' (l. 84)

C Seeing implied connections:

1 What do you suppose Mrs Gregory did after quoting her husband's favourite adage?

2 Why did the guard look at Mrs Gregory '*incredulously*' (l. 10)?

3 According to Mrs Gregory, how did the manager give some people special treatment?

4 '*... he stepped aside*' (l. 24). Why?

5 How is the guard shown to lack the schooling that Mrs Gregory and Mr Lue had?

6 What would you say was the guard's attitude to the crowd of women in the supermarket?

7 How did Mrs Gregory show that she felt superior to Mr Lue?

8 Which sentences of Mr Lue show that he would sell Mrs Gregory what she wanted?

9 Say what you think Mrs Gregory's attitude was to the people in the supermarket.

To Enrich Your Word Bank

Using words you read

In teams of three or four consider which one of these words fits into each sentence.

*incredulously   reluctant   hoard
inscrutable   indicate   adequate
persuade   adage*

1 Do you know the old _____ 'Grasp all, lose all'?

2 Misers _____ their money and refuse to spend any.

3 The directions you gave me were not _____ enough.

4 When I saw the risk I was _____ to take the chance.

5 People use various tricks to _____ others to agree with them.

6 The painting of the Mona Lisa shows her with an _____ expression on her face.

7 You must give me some sign to _____ when the teacher is coming.

8 They were staring _____ at the limbo dancers.

Words related in meaning

Discuss what word, related in meaning to the one in brackets after the sentence, best fits into the gap in the sentence.

1 It seems that the set was stolen by a clever _____. (*theft*)

2 My sister always needs a _____ to go shopping with her. (*company*)

3 The _____ of the water made it sparkle. (*pure*)

4 We must not be _____ of those who succeed. (*envy*)

5 The postman makes an early _____ on Monday mornings. (*deliver*)

6 Taking all things into _____ it was not a bad effort. (*consider*)

7 My uncle had to take over the _____ of the store. (*manage*)

8 In some places the _____ give helpful and polite service. (*attention*)

9 The park is used by all the _____ of the area. (*residence*)

10 If you help a wrongdoer you are just as _____. (*culprit*)

Choosing the right word

Discuss together which one of the four words given with each sentence best fits into the sentence.

1 Mark was told not to _____ into Mr Singh's business.
invade   control   intrude   dare

2 Stephanie was so _____ she fooled most people.
inadequate   cunning   expensive   agile

3 There was an _____ amount of damage done by the storm.
extensive   incredulous   annoyed   elevated

4 Many people have cages to keep birds in _____.
creativity   scarcity   inscrutability   captivity

5 She showed how _____ she was by dodging the falling branch.
superior   insensitive   agile   persuasive

6 I wonder if they really feel _____ concern for me.
suspicious   genuine   typical   scarce

7 One of the boys made a serious _____ against a girl.
accusation   plea   confession   omission

8 I came to the _____ that he was dishonest.
responsibility   temptation   conclusion   corruption

GRAMMAR

Grammatical Sentence Patterns

Using 'could have' with 'had'

Look at this sentence:

Before I could have *said Jack Robinson he had shinnied up that tree.*

1	2	3	4	5	6
Before		could have	turned around said anything opened my mouth put it down decided what to do		had shut the door had broken the seal had swallowed the pill had removed the cover

Now use the table to say as many sentences as you can using *could have*, putting your own words or phrases in columns 2 and 5.

Using a Dictionary

Words with several meanings
If you look for the word *bowl* in a dictionary you would see that at least two meanings are given for it: (1) a round, deep basin; (2) deliver a ball.

Many words in English carry more than one meaning, and when you use a dictionary to look for the meaning of a word that you read in a book you have to take the meaning that fits the context where you found the word.

As an exercise, arrange these words in alphabetical order and find at least two meanings for each in a dictionary.

gear   desert   beat   point   dash
entrance   brake   pound   pass   suspect
raise   fly

Writing a Conversation

In dialogue form
One way of writing a conversation between people is to set it down in the form of a dialogue, like this:

Mrs Gregory: Good morning, Mr Lowe. I'm sorry about this little trouble you're having.

Mr Lue: Lue, not Lowe. Good morning, Mrs Gregory.

Mrs Gregory: You know, Mr Lue, the one thing that's wrong with this country is that it's overpopulated.

Notice that the names are in a margin by themselves and that after each name there is a colon (:).

Writing a dialogue or conversation between people is easy to do and can be good fun. To get some fun doing it divide yourselves into groups of six and make up a short conversation in your group between the security guard, Mrs Gregory and Mr Lue. Then go back to your desks and write it in the form of a dialogue.

Or write, in the form of a dialogue, the part of the conversation between Mrs Gregory and Mr Lue beginning with '*Oh, I have lots of the tinned stuff*' and ending with '*Nothing tried, nothing done*'.

About the Language

Subject and predicate

Every sentence has two main parts: a part which tells what the sentence is about, called the *subject* part, and a part which says something about whatever the sentence is about, called the *predicate* part.

The predicate part has the verb or 'doing word' in it. Consider this sentence:

A bunch of the boys whooped it up.

It can be divided into its two parts like this:

a   *A bunch of boys* (subject part)
b   *whooped it up* (predicate part)

Sometimes a sentence is turned around or inverted like this:

The last to drink was Dangerous Dan McGrew.

In the normal or usual way that would be:

Dangerous Dan McGrew was the last to drink.

So its two parts are:

c   *Dangerous Dan McGrew* (subject)

d   *was the last to drink* (predicate)

Very often the subject part is somewhere inside the sentence, as in:

Then all of a sudden the music changed.

The subject there is *the music* and the predicate is *changed then all of a sudden*.

How do you find the subject part in sentences? Well, usually it is a matter of common sense, but if you are in doubt use this rule:

Find the verb and put who or what before it to ask the question Who –? or What –?

For example, with the sentence *Then all of a sudden the music changed*, ask *What changed*? The answer will be the subject of the sentence.

Why do you have to know the subject and predicate of a sentence?

- for better comprehension
- to use the correct forms of verbs
- to see if a sentence is complete.

Now, for practice, divide these sentences into their subject and predicate parts by finding the verb and asking the question *Who* (+ *verb*)? or *What* (+ *verb*)?

1   I turned my head.
2   His eyes went round the room.
3   The stranger stumbles across the room.
4   There stumbled a miner fresh from the creeks.
5   Back of the bar, in a solo game, sat Dangerous Dan McGrew.
6   The rag-time kid was having a drink.
7   Then with a crash the music stopped.
8   Till at last that old piano came into his gaze.
9   On the bar he tilted a poke of dust.
10 Out went the lights.
11 The thought came back of an ancient wrong.
12 In the end the two men paid with their lives.

10 A Desperate Plan

Everyday Life

Saying words correctly

Whenever you have some spare time, give your attention to this.

There are two ways to say *protest*, two ways to say *progress*, and two ways to say *contest*. One way is to put the stress or emphasis on the first syllable, as in these sentences:

We wanted to take part in the cóntest. (Noun)
You are making good prógress. (Noun)
He's lodging a prótest against the decision. (Noun)

The other way is to put the emphasis or stress on the second syllable, as in these sentences:

You must not contést the umpire's decision. (Verb)
If you progréss quickly you will save time. (Verb)
What do you want to protést about? (Verb)

You have to get the habit of saying each one in the right way when you speak, and the right way depends on whether you use the word as a noun (name) or as a verb (doing word).

Read these sentences aloud to practise putting the stress on the correct syllable.

1 The cóntest is being held in the school.
2 Several calypsonians will contést for the prize.
3 What prógress are you making?
4 Try to progréss as fast as you can.
5 A prótest was sent in to the judges.

6 Why do you protést so much about the marks?
7 There is an annual cóntest to choose the best costume.
8 All the candidates will contést against one another.
9 The results show you what prógress has been made.
10 The traffic will progréss very slowly on that road.
11 There was a loud prótest against the referee's decision.
12 Everybody will protést against a higher price.

Take note that Americans and many Canadians now put the stress on the second syllable of all such words. In American English many words are pronounced in an un-English way and spelt in an un-English way. For example Americans pronounce *route* as rowt not as root, and spell *labour* as *labor*.

Reading to Enjoy a Story

Getting ready

In this part of a story Sunny's mother, Rannie, seems to be dying of thirst because they had no water in their village for months, except in Rampersad's well where they could not get it.

Sunny's father, Manko, sets out to do something very risky without telling Sunny about it.

See what happens.

brooding (l. 1) = thinking sadly
delirious (l. 18) = raving like a mad person

desperate (l. 24) = reckless because there is no choice
intrusion (l. 48) = unwanted entry
cautiously (l. 59) = very carefully

All day, Sunny sat in the hut brooding over the matter, trying hard to understand why his mother should die from lack of water when a well was filled in another man's yard.

5 It was late in the evening when Manko returned. As he had expected, the river was nearly dry, a foul trickle of mud not worth drinking. He found the boy quiet and moody. After a while, Sunny went out.

Manko was glad to be alone. He didn't want Sunny to see him leaving the hut later in the night, with the bucket and the rope.
10 It would be difficult to explain that he was stealing Rampersad's water only because it was a matter of life or death.

He waited impatiently for Rannie to fall asleep. It seemed she would never close her eyes. She just turned and twisted restlessly, and once she looked at him and asked if rain had
15 fallen, and he put his rough hand on her hot forehead and said softly no, but that he had seen a sign that evening, a great black cloud low down in the east.

Then suddenly her fever rose again, and she was delirious. This time he could not understand what she said. She was
20 moaning in a queer, strangled way.

It was midnight before she fell into a kind of swoon, a red flush on her face. Manko knew what he must do now. He stood looking at her, torn between the fear of leaving her and the desperate plan that he had made. She might die while he was
25 gone, and yet – he must try it.

He frowned as he went out and saw the moon like a night sun in the sky, lighting up the village. He turned to the east and his heart leapt as he saw the cloud moving towards the village in a slow breeze. It seemed so far away, and it was moving as if it
30 would take days to get over the fields. Perhaps it would; perhaps it would change direction and go scudding down into the west, and not a drop of water.

He moved off towards the well, keeping behind the huts and deep into the trees. It took him ten minutes to get near the
35 barbed wire fence, and he stood in the shadow of a giant silk-cotton tree. He leaned against the trunk and drew in his breath sharply as his eyes discerned a figure on the other side of the well, outside the barbed wire.

The figure stopped, as though listening, then began clambering
40 over the fence.

Even as he peered to see if he could recognise who it was, a
sudden darkness fell as the cloud swept over the moon in the
freshening wind.

Manko cast his eyes upwards swiftly, and when he looked down
45 again the figure was on the brink of the well, away from the
sleeping watchdog.

It was a great risk to take; it was the risk Manko himself had
to take. But this intrusion upset his plan. He could not call out;
the slightest sound would wake the dog, and what it did not do
50 to the thief, Rampersad would do with his shotgun.

For a moment, Manko's heart failed him. He smelt death very
near – for the unknown figure at the well, and for himself, too.
He had been a fool to come. Then a new frenzy seized him. He
remembered the cruel red flush on Rannie's cheeks when he had
55 left her. Let her die happy, if a drop of water could make her so.
Let her live, if a drop of water could save her. His own thirst
flared in his throat; how much more she must be suffering!

He saw the bucket slide noiselessly down and the rope paid out.
Just what he had planned to do. Now draw it up, cautiously, yes,
60 and put it to rest gently on the ground. Now kneel and take a
drink, and put the fire out in your body. For God's sake, why
didn't the man take a drink? What was he waiting for? Ah, that
was it, but be careful, do not make the slightest noise, or
everything will be ruined. Bend your head down ...

65 Moonrays shot through a break in the cloud and lit up the
scene.

It was Sunny.

From a short story *A Drink of Water* By Samuel Selvon, TRINIDAD

Discussion for developing comprehension skills

A Understanding explicit statements:

1 What was Sunny 'brooding' (l. 1) about?
2 'Manko was glad to be alone' (l. 8). Why?
3 Say what 'torn between' (l. 23) means.
4 What lit up the village?
5 Where was Manko when he 'discerned a figure' (l. 37)?
6 What prevented Manko when he tried to 'recognise who it was' (l. 41)?
7 'He could not call out' (l. 48). Why not?
8 'Manko's heart failed him' (l. 51). What do you think that means?
9 What did Manko see the figure of the person do?
10 What happened when 'moonrays ... lit up the scene' (ll. 65–66)?

B Using context clues:

1 Why is the phrase 'his eyes' (l. 37) a clue to the meaning of 'discerned' (l. 37)?
2 How does 'over the fence' (l. 40) serve as a clue to the meaning of 'clambering' (l. 39)?
3 Whether you know what these words mean or not, find clues that would help someone to make a guess at their meanings:
'moaning' (l. 20)   'swoon' (l. 21)
'frenzy' (l. 53)

C Seeing implied connections:

1 What was Manko's 'desperate plan' (l. 24)?
2 Why didn't Manko 'want Sunny to see him leaving the hut later in the night' (ll. 8–9)?
3 Why did he frown when he saw the moon?
4 '... his heart leapt' (ll. 27–28). Why?
5 When he saw a figure why did he draw in his breath sharply?

6 Why did Manko feel 'a new frenzy' (l. 53)?
7 Find sentences where Manko is silently giving advice to the person at the well.
8 What was Sunny planning to do when he was 'quiet and moody' (l. 6)?
9 Where did Sunny go when he 'went out' (l. 7)?
10 Why do you suppose Sunny and Manko kept their plans from each other?

To Enrich Your Word Bank

Using words you read

Put your heads together and find the sentence into which each of these words fits.

*foul   restless   delirious   swoon
desperate   discern   clamber   intrusion
frenzy   cautious*

1 She was a _____ person who never took risks.
2 Passing the swamp I was aware of a _____ smell.
3 When they heard the news she got into a _____.
4 The children were so _____ they could not sleep.
5 To escape from the dog I had to _____ up a tree.
6 If you do not eat for days you would probably _____ from weakness.
7 In the dark I could not _____ anything clearly.
8 The man was so _____ he was ready to risk his life.
9 It is an _____ to enter where you are not invited.
10 From his wild talk I concluded he was _____.

Word relationships

Get into groups and use your ideas and common sense to find the missing words for each of the columns. The first one is done for you.

Verb	Noun	Adjective
expect	expectation	expectant
intrude	_____	intrusive
explain	_____	explanatory
live	life	_____
_____	sharpness	sharp
conclude	_____	conclusive
act	action	_____
create	creation	_____
lose	_____	lost
_____	circle	circular
_____	strength	strong

The prefix pre-

The prefix *pre-* in a word tells that something comes or goes *before* something else, as in the words *prefix* and *preliminary*.

See if you can spot what comes or goes before something else in the meaning of each of these words:

precede   prepare   prevent   prefect
predict   prefer   premier   preliminary
prejudice   premature   prescribe
preface   presume   preview   preserve

that would not be a complete sentence. It does not say what happened as he had expected.

But quite often a clause like *As he had expected* is written by students and others as if it is a complete sentence. So, writing complete sentences is one of the main things you should have been learning to do.

If you have not yet mastered that, the exercise below is to help you to get the habit of making complete sentences.

The beginning of a sentence is given. Say it and add your own ending to complete it, saying each complete sentence loudly for everyone to hear. Take turns around and around the class until the time is used up.

1 Then suddenly a figure _____.
2 Before leaving the hut _____.
3 Keeping near the trees _____.
4 As she tossed on the bed _____.
5 In a mad frenzy _____.
6 As if he was not afraid _____.
7 Now and again as the clouds moved _____.
8 But what he saw _____.
9 Not having any water _____.
10 With the bucket down the well _____.

Grammatical Sentence Patterns

Completion of sentences

Read this sentence:

As he had expected, the river was nearly dry.

If someone writes just

As he had expected

Spelling

Some words you need

These are some words used in the excerpt about Manko that you must be able to spell since you will need them when you write.

If at first you cannot 'see' the missing letter or letters in your mind, find the word in the excerpt and then try to 'see' it with your eyes closed again and again until you can.

mat_er   qu_ _t   st_aling   r_ _gh   sof_ly
fev_r   desp_rat_   vi_ _age   min_tes
su_ _en   ri_k   s_ _zed   k_eel   n_ _se
s_ene   th_rs_

A 'battle' with -able and -ible

Look carefully at the words in the columns below so that you can write them when necessary. Then have a 'battle' between two teams, shooting words at each other to be spelt.

Here's how to battle:

No. 1 of Team A asks No. 1 of Team B to spell a word. If he or she spells the word correctly he or she wins a point for Team B, and then asks No. 1 of Team A to spell a word to win a point for Team A. If both spell the word asked, the action moves on to the next pair. However, if someone fails to spell a word correctly, the person who asked the question must spell it to win the point.

-able

valuable   reliable
movable   agreeable
believable   reasonable
desirable   provable
noticeable   indispensable
observable   indescribable

-ible

visible   digestible
sensible   incredible
possible   indelible
responsible   flexible
edible   flexible
divisible   legible

Writing a Story

Completing what happened

Here is the first paragraph of a short story. Read it and exchange ideas about what could have happened after Mark stood at the door. You may have the discussion in small groups.

Then return to your desks and sit quietly and think how you yourself would prefer to carry on the story.

When you have the things happening fixed in your mind, begin to write the rest of the story and finish it at home.

The school was settling down to a quiet buzz. The bell had been rung a long time before. Classes had assembled and marched in. Mark ran up the steps two at a time and stood at the door wondering what to do. He felt like pelting away and going back home or somewhere. He could see the eyes of some of the students looking at him. He was late again.

Words in Literature

Accents and rhythm

Remember that certain words or syllables are stressed or emphasised or accented on speaking English, as you saw in Unit 7.

In reading these lines from a poem you would probably put the stress or emphasis in your voice on the words with the accent mark (´).

> Me óne, wáy oút in the crówd,
> I blów the soúnds, the páin
> but nót a sóul
> would cóme insíde my wórld
> or téll me hów it trúe

From *Valley Prince* By Mervyn Morris,
JAMAICA

If you change the words to
ti TUM, TUM TUM ti ti TUM,
ti TUM, ti TUM, ti TUM

and so on, you would hear the rhythm the poet has put into the poem.

Now, see if you can pick out the words or syllables where the beat or accent falls in each case below, and hear the rhythm the writer has put into the lines.

a   Sweet day, so cool, so calm, so bright
    The bridal of the earth and sky.
    George Herbert, ENGLAND

b   All that I know
    Of a certain star
    Is, it can throw
    (Like the angled span)
    Now a dart of red,
    Now a dart of blue
    Robert Browning, ENGLAND

c   Tiger! Tiger! burning bright
    In the forests of the night
    William Blake, ENGLAND

d   The sea is calm tonight.
    The tide is full, the moon lies fair
    Upon the straits; – on the French
    coast the light
    Gleams and is gone; the cliffs of
    England stand,
    Glimmering and vast, out in the
    tranquil bay.
    Matthew Arnold, ENGLAND

11 Too Much, Too Little

Everyday Life

The point in a comic strip

You and your friends might talk about this comic strip during a recess. What is it saying?

Reading to Learn Things

Getting ready

Like air to breathe, we need some kind of food to eat. Do all people in the world have enough food? What do you think can be done so that everybody in the world can get enough to eat?

See what the writer of this article suggests, and compare his ideas with yours.

problem (l. 2) = something that causes difficulty or hardship
technology (l. 13) = ways of making or doing things
hectare (l. 17) = an area of land, about 2.471 acres
protein (l. 38) = a component needed in our food, especially for making and repairing our flesh

If there are more people in the world, then there must be more food to feed these people. But food is already a problem in today's world. A third of the world's population (30%) is starving, because there is not enough food. Ten thousand
5   people die of hunger every day, in some parts of the world. But in other parts of the world, people become ill or die because they eat too much food, and they are too fat. Some countries have no food, but others have too much, and they throw it away. How can Tomorrow's World feed its people?

10   The world needs to produce more food than it produces now. Scientists say that there are many parts of the world which could use their land better and grow more food. They say that there will be new technology and new ways to grow food in the next 50–100 years. These are some of the things that they say
15   the world can do about the food problem in different countries:

Brazil – if we make the soil better and stop the rain washing it away, then there will be 450 million hectares to use for food.

Peru and Chile – if we use water from the sea, then 50 million hectares of land along the coast could produce food.

20   United States of America – if we pay higher prices to the farmers, they will grow more food and use more land. In the USA there are 100 million hectares of land to use.

The Sahara Desert, Africa — 500–700 million hectares of land could produce food if we bring water to the desert.

25 **Factory food**

We can grow food in tall glass buildings. We don't need soil. We can use pipes which take food to the plants. The sun will give heat for the plants to grow all the year round, especially if the buildings are in the desert or on high ground.

30 **The sea and fish farming**

We will grow fish like plants in fields. The water will not be very deep. The water heat will make the fish grow bigger and faster. Farmers will put oxygen into the water, and planes will drop food on the sea. Scientists say that there are already
35 enough fish in the Indian Ocean to feed all of India for a hundred years, and in the Antarctic Sea there are so many tiny fish called 'krill' that it is impossible to use them all.

Protein

With protein, we can feed the world. If we can't get enough
40 protein from meat or fish, then the scientists say they can make it from almost anything. We can see a future without meat. Real meat will disappear and slowly people will stop liking it – they will find the taste of animal meat too strong.

A writer who lived in the 18th century said that the more food
45 we have, the more people we will have to feed. Because of this, there will always be hunger. Many people still believe this. Others say that the plans to grow more food are impossible and they ask 'Who will give the money for the new farms? Who will control the food? Who will sell it? and who will keep the
50 money?' The governments of different countries need to work with each other but they cannot agree now, so how can they agree in the future?

From *Spotlight on Tomorrow's World* By Clive Riche, ENGLAND

Discussion for developing comprehension skills

A Understanding explicit statements:

1 What is meant by '*the world's population*' (l. 3)?

2 According to the article, how much hunger is there in the world?

3 While some people starve, how does food kill people in other parts of the world?

4 How do scientists think all people can get enough food?

5 What do scientists say should be done in Brazil? (Find Brazil on a map.)

6 Using water from the sea, what would happen in Peru and Chile? (Find Peru and Chile on a map.)

7 A desert is a place where little or nothing grows. What could make the Sahara Desert give people food? (Find the Sahara Desert on a map of Africa.)

8 '*We don't need soil*' (l. 26). How could food be grown without soil?

9 How could people get enough fish as food?

10 Why did an 18th century writer say there will always be hunger in the world?

B Seeing implied connections:

1 Which two reasons are given for why the world needs to produce more food than it produces now?
2 Where do we now mostly get protein?
3 What does the writer say US farmers would do if they were paid more money?
4 Why do you think so many people are left to die of hunger every day?
5 How do plans to grow more food get stopped?
6 What do you think prevents countries with too much food giving some to those without food?

To Enrich Your Word Bank

Words related to topics

1 Here are some words related to food and starvation:
nourishment famine drought production agriculture farming yield vitamins

Try together to add at least 12 words to this list.

2 These words are related to health and disease:
diet nutrition infections immune medicine microbes bacteria resistance

Try together to add as many words as you can to this list, as long as each one can be used particularly in talking about health and disease.

3 Here are some words having to do with life in school:

attendance assembly discipline report principal detention attention recess

Take turns around the class to add at least one word each to the list.

Words related in meaning

Discuss which word related in form and meaning to the one in brackets after the sentence fits into the blank space in each sentence.

1 Heavier air _____ on lighter air. (*pressure*)
2 The gas station _____ puts pressure into the tyres. (*attended*)
3 Some nations were divided by _____ warfare. (*tribe*)
4 Hannibal wanted to be _____ of many places. (*conquest*)
5 The factory is used for the _____ of furniture only. (*product*)
6 It was the custom to _____ captured enemies. (*slave*)
7 The slaves stumbled in a long _____ down the avenue. (*process*)
8 They said it was _____ to sacrifice some slaves. (*custom*)

GRAMMAR

Grammatical Sentence Patterns

Words in the right order

This is a sentence with the words properly arranged:

We will grow fish like plants in fields.

The words of that sentence could be scrambled or mixed up, like this:

fish like – in fields – plants – grow – we will

Now look at these scrambled words of a sentence:

more food – needs – the world – to produce

What sentence do you get when you put those words in the right order?

Here it is:

The world needs to produce more food.

Now, here are some sentences that have got scrambled up and need to be straightened out. See if you can unscramble them and put the words and phrases in the right order to make grammatical sentences.

Work together in teams of about six or eight.

1 survive – to – must – struggle – people
2 vapour – into – the – turns – water
3 live – she – but – does – where
4 is – called – in a secure – the gold – vault – kept – place – a
5 which – but he – backgammon – game – plays – always – is – a silly
6 burned – the petrol – to the – to be – has – pumped – carburettor – to be – cylinders – in the – burned
7 excites – a story – just as – condiments – a meal – more details – carries – flat and unpalatable – so – if – it tastes – better – needs – if it – or amuses
8 of the world – called cartons – the parts – are sent – cardboard boxes – in large – the imports – of the countries – through

Punctuation Signals

Commas

If you are tempted to think that you need not spend time practising using punctuation marks, or that you could leave it until you have to do your school-leaving examination, look at the comic strip on page 84.

A little comma could make something you write become clear or could change what you want to write into something else.

Look at what the commas do to the two sentences (a and b) on page 84:

Peanuts

a   I can tell you, as president of the club you'll get a hearty welcome.
b   I can tell you, as president of the club, you'll get a hearty welcome.

Sentence a means the president of a club is being spoken to.
Sentence b means the president of a club is speaking.

Where should commas be put in these sentences?

1   There was a big tree at the corner of the path and kneeling there in a patch of tall grass weeds and flowers they could observe all that was happening.

2   The children's friend Barry sat and wrote his letters there and the boys could see him sitting which meant he did not want to be disturbed.

3   The bright lights had been put on but there was still a dim vague shadowiness in the corner and the place looked dangerous.

4   The moon was brighter now gleaming on the stones the water and the leaves turning the thick grass the tall branches and the smooth tree trunks into silver.

Commas with names of persons spoken to

What do you notice about the commas in these sentences?

1   'But she'll catch us, Roy.'
2   'It's not me, ma'am.'
3   'Come on down here, you little monkey.'
4   'It's you, Roy,' I accused him.
5   'Answer me, boy!'

In each case the name or name phrase for the person spoken to is separated from the rest of the sentence by a comma. Look again and see.

Now, where are commas missing in these sentences?

1   'I think we'll be late John.'
2   'I didn't do it Sir.'
3   'This is yours Merle,' she pointed out.
4   'Get away from there all of you.'
5   'Put it down girl.'
6   'I'm listening to you Miss.'
7   'Look Mike the sun is setting.'
8   'Class get out your folders.'
9   'Take your turn you disorderly ruffians.'
10   'You're just in time Lena,' I said.

Commas, apostrophes, quotation marks

Pick out the commas, apostrophes and quotation marks in these sentences and discuss what each one is there for:

1   'It's not me, ma'am,' he said.
2   'I'm sure he didn't take what's yours,' Mrs Mark stated.
3   'You're making sure we'll be late for John's party,' Maxine cried.

4 'He's here, but she's not, so we'll all have to wait,' I complained.

Writing a Letter to a Friend

To give information

Suppose a friend attending another school had to write a report for his or her class and wrote to you asking you to tell him or her what you know about an organisation of people that helps other people, like the Salvation Army or the Red Cross.

You should get together with one or two of your friends in your class and talk about the questions you have answers for, and write those questions down in the order in which they should be answered. For example, *What is the name of the organisation? What does it do? How does it get money?* and so on.

When you have all the questions in the right order and the information to answer each one, you may begin to write the letter.

Remember how to put your address and the date in the right place, and *Dear …* on the other side. End up with something like:

Your friend,   *Sincerely,*   *As ever,*
Josie   *Bob*   *Rick*

Words in Literature

Rhythm

The feeling or mood that a poem makes us get is partly, if not largely, brought to us by the rhythm or beat in the words. That is why it is important to be able to let the words bring you their rhythm.

Here is a line marked where the accents or stresses in the voice would fall:

I have seén old ships sáil like swáns asléep.

It goes:

ti ti TUM ti ti TUM ti TUM ti TUM

Which syllables or words would your voice give the stress to in this line?

I come from haunts of coot and hern.

Now, to get your ear more sensitive, say each of these bits of poetry aloud to find the syllables or words that must get greater stress than the others so that you feel the rhythm of the words.

1 If, in response to the sobbing
   Of wheels consuming miles of rail

   Cecil Herbert, TRINIDAD

2 Steel drum steel drum
   hit the hot calypso dancing
   hot sun hot sun
   who goin' stop this bacchanalling?

   Edward Braithwaite, BARBADOS

3 From a church across the street

   Children repeat
   Hail Mary, full of grace
   Skipping the syllables; Follow-the-leader pace.

   Barbara Ferland, JAMAICA

4 Nothing can soak
   Brother Joe's tough sermon
   his head swollen
   with certainties

   When he lifts up a s'liff
   you can't stop him,
   and the door to God, usually shut
   gives in a rainbow gust.

   Anthony McNeill, JAMAICA

5 Walking from that corner
   where the street butts the Square
   you could pass an entrance
   armoured with cobblestones
   and not know it was there.

   Cecil Gray, TRINIDAD

6 Here in this remote corner,
   This neglected fringe of a fishing village,
   Bare with the sea-blast, where only
   Cactus flaunt their flagpoles in the sun.

   Frank Collymore, BARBADOS

12 Fighting A Bully

Everyday Life

Hardship happens

Do you agree with the opinion that what happens in real life should be hidden from young people like yourselves? In your spare time consider what this poem is saying.

Lies

Telling lies to the young is wrong.
Proving to them that lies are true is wrong.
Telling them that God's in his heaven
and all's well with the world is wrong.
The young know what you mean. The young are people.
Tell them the difficulties can't be counted,
and let them see not only what will be
but see with clarity these present times.
Say obstacles exist they must encounter,
sorrow happens, hardship happens.
The hell with it. Who never knew
the price of happiness will not be happy.
Forgive no error you recognise,
it will repeat itself, increase,
and afterwards our pupils
will not forgive in us what we forgave.

Yevgeny Yevtushenko, SOVIET UNION

Reading to Enjoy a Story

Getting ready

Have you ever known someone who was a bully, forcing others like him or her to do what he or she wanted? How did you feel about it? Did you have a fight with the bully?

The excerpt you are going to read comes from a novel in which a boy, Jester, used his strength against others. Milton and his brother had left their fish pot in the river overnight to catch fish. What do you think happened?

jester (l. 10) = joker or comic
bung (l. 15) = stopper for a hole

The next morning Milton and I woke a bit before dawn and
went down to the river where we had put the pot in the
previous evening. There was fog lying in the valley and it
looked like a swab of cotton and the trees lacked sharp outlines
5 in the thin darkness. We squatted in a clump of shrubs and
waited. That someone who was drawing our pot couldn't have
been earlier than us. We didn't have to wait long either before
our quarry came along. And who was that quarry? Thank you
very much: that's as good a guess as any I have ever heard.

10 Jester indeed!

He was sure of himself, sure that he was minutes ahead of me,
because he didn't waste time with such preliminaries as
looking around him for anyone. He proceeded straight-away to
draw the pot. We allowed him to do so and to start pulling the
15 bung out. Then Milton said, 'Drop it!'

Sure he was frightened, this Jester, at being caught red-
handed, but he wasn't the one to run. He did not drop the pot
either, but when Milton and I stood up and walked out of our
hiding place, Jester's face underwent a change. Fright changed
20 into belligerence on that round dirty face.

'Who you talkin' to?' he asked.
'You,' Milton said, walking towards him. 'That pot is not yours.
You are a thief!'

'You callin' me a thief?'

25 'Yes,' Milton said. 'You are a sneak thief.'

This I considered strong language for Milton to use to Jester,
because he was no match for the bully. Milton was thirteen and
Jester, if anything, must have been fifteen and going on
sixteen.

30 To understand Jester's power one would have to have a
knowledge of his capacity. He wasn't called Jester because he
was a joker or a comedian. No, he got his name from a special
kind of pot called a jester pot. The story went that the bully
had eaten off, in a single go, all the yam boiled in a full jester
35 pot that boasted a six-man capacity. Since this feat he had been
nicknamed Jester.

But the fact that Jester was a champion eater also meant that
he was strong. He must have beaten up nine out of every ten
boys in Boswell at some time or another. No one playing a
40 game with Jester could win. What I mean is, if he won, he'd
still be beaten up and, knowing this, he purposely lost to Jester
to spare himself. A boy could get beaten up by just looking at

Jester, who would say, 'Hey! What you lookin' at me for?' And he'd proceed to hit the boy. Some boys, knowing this, took steps
45 not to look at him, but this didn't save them from the all-mighty Jester. He'd demand to know what was the matter with him, why he wasn't looked at, and he'd start throwing punches even before he got an answer.

Jester was the most well-fed boy in all Boswell because so
50 many boys paid him hands-off dues in the form of food. I had seen many a boy give up his choicest fruit to Jester as a peace-offering. So I was more than surprised to hear Milton talking to Jester in such harsh terms.

He would fight, as I expected.

55 He made fists and came at Milton and the latter went on guard to meet the challenge. Jester got in a few early blows and, frankly, I feared greatly for Milton; but Jester had never learnt to organise anything, not even his strength. Milton, skipping around nimbly, avoided most of his sledge-hammer blows. Soon
60 Jester was snorting from weariness, and the fact that his punches were not going home seemed to madden him and he rushed at Milton wildly. But he didn't demolish Milton, who now began to go on to the offensive, getting in a punch or two of his own. Milton's face was blazing with concentration and I
65 cheered him on.

'Hit him, Milt! Hit him!'

Though Milton was bleeding in the nose, he was landing a few punches. He put down one on Jester's ear and it went red, and then he got another into his mouth and the foolish Jester went
70 off guard to spit and determine if he had lost a tooth or sustained a cut mouth. Milton got his opportunity to demolish his opponent and he made ample use of it at that. He let loose with a trio of swift block-busters – one to the stomach, another whammed into Jester's right cheek, and the third found a
75 landing place in the left eye. Jester squirmed and covered his eye with one hand and, excited now by his success, Milton continued to rain blows on his opponent. In the head, on the neck, on the point of the chin ... wham! and wham! and wham! The bully could take no more. He turned and showed us a pair
80 of dew-wet heels as he skimmed away.

From *The Cloud with the Silver Lining* By C. Everard Palmer,
JAMAICA

Discussion for developing comprehension skills

A Understanding explicit statements:

1 '... *our quarry came along*' (l. 8). Who or what was '*our quarry*'?
2 What was Jester '*caught red-handed*' (ll. 16–17) doing?
3 In what ways did Jester show he had power?
4 What happened when a boy played a game with Jester?
5 Which was riskier, looking at Jester or not looking at him?
6 '... *the latter*' (l. 55). Who or what does that refer to?
7 How did Milton get away from Jester's blows?
8 What made Jester rush wildly at Milton?
9 Explain what you think is meant by '*began to go on to the offensive*' (l. 63).
10 What do you understand by '*a trio of swift block-busters*' (l. 73)?
11 '... *continued to rain blows on his opponent*' (l. 77). Put that phrase into your own words.

B Using context clues:

1 How is the phrase '*had put*' (l. 2) connected with the meaning of '*previous*' (l. 3)?
2 What happens soon after the word '*belligerence*' (l. 20) that tells you what '*belligerence*' is?
3 What part of the word '*preliminaries*' (l. 12) helps to tell you what '*preliminaries*' are?
4 Find a clue to the meaning of '*feat*' (l. 35).
5 Whether you knew any of these words before or not, discuss what there is in the excerpt that helps a reader to know what each one means:

'*capacity*' (l. 35)   '*harsh*' (l. 53)
'*nimbly*' (l. 59)   '*snorting*' (l. 60)
'*demolish*' (l. 71)   '*offensive*' (l. 63)
'*sustained*' (l. 71)   '*opponent*' (l. 72)
'*ample*' (l. 72)

C Seeing implied connections:

1 Can you suggest why Jester's fright turned to '*belligerence*' (l. 20)?
2 '... *he was no match for the bully*' (l. 27). Why did the narrator think so?
3 Why did the narrator tell how Jester got his name?
4 How would you explain what '*hands-off dues*' (l. 50) are?
5 Why were Jester's punches '*not going home*' (l. 61)?
6 What gave Milton his big chance to win the fight?
7 How did Jester show in the fight that he was not very smart?
8 What kind of boy is Milton shown to you as?
9 In what way is the writer saying something about everyday life in general?

To Enrich Your Word Bank

Using words you read
Think together and find the sentence below into which each of these words fits.

previous   preliminaries   sneak   feat
demand   harsh   organise   nimbly
demolish   ample

1 He did not deserve such _____ punishment for what he did.
2 Let us _____ ourselves into a good team.
3 In the _____ of the competition our steel band did well.
4 The girl received an _____ share of the ice cream.

5 That game was not as exciting as the _____ one.
6 He got out of the way as _____ as a cat.
7 Dinah was highly praised for the _____ she performed.
8 When I hold the dog you must _____ through the gate.
9 The bulldozers were used to _____ the squatter's hut.
10 You are making a heavy _____ on my patience.

Analogies
Put on your thinking caps and supply the missing words for the spaces.

1 *madden* is to *enrage* as *concentrate* is to _____
2 _____ is to *squat* as *build* is to *demolish*
3 *defensive* is to *offensive* as *harsh* is to _____
4 *nimbleness* is to *nimble* as _____ is to *belligerent*
5 *capacity* is to _____ as *ability* is to *able*
6 _____ is to *organise* as *determination* is to *determine*
7 *full* is to *ample* as *refuse* is to _____
8 *sustain* is to *sustenance* as _____ is to *opposition*
9 _____ is to *challenge* as *cheer* is to *praise*
10 *widow* is to *widower* as *proceeded* is to _____

Talking about a fight
Here are some words used in telling about a fight. See how many of them you can use in sentences of your own.

spectators urged challenge excitement attack defend rivals confront champion dare powerful force contest conflict guard onslaught assail enraged squirm wrestle wince feint weave avoided evaded opponent stunning desperate exhausted knock squeeze twist punch blows cheer swing ducked grabbed defeat victory

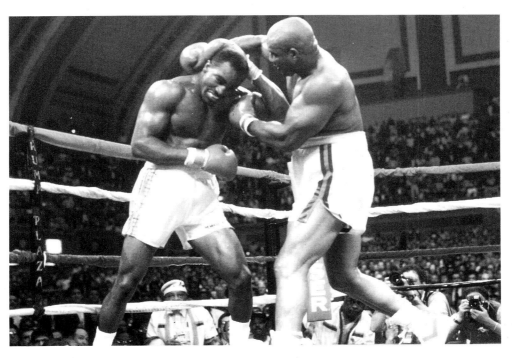

Grammatical Sentence Patterns

Putting words in the right order

Look at these phrases:

a clump   and waited   we squatted in of shrubs

They can be put together to make this sentence:

We squatted in a clump of shrubs and waited.

In the same way, see if you can say each set of phrases given below in the right order to make proper sentences.

1 in the valley – fog – there was – lying
2 his name – a special kind – he got – from – of pot
3 in the village – must have – three of every four – stolen – fish pots – he
4 fatigue – moaning – soon – she was – with
5 his chance – his enemy – to defeat – he got
6 continued – his friend – letters – Jeff – to write – to
7 for Christmas – to compete – plants – with one another – seem – in flowering
8 only vegetable food – such as grass – eat – farm animals
9 a common thing – slavery was – in ancient times – very – throughout the world
10 the body – digestion – from food – by which – the process – is – nourishment – gets

What's True and What's Not

Opinions you hear

In talking and writing, people use words that say something good or something bad about someone or something. They use certain words if they like something, but different words if they do not like it. What they say with such words cannot be proven to be true or untrue.

Listen to what two girls said about Geraldine:

a Geraldine is so quiet and shy, she just looks in a silent, innocent way at you.
b Geraldine is so sly and sneaky, she just looks in a cunning, deceitful way at you.

One person's view or opinion is expressed in the words *quiet, shy, silent* and *innocent*. They are saying good things. The person approves of Geraldine.

The other person looks at the same things Geraldine does and expresses her opinion in the words *sly, sneaky, cunning* and *deceitful*. They are saying bad things. The person disapproves of Geraldine.

To describe the same person, thing, or action people may use words with opposite feelings. So one person might say *unafraid* and *confident* but another might say *haughty* and *conceited*.

You have to become very alert to the everyday use of words, especially when you read newspapers and watch television.

Start getting more alert now by taking a word in list **A** that expresses approval and pairing it with the word in list **B** that someone who did not like the person would use.

A		B	
skinny	plump	foolhardy	hasty
careful	quick	harsh	interfering
strict	save	bony	overdressed
shy	regularity	stubborn	hoard
brave	fashionable	fat	sameness
courageous	helpful	fussy	secretive

Writing a Story

A fight

Read the paragraphs describing the fight between Milton and Jester. Begin at '*He made fists and came at Milton*' (l. 55) and go on to the end of the excerpt.

Notice how the writer tried to make you see the action of the fight in your imagination with sentences like '*He rushed at Milton wildly*' (ll. 61–62).

Notice also that everything that is said there could have been said by you if you had seen that fight. The things written by that writer are things you can write yourself.

Now try to remember or imagine a fight you saw, and try to write a description of it in a way that would help a reader to see the action as you see it in your own imagination.

Drama for Fun

A snippet to act

A very small part of a play might be called a snippet. It could be used to have fun with as you pretend to be the characters in it. Here is one to do that with in small groups in your auditorium or outside somewhere.

First you may sit for a few minutes and read the script, getting as familiar as possible with the dialogue. Then choose the persons to play the parts or characters, and someone to direct or be in charge. You can change the players around to give everybody a chance.

As soon as you get a good idea of what is to happen get up and begin to act it with the book in your hand, remembering to move from one place to another at the right time; and remembering, too, to put pauses into what you are saying in places where they would help to make it sound more convincing.

When you have practised enough put down the script and do the scene without it as many times as you can.

The threat

In the school gym or hall, Laura, Gail, Henry, Ritchie and Susan are in a scattered group, looking very worried and serious. Laura is leaning against a post. Gail is standing near a door opposite to her. Henry and Susan are sitting on a bench towards the back. Ritchie is sitting on the floor a little distance away from Laura.

LAURA: I think we can get her to co-operate if we …

GAIL: She comin'! Don't say anything. (*Everybody falls silent and becomes tense.* BRENDA *enters.*)

BRENDA: (*Coming towards the centre and looking around at them.*) Hi! What's happening?

HENRY: (*Getting up and moving to the right of* BRENDA.) Like what?

RITCHIE: (*Standing up.*) Nothing happenin'. We just want to talk to you.

BRENDA: (*Backing away a little towards the door.*) Talk to me? What about?

GAIL: (*Getting between* BRENDA *and the door.*) Look, Brenda, we know you know what we want to do. But if you go and talk everything will spoil.

SUSAN: (*Moving to stand a little behind* BRENDA.) So we want yuh to promise to keep yuh mout shut.

BRENDA: (*Looking at them all, a little frightened.*) I … I mean … I can't really promise that.
(HENRY *moves away and goes nearer to* RITCHIE *and* LAURA.)

LAURA: (*Coming closer to* BRENDA.) Brenda, yuh realise that we all in trouble if yuh open yuh big mout?

BRENDA: Well, in a kind of a way, yes. But … but yuh see … well, I mean … what you want to do is not right.
(*She tries to get from between* GAIL *and* LAURA.)

RITCHIE: Gail, Laura, leave her. Move. Let her go if she want.

GAIL: What?

RITCHIE: If she want to go let her go. She will be sorry.

LAURA: What yuh mean?

RITCHIE: I mean Brenda know I can tell her farder someting dat she wouldn like him to know. So if Brenda tell anybody about anything she in for a lot of trouble.

BRENDA: (*Taking a step towards* RITCHIE *and holding out her hands as if she is going to touch him.*) No, Ritchie! You wouldn't do that? You know it's not true.

HENRY: (*Slowly.*) So yuh ready to co-operate now, eh?

SUSAN: Yuh will come to yuh senses now then?
(*They all wait in silence as* BRENDA *looks around confused. Then she straightens up and looks at them in defiance.*)

BRENDA: No. You can do what yuh like. I am not getting involved in what you are trying to do. If you want to be dishonest and cheat people that is your business. But don't expect me to keep quiet. And you can do what you damn well like.
(*She strides through the door, leaving them all in stunned silence.*)

13 For Self-Expression

Everyday Life

Polite exchanges

Some young people in their teens feel awkward and uncomfortable in certain situations, not sure of what to do or how to behave, and sometimes that makes them become hostile and belligerent to adults. They need to get what is called poise, the feeling of being comfortable because of knowing how to behave.

You can use your spare time with some friends to improve that by doing some role-playing.

Memorise and dramatise these brief dialogues, pretending to be a person of a certain age, occupation, and so on.

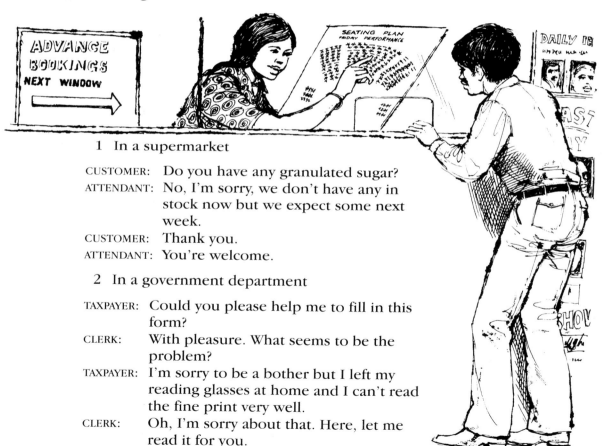

1 In a supermarket

CUSTOMER: Do you have any granulated sugar?
ATTENDANT: No, I'm sorry, we don't have any in stock now but we expect some next week.
CUSTOMER: Thank you.
ATTENDANT: You're welcome.

2 In a government department

TAXPAYER: Could you please help me to fill in this form?
CLERK: With pleasure. What seems to be the problem?
TAXPAYER: I'm sorry to be a bother but I left my reading glasses at home and I can't read the fine print very well.
CLERK: Oh, I'm sorry about that. Here, let me read it for you.

3 At a booking office

PATRON: Could I get two front seat tickets for Friday night, please?

CLERK: I'm sorry, I'm afraid we have no front seats left for Friday. Would you like two just at the back or two for some other night?

PATRON: Well, I would like two good seats and I can only come on Friday night.

CLERK: The seats at the back are quite good, I assure you. I have some that give you an excellent view.

PATRON: On second thoughts, I'd better not. My wife insists on front seats. Thank you very much all the same.

CLERK: You're welcome.

Reading to Learn Things

Getting ready

Do you have a camera, or know somebody who uses one? Do you know anyone who takes photographs as a hobby? Do you know we would have no television if the camera had not been invented long before? Can you guess when people first began using cameras?

The excerpt you are going to read tells the story of the early days of photography. The first photograph ever was taken by a Frenchman, J. N. Niepce, in 1826. It took him several hours to take it. As you read the excerpt compare those early days with what happens today.

process (l. 5) = method or way
projected (l. 27) = sent outwards
permanent (l. 40) = without any change

Long ago, around 1840, people who wanted to have their photographs taken had to sit very still for almost 20 minutes with their heads held by a clamp. After that, a portrait or picture called a daguerreotype (da-GAIR-ah-tipe) was made. It
5 was done by a process invented by a Frenchman named J. M. Daguerre.

The craft of photography has come a long way since the daguerreotype was popular. Today, with the use of electronic flash and fast films, pictures are taken in a split second.

10 Now, too, photography plays a very important part in our lives. Can you imagine how boring newspapers and magazines would be without pictures? Moreover, without the invention of photography there would be no television. Today, pictures record for history all the important events that take place. And
15 photography has become one of our most popular hobbies.

One reason why photography is so popular is that it is a means of self-expression. It gives us a chance to be artistic and creative. It helps us see the beauty in nature.

It's also a lot of fun to take pictures. And the more we know
about photography, the better are the pictures we take.

Photography is a Greek word that means 'to draw with light'.
Its history started when someone discovered the camera
obscura (KAM-er-ah ob-SKEW-ra). This happened more than
200 years before Mr Daguerre was alive. The camera obscura
was a darkened tent or room with a small hole punched in an
outside wall. The light that came through this pinhole
projected an image of the scene outside on a white screen
inside the tent. Artists who sat in this darkened room could
trace the image on pieces of paper. They were able to make
very good drawings of the scene outside the wall. Some artists
wished they could capture this image without tracing and
drawing it.

In 1727 a man named Johann Schulze (YO-hon SCHOOLTZ)
discovered that if he coated a piece of paper with silver
chemicals, the paper became sensitive to light, that is, it
darkened when light touched it. By placing leaves and other
things on this paper exposing it to daylight, Schulze made
what were called 'prints.' As a result of his discovery, he was
named the inventor of photography. But he could not find a
way to make his prints permanent. When they were exposed to
more light, they quickly darkened all over.

It was almost a hundred years before a chemical was discovered that would 'fix', or make prints permanent. In 1819 a scientist named John Herschel (HER-shul) found the right
45 chemical and called it 'hypo'. It was by using this chemical that Mr Daguerre was successful in producing his daguerreotypes. But his photo plates (light-sensitive pieces of glass) had to be prepared in a dark room and then very quickly placed in his camera. This was not easy to do.

50 In 1889 George Eastman invented an easier method. He invented film. Eastman's film was a light-sensitive strip of a plastic substance called celluloid. Two years later he invented a camera that could be loaded in daylight. This invention brought photography within the reach of everyone. Thus, we
55 can say that George Eastman was really the father of modern-day photography.

From *Photography* By Phil Steinberg, USA

Discussion for developing comprehension skills

A Understanding explicit statements:

1 What did J. M. Daguerre do?
2 Explain simply what is meant by the 'craft of photography' (l. 7).
3 Give another phrase for 'come a long way' (l. 7).
4 How long did it take at first for a photograph to be taken?
5 Where did the word 'photography' come from?
6 Which sentence describes the 'camera obscura' (ll. 22–23)?
7 What did Johann Schulze find out?
8 What made the paper darken when touched by light?
9 Why was Johann Schulze named as the inventor of photography?
10 What does 'fix' in photography mean?
11 Of what use is hypo?
12 What was invented in 1889?
13 What is 'celluloid' (l. 52)?
14 Who was George Eastman?

B Seeing implied connections:

1 Which two reasons does the writer suggest for the popularity of photography?

2 How long did a print made by Johann Schulze last?
3 Give an explanation of what 'light-sensitive' (l. 51) means.
4 What was the problem with photo plates?
5 What would you think 'loaded' (l. 53) means?
6 Together with giving facts that can be checked, the excerpt tells some of the writer's opinions. Can you find six or more places where an opinion is given, not a fact?

To Enrich Your Word Bank

Using words you read
Find the sentence below into which each of these words fits.

craft invention discovery artistic projected sensitive chemicals permanent substance strip

1 We used a _____ of cloth as a bandage.
2 Some scientists use _____ in their experiments.
3 Marconi is associated with the _____ of the radio.
4 My uncle is proud of his _____ as a cabinet-maker.
5 The _____ used for making celluloid is called plastic.
6 As a painter he was praised for his _____ brilliance.
7 Harsh remarks like that will damage a _____ person.
8 Some of the actors _____ their voices to the back of the auditorium.
9 One of the applicants is looking for a _____ job.
10 Finding how to record sound was an important _____.

Words related to topics

Discuss which of these words are related to mathematics and which to science:

*nuclear   rectangular   experiment
gravity   equation   radius   laboratory
glands   multiple   symmetry   ratio
magnetism*

Words related in meaning

Discuss which word, related in form and meaning to the word in brackets after the sentence, best fits into the blank space in the sentence.

1 She was so _____ I finally agreed. (*persist*)
2 They were behaving like _____ old ladies. (*irritate*)
3 We used a _____ to destroy all the germs. (*infect*)
4 What will happen in the future is not _____ by the nonsense called astrology. (*predict*)
5 He was in charge of the _____ of the crowd. (*disperse*)
6 The _____ I showed was not because I was afraid. (*hesitate*)
7 The old lady's behaviour was quite _____ and I will long remember it. (*impress*)
8 Advertisements often use dishonest means of _____ people to buy things. (*persuade*)
9 You must make a quick _____ if you find yourself in the wrong place. (*withdraw*)

GRAMMAR

Grammatical Sentence Patterns

Notes and complete sentences

There are many occasions when people have to write or understand shortened forms of complete sentences – for example, reading and sending telegrams, and writing notes about something you are reading or hearing about.

Can you tell what each of the following shortened sentences is saying? Put it in the pattern of a complete sentence. (Do it orally.)

a Hope see you Christmas.
b Send money next letter.
c Caribs nothing wrong naked bodies.
d Arawak women maize after ground cleared men.
e Mary seen talking Ken Harry Mildred corner.
f Pull objects depends mass distance.

Below are sentences written as notes or telegrams. What does each mean?

i Oxygen travels blood all parts body.
ii Lungs enclosed bony cage: thorax.
iii Saw father. Gave message. Awaiting answer.
iv Need funds. Send urgently. Fees due.
v Breathe get oxygen air.
vi Put hands side above waist feel ribs form cage.

vii Lost sample. Replacement needed.
Exhibition tomorrow.

Now take these complete sentences and shorten them into note or telegram form:

1 The children were kept busy driving away the birds.

2 I will be arriving at the airport on Thursday at 8 p.m.
3 The villages were usually on high ground where the air was cooler.
4 We regret we cannot come to meet you at the airport.

Spelling

From the excerpt

Can you 'see' the missing letter or letters in these words? If you cannot do this easily find the word in the excerpt and try to make a picture of it in your mind.

imagin_   telev_s__n   p_otogra__y
hist_ry   popul_r   cr__tiv_   imag_   ser__n
p_eces   capt_r_   perm_n_nt
s___ntist   su__e__ful   sens_t_ve
cel_ul__d   l_aded

Words beginning with ph-
Complete these words

phant__   pharm___   phas_   phon_
phonogr___   phras_   physi__l
physic__n

Words about artistic expression
Spend some time fixing the letters of these words in your mind.

craft   design   graphic   manual
architecture   artistry   portrait
illustration   sketch   style   scene
canvas   studio   sculpture   model
literature

Writing to Give Information

Instructions

Suppose a friend wrote this explanation for you when you asked him how a camera works. What would you tell him to do about it to make it clearer to you?

While the shutter is open the lens focuses light on the film. That is why there is a shutter in the camera. Light must fall on it for a fraction of a second. Use the shutter release gently but firmly. When this happens the film is changed into a negative. Only light coming through must reach the film. The lens focuses light on the film. Behind the lens there is a photographic film. Make sure you look through the viewfinder to frame the picture.

Now, bearing in mind that every necessary bit of information must be given at the right time and in the right place, get some practice yourself by writing some sentences instructing someone how to make or do something. Choose something that you do very well yourself.

About the Language

Nouns and verbs

In these sentences the word *glare* is used as a noun or name:

The miner came into the glare of the light.
He gave me an angry glare because I was late.

But in these sentences *glare* is used as a verb or doing word:

You glare at me every time I come in.
I wish you would not glare like that.

1 Discuss whether the word underlined in each of these sentences is used as a noun or as a verb.

a The open door was a <u>clue</u> that someone had entered.
b I don't understand, so you'll have to <u>clue</u> me in.
c Do not <u>despair</u> at any time.
d His heart was filled with <u>despair</u>.
e The burglars got away with the <u>loot</u>.
f The rioters began to <u>loot</u> the stores.

2 Use each of these words orally in sentences as (a) nouns and (b) verbs.

bar   stumble   load   poke   drinks
face   spell   stare   water   drops   gaze
play

14 Mid-Year Progress Test

If you have been reading books from a library and getting the practice you need with the help of this book, you should be able to score more than 70 marks when you do this test.

Section One: Comprehension
(24 marks)

Read each passage carefully at least twice and then choose answers to the questions.

Write only the number of the question and the letter of each answer you choose.

Passage A

Father was already on his way along the beach, flashing his torch rapidly. Uncle Peter and the two children ran to join him, straining their eyes to pick out Beverley's small figure on the moonlit sand. It was so bright you could see right past the big lagoon, along to where the grove of
5 royal palms stood above the gully, but Beverley was nowhere to be seen. They quickened their pace, the two men well ahead now, using their torches in spite of the bright moon. Peter shouted that they should look for her footprints in the sand, but this was not so easy. The beach slope was covered with tracks made by the children and the
10 hunters earlier in the evening, but most of these went the other way. However, close to the water's edge they soon came to the spot where Alan and Laura had begun to run on seeing the adults, and here they found Beverley's prints, two lines of holes, showing marks of the toes on tiny bare feet, and here a spot where she had squashed a pile of
15 weed. They all turned and sped back, following the tracks which continued in a straight line for about fifty paces. Suddenly, the prints turned up the beach and the men leaped up the slope with big strides, the two youngsters at their heels.

From *Caldong* By Peter Bacon

1 The passage is telling about
   a children playing on a beach
   b a search to find someone
   c how footprints were found.

2 Beverley's footprints were seen
   a where Alan and Laura had run on
   b where they followed the tracks in a straight line
   c when they turned up the beach.

3 It was not so easy to look for Beverley's footprints because
   a the moon was so bright it made them fade
   b the grove of palms made the beach slope down
   c there were many footprints made by others.

4 'At their heels' (l. 18) means
  a falling on their heels
  b standing in one place
  c very close behind them.

5 They all turned and sped back
  a to find where Beverley had gone
  b to get away from danger they saw
  c to climb up the slope of the beach.

[10 marks]

Passage B

The chief crops grown by Arawak farmers were maize, cassava, yams
and sweet potatoes. The men cleared the ground for the maize crop,
but the women did the planting. The workers stood in a row, each
woman having a bag of soaked grain round her neck, and carrying a
5   pointed stick. Stooping down, she made a hole in the ground with the
stick, dropped in a few grains with the left hand and covered them with
her foot. When this had been done, the workers moved a step forward,
and planted another row. As soon as the maize began to grow, the
children were kept busy driving away the birds. The harvest was ready
10   in three or four months.
      Neither Carib men nor women wore clothes, except tight bands of
cotton on the upper arms, below the knee, and above the ankle. They
painted their bodies to protect them from the heat of the sun and from
the bites of insects. A man sat on a stool while his wife painted him. The
15   Caribs took great pride in their long hair which the men gathered into a
tail, with a fringe cut over the forehead. The women parted their hair in
the middle. Sharp-edged grass was used in the place of scissors for
trimming the hair. Hair on the face was plucked out.
      The Carib dwellings were similar to those of the Arawaks. The walls
20   were of woven reeds on a wooden framework, but the thatched roof
often reached nearly to the ground. There were sometimes extra huts
for cooking and storage. The villages were usually on high ground where
the air was cooler, and there was less annoyance from mosquitoes.
Besides the hammocks, the furniture included little stools or seats cut
25   from solid red or yellow wood, 'polished like marble', and also four-
legged tables woven from palm leaves and fibres.

From *History of the West Indian Peoples, Book 3*

1 The first paragraph is about
  a the crops of the Arawaks
  b how the Arawaks grew maize
  c the way workers moved in rows.

2 The second paragraph is about
  a protection from the sun
  b how the Caribs lived
  c the appearance of the Caribs.

3 The third paragraph is about
  a the homes of the Caribs
  b places with Carib villages
  c furniture the Caribs used.

4 The Arawak women made holes in the
  ground
  a to put their sticks in
  b to plant grains of corn
  c to stamp them with their feet.

5 Carib men kept their hair long
   a to protect themselves from the sun
   b for the women of the tribe to part it
   c to win the admiration of others.

6 The homes Caribs lived in
   a were often placed on a hill
   b were different from Arawak homes
   c were extra huts kept for storage.

7 When birds came near the Arawaks' maize plants
   a the workers moved forward
   b the children chased them
   c the harvest was then ready.

[14 marks]

Section Two: Vocabulary, Grammar, Punctuation, Spelling (52 marks)

1 Write a word related in meaning to the one in italics that would fit into each space. Write only the letter of the sentence and the word you think is correct.

Brother
a Let us join together in a _____ to help one another.
b They had the same _____ feeling towards each other.

Horror
c The film was about a _____ monster in a lagoon.
d I was utterly _____ to see such destruction.

Science
e A _____ finally discovered a cure for the disease.
f Some _____ experiments are quite dangerous.

Venture
g I think that Leslie was too _____ in his actions.
h Going up the Amazon was a great _____ for them.

Confide
i She told him those secrets in strict _____.
j Please keep this as a _____ matter between you and me.

Intrude
k He kept the door closed to discourage _____.

l I regard your question as an _____ into my business.

Proceed
m If you follow the proper _____ your name will be listed.
n Sugar is made by a boiling _____.

[7 marks]

2 Write the word in each line which has a different meaning from the other words.

a enormous   gigantic   tremendous   huge   elastic
b glare   lessen   decrease   wane   shrink
c promise   distinguish   pledge   vow   swear
d applaud   raid   attack   assault   ambush
e advise   warn   direct   approve   caution
f villain   veteran   rogue   scoundrel   scamp
g jeer   mock   ridicule   assemble   deride

[7 marks]

3 Write each of these sentences, making the change you are directed to and making all other necessary changes to make sure the sentence is grammatically correct.

a The planes fly at great speed high above us.
   Change *planes* to *plane*.
b A dog was chasing the cat towards the tree.
   Change *dog* to *dogs*.
c Every mother thinks her son is innocent.
   Change *mother* to *mothers*.
d All boys have heroes they admire.
   Change *boys* to *boy*.

e The teacher busies herself preparing each lesson she has to teach.
Change *teacher* to *teachers*.

f My brother does not like school as much as I do.
Change *brother* to *brothers*.

g The students were sitting at their desks reading some books.
Change *students* to *student*.

h I disagree with the reasons that you give for your opinion.
Change *I* to *she*.

i The man goes to work in a factory that makes electronic equipment.
Change *man* to *men*.

j Many of us take what we hear as the truth.
Change *Many* to *One*.

k A record has been set by the school's best athlete.
Change *record* to *records*.

l A person I know was questioned by the police about a robbery.
Change *person* to *persons*.

m What you·do in your spare time shows the quality of your life.
Change *you* to *he*.

n The noise in the yard disturbs us in class.
Change *noise* to *noises*.

[14 marks]

4 Write each of these sentences in the form of a question.

a The music is loud.

b You do the same thing every day.

c The village has a church.

d His mother came to see him.

e I have nothing to do today.

f Some streets in the city are flooded.

[6 marks]

5 Write the following putting in full stops, capital letters, question marks, apostrophes and commas where necessary.

It was a day in january do you know what happened david asked his mother not to send him to school any more would you believe it his mother a very understanding mother asked him what was wrong he didnt answer she knew that david was worried about going to the new school he thought he wouldnt make any friends there

[10 marks]

6 Find the eight misspelled words in these columns and write them correctly.

reveal	precious	fascinate	seperate
peasant	amoung	science	similar
speach	scissors	fashion	fringe
literature	reap	develope	model
curious	aware	genuine	favorite
grammer	language	collapse	controlled
plead	fierce	lable	attempt
system	approche	terrible	omission

[8 marks]

Section Three: Written Expression *(24 marks)*

Imagine that you were given one of these, or something else, as a birthday present.

a watch
a camera
a top
a chemistry set
a flute or recorder

Write a letter to a friend telling the story of what happened on the day you were given the gift, giving the details of things seen, heard, said, touched and so on.

Be careful with the grammar, punctuation and spelling in your sentences. You will lose marks for such errors.

[24 marks]

15 Nadie's Nightmare

Everyday Life

Wisdom in proverbs

In one of your spare moments give some thought to this.

Which proverb on the left matches a meaning on the right?

1 A friend in need is a friend indeed.
2 More haste, less speed.
3 Easy come, easy go.
4 Charity begins at home.
5 The early bird catches the worm.

a Money earned easily is soon spent.
b The person who arrives first has every advantage.
c One who helps you when you really need help is a true friend.
d A task carried out too quickly may be badly done and may have to be done again.
e Kind deeds should start in one's own home.

Reading to Enjoy a Story

Getting ready

Do you remember ever having a nightmare – a bad dream that frightened you? What other things frighten you? Do you believe people's talk about ghosts, devils and demons?

On her tenth birthday Nadie begins to imagine a girl like herself, Gemini, is with her. But before that she has a bad dream.

What do you think her mother said was the reason for the dream?

existence (l.2) = being in the world
loupgarou (l. 36) = a name used for what the people believe is a being who sucks the blood of someone asleep (also called a *soucouyant* or *old higue*)

> Nadie was ten years old when first she became aware of Gemini's existence. In fact, it was the twenty-ninth of May, the day of her tenth birthday.
>
> 5   She had dreamt of a hill the night before. Had stood at the bottom of the hill and looked up. Up and up towards the top almost hidden by the clouds. Or was it the sky? Up there was something bluish. Mist? It may have been the clouds. Nadie had tried to climb the hill. Had walked and walked and walked and when she looked around had realised that she hadn't
> 10   moved. Had closed her eyes and walked faster. Opened them

and found that she still hadn't moved. And the hill must have
become River Hill, up which she walked every morning on her
way to school, only that it was higher than River Hill, but
when she looked to the left there was the same bridge with the
15 boys talking and laughing, some sitting watching her, others
standing with their arms folded leaning back against the big
stone on the corner. Just like they did every afternoon. *She
hadn't moved.*

That was when she had screamed. Or had tried to scream.
20 Because although she knew she was afraid and wanted badly
to scream, she couldn't. She had tried and tried and tried and
struggled against not screaming. And then she had been half
awake, aware that she was still trying to scream, but
something was holding her to the bed; her feet and hands were
25 tied; she was being strangled and her voice couldn't, couldn't …
With an effort bigger than her ten years, Nadie pushed away
the restraining force and sat up, wide-eyed, shivering and
afraid.

Her first waking thought was, Today is my birthday! She stood,
30 walked two steps towards the door, and looked back over her
shoulder towards the bed. Her mouth was slightly opened, the
gap between her front teeth clearly visible; her black eyes were
liquid and weak with fear. People said that when that
happened, when you tried to get up and felt as if someone was
35 holding you down on the bed, it was because you were being

attacked by a loupgarou. Loupgarou was tying you down to suck away your blood. Suppose – suppose – Nadie turned abruptly away from the bed, towards the door. She screamed. Someone was standing there. Nadie put her hand over her
40 mouth, backed towards the bed, sat down and burst into tears.

'What's wrong with you?' her mother asked, moving towards the window and lifting the net curtains on to the nail at the side, so that even more light came into the room. 'What happen? I hear you moving about. It's only half past five,
45 although it so bright outside already. How you get up so early? What happen? What happen to you?'

'I didn't know was you,' whispered Nadie.

'So that's why you crying? What happen?'

'I couldn't sleep.'

50 'You had a bad dream?'

'Yes. Yes, Mai,' Nadie sniffed, 'I had a bad dream.'

'Don't wipe you' nose on you' nightie, Nadie. Come on, you know better than that. There's some toilet paper on the table there. Use that.' Mai stood looking through the window-panes
55 for a moment, lifted the nets off the nail and let them fall gently across the window.

Nadie sniffed and blew her nose.

'You had a nightmare?'

'Yes,' Nadie sobbed. 'Yes, Mai. I had a nightmare. A bad, bad,
60 bad nightmare.'

Mai didn't seem to get more sympathetic because the nightmare had been three or four times as bad as might be expected. 'Is all this green mango you been eating last night. I tell you it would upset your stomach. Go on, lie down. Lie
65 down. You could stay in bed for a while still. Get up by half past six and be in plenty of time for school. Lie down, let me pull the sheet over you.'

'I don't want to sleep again, Mai. It was as if – as if – loupgarou was tying me down to the bed.'

70 'Nonsense. Loupgarou what? You taking all nonsense you hear making it frighten you. Is the green mango riding you stomach that is the loupgarou. Go back to sleep. I will sit down here on the bed for a while. Go to sleep. I will wake you up in time for school.'

From the short story *Gemini* By Merle Collins, GRENADA

Discussion for developing comprehension skills

A Understanding explicit statements:

1 In her dream, where was Nadie trying to go?
2 How did she feel in the dream when she was trying to scream?
3 What did she think as soon as she awoke?
4 What did she remember people said about a dream of not being able to move?
5 'Someone was standing there' (l. 39). Where?
6 What do you understand by 'more sympathetic' (l. 61)?
7 Why did her mother refer to 'all this green mango' (l. 63)?
8 What did her mother say was 'Nonsense' (l. 70)?

B Using context clues:

1 How can someone guess the meaning of the word 'struggled' (l. 22) from the clue 'tried and tried and tried' (l. 21)?
2 How does the word 'voice' (l. 25) help someone who does not know what 'strangled' (l. 25) means?
3 Whether you know what each of these words means or not, point out what is a clue in each case that helps to tell its meaning:
   'effort' (l. 26)   'restraining' (l. 27)
   'attacked' (l. 36)   'sniffed' (l. 51)

C Seeing implied connections:

1 'She hadn't moved' (ll. 9–10). From where?
2 Where do you suppose the bridge in her dream was, in relation to River Hill?
3 'She screamed' (l. 38). What made her scream then?
4 What did she use her nightie to do?

5 What 'nets' (l. 55) do you imagine were lifted 'off the nail' (l. 55)?
6 Did Nadie have the nightmare before? Tell how you know.
7 Suggest words in Nadie's mind to follow 'Suppose – suppose' (l. 37).
8 What is the story saying about superstitious people?

To Enrich Your Word Bank

Using words you read

Put each of these words into the sentence where it belongs.

*aware   exist   realise   struggle
strangle   effort   restrain   attack   sniff
sympathetic*

1 The dog stopped to _____ the smell of the post.
2 She told me something I did not _____ before.
3 He chased the robbers who came to _____ him.
4 Do you want to _____ yourself with that tie around your neck?
5 Their friends felt very _____ when their father died.
6 Although he was warned he was not _____ of the danger.
7 If you make an _____ to do it you would succeed.
8 The two wrestlers were engaged in an even _____.
9 Spirits, demons and devils simply do not _____.
10 The leash on the dog is to _____ him from running off.

Words related in meaning

The word that is missing in each sentence is related in meaning to the word in brackets after the sentence. Discuss what word best fits into the blank space.

1 All knowledge is _____ because it all helps us to understand things. (*use*)

2 One of the rules for enjoying good health is to _____ deeply at all times and take in plenty of pure air. (*breath*)

3 The _____ of cords in the larynx gives the sound that we call the voice. (*vibrate*)

4 When air is pushed through the larynx it _____ the sound we call the voice. (*product*)

5 The molecules of oxygen are carried like _____ in the blood. (*pass*)

6 If we could keep oxygen in _____ in our bodies, we could stay longer without breathing. (*store*)

7 The _____ of pure fresh air is one of the problems of big cities. (*provide*)

8 The alveoli or air-sacs are _____ like balloons. (*collapse*)

9 Normally we breathe in a completely _____ way, not even knowing that we are doing it. (*effort*)

10 _____ drinks have no value as nutrition for our bodies. (*air*)

Some words beginning with ob-

Put your heads together and see how many of these words you have read or heard before. Use a dictionary to check on the meanings of the others.

obeah   observe   obstinate   obstruct
obstacle   obvious   obscene   obsession
obscure   obtrude   objection   objective
obliterate   oblivious   oblique

GRAMMAR

Grammatical Sentence Patterns

Changing the pattern

Consider these sentences:

She had dreamt of a hill the night before.
The night before she had dreamt of a hill.

Notice that the second sentence means the same as the first, although it is worded differently.

Now finish each incomplete sentence below to make it mean the same as the sentence above it. Do each one orally.

Begin each sentence with the beginning words given.

Example:

My exercise book has one page only.
There is …

Completed sentence: *There is only one page in my exercise book.*

a The teacher told us to be quiet.
We …

b Mike can't read as well as Vishnu.
Vishnu can …

c It is enjoyable to read West Indian novels.
West Indian novels …

d My dog is more intelligent than any other.
No other …

e He hasn't come to school for at least a week.
It is …

f 'Would you please leave the room, Frank?' he said.
He asked …

g The place was so hot we could not work.
The place was too …

h Sandra doesn't like school as much as Lutchmin.
Lutchmin …

i She could not go to work because she was ill.
Being …

j His trousers were torn when he got up from the rock.
Getting up …

Some Idioms We Use

Matching meanings

In each of these sentences an idiomatic expression is underlined, and below them is a list of phrases. Discuss which phrase can be used to replace the idiomatic expression in each sentence.

1 The cars passed so close it was <u>touch and go</u>.
2 Although they were brothers they could not <u>see eye to eye</u>.
3 When she heard the news she treated us to her <u>crocodile tears</u>.
4 He claimed that we were lazy but later he had to <u>eat his words</u>.
5 The two old people did not get enough money to <u>make ends meet</u>.
6 <u>I saw red</u> when I heard him tell such a lie.

7 If you do not <u>toe the line</u> you will be asked to leave the club.
8 Learning <u>to play the game</u> is part of growing up.
9 We were sent from <u>pillar to post</u> to find out where to get the information.
10 We had to <u>pay through the nose</u> to get the simplest things done.

became very angry
follow the rules exactly
hand over a lot of money
place to place
pay for what is needed to live
false show of sorrow
a narrow escape from disaster
agree with each other
say he was wrong
to be fair

Writing a Story

A proverb comes to life

Bear in mind the proverb *A friend in need is a friend indeed* as you read this summary of a story.

Maisie went into the schoolyard. She was soon surrounded by a group who were all laughing at her. One of the teachers had called her a nincompoop. The group danced around her, ridiculing her. Then Joan, whom they all liked and admired, came up and said Maisie was smarter than all of them, and that Maisie had taught her a lot of the history they had to study. Some girls in the group said Joan was a nincompoop too. Joan said she did not mind that if her friend, Maisie, was one. The group stopped jeering. They drifted off in shame.

Now, that is only a summary of what happened. It has no details of things seen, said, heard, smelled and felt.

To expand it into a story, putting in the necessary details, you would need to imagine answers for many questions. Here are some questions to begin with:

When did the teacher call Maisie a nincompoop? Why? What did the teacher actually say? How did others in the class behave?

How was she feeling when she went into the yard? Where did she go in the yard? Why? What did she see? What did she hear?

How did the group come around her? How many? Who was the ringleader? What did they actually say? What did Maisie do? How did she look? How did the hecklers look to her? What did she feel like doing?

Those are some of the questions you might imagine answers for to begin telling the details of the story. Now, all together in class make suggestions for other questions that should be answered in telling the story.

Later on, at home or in class, use the list of questions to write the full story and give it a title.

Stories to Read

Visit your school library and any other library nearby and see how many of these books are there for you to borrow.

Remember that the most important thing you must be doing is reading books. So in the next few weeks read as many of them, or any others, as you can.

◆ *The Wooing of Beppo Tate*
  C. Everard Palmer, JAMAICA
◆ *The Sun Salutes You*
  C. Everard Palmer, JAMAICA
◆ *The Hummingbird People*
  C. Everard Palmer, JAMAICA
◆ *Escape to Last Man Peak*
  Jean D'Costa, JAMAICA
◆ *Hurricane* Andrew Salkey, JAMAICA
◆ *Riot* Andrew Salkey, JAMAICA
◆ *Earthquake* Andrew Salkey,
  JAMAICA

◆ *Sixty-Five* Vic Reid, JAMAICA
◆ *The Young Warriors*
  Vic Reid, JAMAICA
◆ *West Indian Folk Tales*
  P. M. Sherlock, JAMAICA
◆ *Three-Finger Jack's Treasure*
  P. M. Sherlock, JAMAICA
◆ *The Lion, the Witch and the Wardrobe*
  C. S. Lewis
◆ *Jet, a Gift to the Family*
  Geoffrey Kilner

UNIT

16 Mas Zeke's Problem

Everyday Life

Speech sounds to make

Learning a language is chiefly a matter of speaking the language correctly, and half of that is making the right sounds – the sounds all other speakers of the language would understand. How do you say words that end with *ing, th, est, act* and *ect*? In your spare time pay attention to that.

West Indians, like some people in other places, often get the habits of saying *in* for *ing, t* for *th, es* for *est, ack* for *act* and *eck* for *ect*.

But when you are in a situation where you need to speak English, those habits could cause you embarrassment if you have them. You also need to have other habits, to be able to switch to saying *ing, th, est, act* and so on as they have to be said in English.

If you need any practice you may use the sentences below in your spare time or in class to get it. Say each sentence aloud at least three times.

1 It is a fact that we select the best of everything on those evenings.
2 Most people thought that the war was coming to an end.
3 We expect to have a club meeting, whether the rest are going or not.

4 I think the best thing is to test out whether the effect is harmful.
5 She suspects that the guests at the wedding were drunk.
6 Who will select the painting for the west wing?

Some other words

Some people seem to think that if they are learning Spanish or French they must learn to pronounce the words correctly, but not if they are learning English. Isn't that odd?

However, if you wish to be understood by persons who do not belong to your little community you would need to say words as they are universally said.

For example, the word *radiator* is pronounced 'raydeeator'.

See if you need to practise saying these words correctly:

radiate (*raydeeate*)   radiator   radiation radiance
definite (*definit*)   definitely definiteness
cháracter (stress the first syllable: *káracter*)
órigin (stress the first syllable)
oríginal (stress the second syllable)
gesture (*jesture*)   gesticulate (*jesticulate*)
gigantic (*jiegantic*)

Reading to Enjoy a Play

Getting ready

Here is an excerpt from Scene 1 of a one-act play set in Jamaica. It takes place in a

lonely spot by the river, a little distance from the village, where Zeke likes to sit fishing. It is a moonlit evening.

See if you can find out what makes him like to get away to that spot. Is it something he wants to get far from?

Choose a reader to read the directions in the brackets, another to read what Zeke says, another what Saphira says, and so on. Change the readers after a while.

Mas (l. 5) = Mr
perdition (l. 52) = damnation
inveterate (l. 96) = with an unbreakable habit
irony (l. 120) = sarcasm, ridicule, mockery
galavanting (as pronounced by Zeke) (l. 20) = *gallivanting* (moving from place to place having fun)

(SAPHIRA *appears at bridgehead with a coal pot on her head and a lantern in her hand. She's a simple peasant girl in a brief dress and with bare feet.*)

FISHERMAN: Oh, it's you.

SAPHIRA: Mas Zekiel, you still here at this hour trailing   5
that silly old line of yours in the river?

FISHERMAN: And you, Saphira Smith, what you doing with
that silly old coal pot on your head?

SAPHIRA: (*depositing coal pot at foot of tree*) Coal pot cooks
dinner anyway. Mas Zeke, we're going to have a   10
feast tonight.

FISHERMAN:	A feast?
SAPHIRA:	A big feast.
FISHERMAN:	But not here? Not at this place?
SAPHIRA:	Same place, right here.

15

FISHERMAN:	Why you can't stay up in the village like sensible, decent human beings?
SAPHIRA:	Because we don't want to.
FISHERMAN:	(*anxiously*) Listen to me, child. This is not such a good place for a feast. If you must go galavanting there's a much better place downstream a little – you know, under the guango tree, near Miss Elsie yard. Now there's a place for a feast.

20

SAPHIRA:	And have Miss Elsie shushing us and preaching at us for having our fun? No sir! Anyway, we like this place the best. Winston choose it himself.

25

FISHERMAN:	(*grumbling and putting up his rod*) Why Winston have to go interfering, I want to know. He was always the interferingest child from he was born.
SAPHIRA:	How you mean? The feast is for himself. You don't remember he's going off into the great wide world tomorrow morning?

30

FISHERMAN:	True, true, I forgot.
SAPHIRA:	Your own nephew. Shame!
FISHERMAN:	Yes, the young eagle spreading his wings. Though why he should want to go interfering with the wickedness of great cities and mighty continents I can't understand.

35

SAPHIRA:	(*tartly*) At least he has a little ambition. That's more than anybody can say of you, Mas Zekiel.

40

FISHERMAN:	(*reproachfully*) Hi Saphira, don't you go turn into that sort of woman too. Keep your simplicity and your youth, my child. Don't go embittering up your sweet tongue with the heartlessness of hardened womanhood.

45

SAPHIRA:	I'm sorry, Mas Zekiel. I didn't mean nothing.
FISHERMAN:	That's all right, that's all right. Child, come here. Hold up your lantern. There, over the water. (*They both kneel on the rock and lean over the river. Then, as though revealing a precious*

50

	mystery) See her there? See her gliding like the dark snake of perdition? Slithering and contorting herself against the bank?	
SAPHIRA:	(*fascinated for a moment*) Yes … I remember once at my auntie's near the sea seeing the men fishing in the night with lights. The water looked just like that.	55
FISHERMAN:	The sea is one thing. Everybody know the sea is vast and foreign. But the river's different. People don't know. They say: 'Oh the river, yes.' But they don't understand.	60
SAPHIRA:	What they don't understand, Mas Zeke?	
FISHERMAN:	Her beauty, Saphira.	
SAPHIRA:	(*gazes a moment, then laughs and moves away*) Lord Mas Zeke, what an imagination a man can have! Fancy you bewitched by that old river! And look at me listening to your great stories and I should be running back up to the village to help bring food for the picnic.	65
FISHERMAN:	Ah yes, the picnic. I forgot. Who and who coming?	70
SAPHIRA:	Most all the young people. Everybody love Winston.	
FISHERMAN:	And you – you love Winston too?	
SAPHIRA:	Oh, Winston never looks at me.	
FISHERMAN:	Foolish boy! You're the pearl of them all, Saphira.	75
SAPHIRA:	Oh go way! Miss Fanny coming too, to help.	
FISHERMAN:	(*chuckling*) Eheh! Since when she counting herself with the young? That's a good one.	
SAPHIRA:	She's your pearl, Mas Zeke.	
FISHERMAN:	(*wincing*) Oh don't mock me, Saphira. I must get out of here quick before all this riotous youth descend on me.	80
SAPHIRA:	You mean before Miss Fan catch you! I think I hear her coming now.	

(*He rises quickly and rips his trousers on a rock as he does so.*)   85

FISHERMAN:	Lord my God, my trousers!
SAPHIRA:	Mas Zeke! What Miss Fanny going say to that now?

FISHERMAN:	They tear bad?
SAPHIRA:	(*looking behind him, laughing and covering her mouth with her hands*) Bad enough! And in such a place.
FISHERMAN:	It's the devil's own work. Let me get out of here fast. (*But it's too late. Two young girls,* ROSE *and* CLEMMIE, *come in laden with trays of food.* ROSE *is a bold forward girl;* CLEMMIE *is an inveterate follower and giggler.*)
ROSE:	There she is, Clemmie, sweetening up old Mas Zeke in the dark. (*Clemmie giggles.*)
SAPHIRA:	Shame, Rose! Poor Mas Zeke!
ROSE:	Mind now, Clemmie, don't laugh so much, you'll go dropping down your tray! (*She puts hers down under the tree.*) Come, Saphira, let us fix up the trays real nice.

(*Several older women and girls follow, carrying a large iron pot and more lanterns. Among these are* MISS FANNY, MAS ZEKE'S *thorn in the flesh, large and formidable, and* MISS MAY, *who is* WINSTON'S *mother and* MAS ZEKE'S *sister-in-law. They at once busy themselves lighting the coal pot. They are followed presently by a group of men, mostly young, among them* WINSTON, *carrying rum,* MAS CHARLIE, *an old farmer, and two or three musicians.*)

MISS FANNY:	Come on, Miss May. Make us get the pot boiling quick time. This curry goat won't be no good if we let it cool off.
MISS MAY:	Right, Miss Fanny. My Winston's crazy bout good hot curry goat. (*Seeing fisherman who is standing with his back to the rock*) Eheh, Miss Fan, look who here.
MISS FAN:	(*with terrible irony*) Ah, is the fisherman, eh? What you doing here, may I ask? I haven't seen you all day.
FISHERMAN:	Nothing, Miss Fan. Nothing.
MISS FAN:	Nothing. That I can well believe, for you never yet done nothing useful or that don't vex a woman to death.
FISHERMAN:	(*sidling upstage*) I going right now, Miss Fan.
MISS FAN:	Wait a bit. What you walking sideways for like a crab?

FISHERMAN:	I walking sideways? I didn't notice.	130
MISS FAN:	You hiding something. Turn round!	
FISHERMAN:	I wouldn't hide nothing from my own Miss Fan, you should know that.	
MISS FAN:	Don't give me none of that talk. Turn round!	
FISHERMAN:	(*suddenly vexed; bluffing*) I not turning round. Why you always have to think the worst, eh? Suppose I had a surprise for you, what then? But no. You would always expect to find a serpent in place of a rose.	135
MISS FAN:	(*astonished*) Zeke, what come over you now?	140
FISHERMAN:	(*following up his advantage*) Now leave me woman, while I go to me home in peace with the world.	
MISS FAN:	(*with sudden inspiration and hope*) Wait! I know! Don't tell me. You caught a fish! You hiding it there, behind your back, to surprise me! You caught a fish, Zeke, and you know how I love a nice piece of curry fish and you have it there hiding for me behind your back! Zeke! Turn round!	145 150
FISHERMAN:	(*warding her off*) Now, now!	
MISS FAN:	(*swinging him vigorously round*) Turn yourself round man, and show us.	

(*Everybody sees the torn trousers. There is a burst of laughter. But* MISS FAN *gazes with bitter anger and disappointment.*) 155

From *The Creatures* By Cicely Waite-Smith, JAMAICA

Discussion for developing comprehension skills

A Understanding explicit statements:

1 '... *trailing that silly old line*' (ll. 5–6). What was Saphira talking about?
2 Why did she come down to the river?
3 For what reason was a picnic to be held?
4 Where was Winston going?
5 '*See her there*' (l. 51). See whom?
6 '*Her beauty, Saphira*' (l. 63). Whose beauty?
7 What made Saphira say Zeke was '*bewitched*' (l. 66) by the river?
8 '*She's your pearl, Mas Zeke*' (l. 79). To whom is Saphira referring?
9 What happened when Zeke got up quickly?
10 Say what you think a '*thorn in the flesh*' (l. 107) is.
11 Why did Miss Fan say '*You hiding something*' (l. 131)?
12 What did she think Zeke was hiding?

B Using context clues:

1 The word '*snake*' (l. 52) is a clue to the meaning of '*gliding*' (l. 51) and '*slithering*' (l. 52). How?

2 Find a remark Saphira made that helps someone to know what '*tartly*' (l. 39) means.

3 Which phrase said by Miss Fan and then Mas Zeke gives the meaning of '*sidling*' (l. 127)? (From *sidle*.)

C Seeing implied connections:

1 '*Oh, Winston never looks at me*' (l. 74). What does that answer tell about Saphira's feelings?

2 Why did she speak '*tartly*' (l. 39) when she said '*At least he has a little ambition*' (l. 39)?

3 What did she think showed ambition?

4 What did Mas Zeke mean by '*don't you go turn into that sort of woman too*' (ll. 41–42)?

5 How do you tell Miss Fan's feelings about Mas Zeke's fishing?

6 '*Don't give me none of that talk. Turn round!*' (l. 134). What does that remark show you?

7 What '*astonished*' (l. 140) Miss Fan?

8 Who did Mas Zeke think had '*the heartlessness of hardened womanhood*' (ll. 44–45)?

9 Why do you think Mas Zeke said '*don't mock me, Saphira*' (l. 80)?

10 '*I haven't seen you all day*' (ll. 121–122). Why do you suppose Mas Zeke spent a lot of time by the river?

11 What kind of voice do you think the actress playing Miss Fan should use?

12 What must be made clear to the audience by the actress playing Miss Fan?

To Enrich Your Word Bank

Using words you read

1 The word *festive* is an adjective related in meaning to the noun *feast*.

Similarly the word *decency* is a noun related in meaning to the adjective *decent*.

What words can you think of related in meaning to each of these?

sensible   ambition   simplicity fascinated   riotous   astonish advantage   inspiration

2 Find the word in each line that is similar in meaning to the first one.

a precious   mysterious   dear disgraceful

b gliding   existing   coasting ascending

c slithering   sliding   trotting   blurting

d contorting   stretching   grasping twisting

e fascinated   charmed   drunk performed

f bewitched   protective   enchanted alert

g inveterate   valid   open   constant

h astonished   amazed   rummaged puzzled

i wincing   overpowering   grinning flinching

j inspiration   ridicule   encouragement residence

k presently   fiercely   soon   slowly

3 Pair a word from list **A** with a word of opposite meaning from list **B**:

A tartly   reveal   formidable   vast foreign   relations   embitter gallivant

B small   quiet   stay   hide   local weak   sweetly   sweeten

Fun with a puzzle

Here is a crossword puzzle for you to try to solve in your spare time, or together in class if you wish.

Some letters are put in to help you.

13 The letters used for United States
14 Change oneself to fit a situation
15 Look at carefully to pick out parts
17 Spanish for *yes*
18 Type of fish
20 Spanish for *the*
21 Pronoun for a thing
22 Precious valuables kept in a safe place

Down

1 Type of creature, e.g. fish, birds, etc.
2 Get service from something
3 Extinct creatures about 16 metres long and 7 metres high
4 Leave
5 Not in active existence
7 You and I
8 Bones, etc., found in the earth after thousands or millions of years
10 What many children call their father
14 One who helps another
16 An animal that does not often get on with dogs
17 What your eyes do
19 Either take it _____ leave it

Across

1 Places and things around you
5 A female lamb
6 Not old at all
9 Try to encourage someone to do something
10 Carry out or act
11 Opposite of *from*
12 Just then

Grammatical Sentence Patterns

Using an alternative pattern

Look at this sentence:

The tall man had told them that the mule was mad and dangerous.

You can change the pattern of that sentence by beginning with *They had been*, and still say the same thing, like this:

They had been told by the tall man that the mule was mad and dangerous.

Now, change the pattern of each sentence below, making a new sentence that tells the same thing, but beginning with the words you are told to begin with.

1 The mule snapped at anyone who came near.
   Begin: *Anyone who came near …*

2 A thin, lanky man came out of one of the houses overlooking the street.
   Begin: *Coming out of …*

3 He looked down to find himself confronted by a tiny old woman in a crisp dress of printed cotton.
   Begin: *Looking down …*

4 Sprat, who was being held back by his father, could not hear anything.
   Begin: *Being held back …*

5 He set to work and soon had the tangled harness cut away from the mule.
Begin: *Setting to work …*

6 Half-lying, half-sitting between the broken shafts was a very cross mule.
Begin: *Between the broken shafts …*

7 The tall man, assisted by Mr Morrison and two burly truck drivers, persuaded most of the crowd to disperse.
Begin: *Mr Morrison …*

8 So it was some time before they could see what was happening.
Begin: *To see what was happening …*

9 They found their way blocked by a broken-down wagon.
Begin: *They found a broken-down wagon …*

10 Before the tall man had time to say a word, he was being towed along right up to the mule.
Begin: *The tall man …*

Spelling

Words connected with plays

Here are some words that are used in talking and writing about plays. Can you 'see' the missing letter or letters in each one? If not, find out what it is and fix the spelling of the word in your mind.

s_ene   theat_ _   dialog_ _   tra_edy
hum_ _r   char_ct_r   p_rform_nce
set_ing   a_di_nce   c_rt_ _n   amat_ _r
pag_ _nt

Picnic words

When you have talked about how to spell each of these words, close your eyes and 'see' it.

a   people at a picnic   picnic_ _ _ _
b   something taken on a picnic
sand_ _ _ _
c   these might be eaten there
bis_ _ _ _ _
d   something to carry picnic food
bas_ _ _
e   this goes between slices of bread
let_ _ _ _
f   do this with a tablecloth on the ground
spr_ _ _
g   you might drink this   ju_ _ _
h   these might bother you a bit
ins_ _ _ _
i   where we usually go to have it
c_ _ntry

Spotting errors

In each of these words there is a misspelling. Find it and write the word correctly. The words are in the play excerpt you read.

apears   faest   vilage   desent
preeching   tommorrow   nehpew
yuoth   tongeu   fareign   decsend
musicains   beleive   suppuse   peice

Writing What Characters Say

Part of a play

Have you noted well how the dialogue and directions of a play are set down in writing?

The name of the character or person in the play is put near the margin (usually) and then the 'lines' or what the character has to say follows. The name of the character may be written in capital letters or may be underlined, and a colon or a full stop comes after the name. Any directions that the author wants to give the players are put into brackets here and there.

Now, one good way of making up a play before trying to set it down in writing is to improvise the actions and conversation that could take place in a certain situation. For example, suppose a boy wanted to make friends with a girl and the girl wanted it too but didn't want to show it because she was with two of her girl-friends. You can take a situation like that and improvise (i.e. make up dialogue and actions as you act it). Each character will be played by one of you. Then you can set down the scene in writing, following how you see it in the excerpt from *The Creatures*.

Divide yourselves into groups of four or five. Each group must go by itself somewhere and choose a situation to improvise. Then you will return to your desk and write out the scene that was improvised as if you were a playwright writing a play.

Put the best written scene from each group with the others to make a little booklet and give the booklet a title like *On Stage* or *Young Playwrights*, or some title you prefer.

Some Mix-Ups to Avoid

Grammar, punctuation, spelling

1 *It's* means *it is*; *its* means belonging to *it*.

2 *Each other* tells of two people; *one another* tells of more than two people.

3 *Between* tells of two people; *among* tells of more than two people.

4 *Practise* is to do; *practice* is something done.

5 *Every day* (two words) means each day; *everyday* (one word) means usual, common, ordinary.

6 *Presently* still means *soon* for most speakers of English, but Americans and some others use it to mean *now*; to mean *now* most people still say *at present*.

7 *As regards* (*regards* has an s) is used to mean *with regard to* (*regard* has no s).

8 *Alternate* means go from one to the other and back; an *alternative* is a choice you can make (Americans use *alternate* for *alternative*).

Choose the correct form in the brackets:

a It is not wise to follow such a (*practise/practice*).

b The dog keeps wagging (*its/it's*) tail.

c It was just an ordinary (*everyday/every day*) mango.

d Observe how those two people look at (*each other/one another*).

e Let us wander about (*among/between*) the crowd.

f That road is closed but there is an (*alternate/alternative*) route you can choose.

g I want to speak to you (*with regards/with regard to*) your homework.

h I think (*its/it's*) too late to get the bus now.

i Boys and girls will (*alternate/alternative*) in carrying the flag.

j The sun appears (*everyday/every day*).

17 A Well-Kept Garden

Everyday Life

Matters to talk about

To use some of your spare time in a beneficial way, get together with a friend or two and share your ideas on the following matters.

What, would you say, makes a neighbourhood a pleasant place to live in?

As you move from place to place, what do you feel when you see that people have littered their environment with cigarette ends, cardboard boxes, used cartons, empty cans, old newspapers and so on?

What is the purpose of having flowers and flower gardens around you? Do you see a lot of them? If not, why not?

Apart from litter dropped by people, do you know of any other way your environment may be spoiled and made unpleasant or unsafe?

Reading to Learn Things

Getting ready

In certain ways Barbados is different from other West Indian islands and in certain ways it is just like other islands.

As you read the excerpt ask yourself what it is telling you about Barbados that you did not know before.

volcanic (l. 4) = coming from a volcano
serenely (l. 31) = calmly
casuarinas (l. 33) = tall trees with feathering branches (as all Barbadians know)
revive (l. 17) = bring to life again
foliage (l. 33) = branches and leaves

Barbados is indeed an island of which the utmost has been made. But the Barbadian soil and climate are not really suited for the cultivation of fruit trees on a large scale. Our soil is not

of volcanic origin, as is the case with other West Indian islands
which produce fruit in abundance. Being made from the
underlying limestone, it contains too much lime and this
prevents our fruit trees from bearing well. Moreover, these
trees do not get enough water because our rainfall is not
sufficient for this purpose.

Such fruit trees as grapefruit, orange, sapodilla, cashew and
guava have to be planted in places that are shady and moist
and protected from the trade winds. It is not surprising,
therefore, that the fruit grown in Barbados is far from
adequate for the needs of its population and consequently not
sufficient to develop an export trade.

Thus it is that sugar has continued to be the staple crop of the
island. Attempts have been made from time to time to revive
cotton as a major crop. But when the U.S.A. began the
cultivation of cotton on a large scale in the nineteenth century,
Barbados was forced to give even more attention to sugar as its
principal product.

When you walk or drive through the countryside, you will enjoy
the many charms with which nature had endowed the island.
You will be fascinated by the many tints and hues of the
hibiscus, the white, pink and mauve of the queen of flowers,
the cobalt-blue of the morning glory and the rich crimson of the
sweet william. You will see the sun shining on green cane fields
and feel the rustling of the wind as it whistles through the

waving cane arrows. At night, when the moon is shining in all
30 its brilliance, you will see the tall, majestic cabbage palms
waving their branches serenely from side to side and you may
hear the strange music the trade winds seem to play, with the
foliage of the casuarinas as their delicate instrument. And
always you will savour the fragrance of the many scents that
35 come from the trees, the shrubs and the flowers that give the
island the appearance of a trim, well-kept garden.

From *Barbados, Our Island Home* By F. A. Hoyos, BARBADOS

Discussion for developing comprehension skills

A Understanding explicit statements:

1 Say what you think '*the utmost has been made*' (ll. 1–2) means.
2 Suggest a phrase of your own for '*on a large scale*' (l. 3).
3 What does to '*produce fruit in abundance*' (l. 5) mean?
4 '*Being made from*' (l. 5). What is it that is made?
5 What prevents fruit trees from '*bearing well*' (l. 7) in Barbados?
6 Would it be true or false to say Barbados only grows the fruit the people need?
7 You met the word *export* in Book 1. Why does Barbados not have a fruit export trade?
8 What is the staple (main) crop of Barbados?
9 Which other crop was once widely grown?
10 Tell some of the '*charms*' (l. 23) mentioned.

B Using context clues:

1 Why is '*underlying*' (l. 6) a clue to the meaning of '*limestone*' (l. 6).

2 You met the word '*adequate*' (l. 14) before, in Unit 9. How do the phrases '*far from adequate*' (ll. 13–14) and '*not sufficient*' (ll. 14–15) help someone to know the meaning of '*consequently*' (l. 14)?

3 After the phrase '*tints and hues*' (l. 24) some flowers are mentioned. How does that help a reader to guess what tints and hues are?

4 How does the word '*scents*' (l. 34) help to tell the meaning of the words '*savour*' (l. 34) and '*fragrance*' (l. 34)?

5 How could you tell the meaning of '*endowed*' (l. 23) if you had not known it before?

C Seeing implied connections:

1 What kind of soil is best suited to grow fruit?
2 Why does the writer say '*It is not surprising, therefore*' (ll. 12–13)?
3 How do you suppose people in Barbados can get enough fruit to eat?
4 What happened when Barbados tried to revive the growing of cotton?
5 Why is the foliage of the casuarinas described as an '*instrument*' (l. 33)?
6 How does Barbados resemble '*a trim, well-kept garden*' (l. 36)?

To Enrich Your Word Bank

Using words you read

Working together, find the sentence into which each of these words fits:

abundance purpose adequate
consequently revive major endowed
hues serene foliage savour
fragrance

1 He spends the _____ part of his spare time reading.
2 My strength was not _____ to the task of moving that desk.
3 As they walked they were surrounded by flowers growing in _____.
4 The _____ of the sunset sometimes take my breath away.
5 The ambulance crew tried to _____ the girl who had fainted.
6 What a pleasant _____ comes from that rose!
7 There seemed to be no reason nor _____ for doing such a thing.
8 Through the thick _____ of the trees the sun peeped.
9 After the storm the sea had a calm and _____ face.
10 In my mother's kitchen you can _____ the smell of good cooking.
11 Some people are _____ by nature with high intelligence.
12 He was careless and should be blamed for what happened _____.

Odd one out
Discuss the words in each line and decide on the one that does not fit in with the rest.

1 Barbados Guyana Trinidad Jamaica
2 bananas cane pineapples mangoes
3 hibiscus bougainvillaea chrysanthemum cassava
4 scent weight fragrance smell
5 strange foreign silent alien
6 majestic royal regal cautious
7 foliage cement vegetation crops
8 volcano earthquake moonlight hurricane
9 fascinated charmed enchanted traded

10 scarce adequate sufficient enough
11 develop escape mature grow
12 brilliance brightness politeness radiance
13 hastily serenely calmly peacefully
14 delicate fragile frail typical
15 instrument equipment government gear

Talking about a country
Here are some words used in talking about a country. See how many of them you can use in sentences of your own.

climate agriculture cultivation vegetation industries population resources culture education environment fertile season government independence production prosperity tropical natural development migration

Grammatical Sentence Patterns

Combining sentences
In the excerpt you read there is this sentence:

Barbados is indeed an island of which the utmost has been made.

That sentence is putting together two ideas which could have been these two sentences:

Barbados is an island.
The utmost has been made of Barbados indeed.

Below are pairs of sentences for you to put together as one correct sentence. Do not use the word *and*, nor the word *but*, to join them.

1 We come to our own times. We find several species in danger.
2 The mother turtle has laid the eggs. Someone digs them up.
3 Another animal is in danger from man. It is the orang-utan.
4 The tiger has stripes. They make it hard to see in the jungle.
5 We want the species to survive. What does an animal need?
6 The young fish get attacked by many enemies. It does not matter.
7 There is the box. We put the letter in it.
8 The person does not live here. The dog belongs to that person.
9 We do not do anything about it. The school will become shabby and dirty.
10 The article we ordered did not arrive. We paid for it.

Punctuation Signals

Commas for phrases and words put in

Look at these sentences:

a *The road was only another track.*
b *The road was only another, but broader, track.*

In b the phrase *but broader* is inserted into the main pattern of the sentence. Notice that it is separated from the rest of the sentence by commas – one before it and one after it.

When such a word or phrase is put at the end of the sentence only one comma is necessary, because a full stop has to be put at the end, as in this sentence:

'Hai, hai!' he shouted, tugging the reins.

Only one comma is used, also, when such a word or phrase is put at the beginning of a sentence, as in this sentence:

Looking back, he could see she was scolding Manko.

For practice, write the sentences below, putting in the word or phrase given in brackets in a suitable place in the sentence.

Example

He saw Sookdeo's son carrying a bucket of water. (Govind)
He saw Sookdeo's son, Govind, carrying a bucket of water.

1 Manko's neighbour came into the yard. (*Sookdeo*)
2 He tiptoed to the window and looked out. (*feeling afraid*)
3 The boy tried to push the animal. (*grabbing the horns*)
4 He started off. (*glad that the sun was setting*)
5 He would have liked to pass them. (*but there was no room*)
6 She must have gone about half a mile before she saw any signs of a house. (*scrambling over rocks and parting bushes*)
7 He dangled his legs as if he had been driving a cart all his life. (*swinging them as he had seen his father do*)
8 Manko came in from his plot of land with a worried expression on his face. (*after trying to break up the hard earth*)

Look at how these sentences are punctuated. Where are commas used? Why?

a An Ice Company wagon, <u>packed with rioters</u>, drove into Cross Roads.
b <u>At that moment</u>, Gerald was in the look-out with Shifty and Fu Manchu.
c The vendors, <u>screaming and running</u>, stampeded out of the place.
d The wagon moved off, <u>loaded with stones and sticks</u>.

In each sentence something is inserted with the main idea of the sentence, something which can be left out. It is underlined to help you to see it. In a and c the insertion is in the body of the sentence. In b it is at the beginning, and in d it is at the end.

In each case a comma or commas are used to separate what is inserted from the main idea of the sentence. When the insertion is in the body of the sentence, two commas have to be used, as shown. When it is at the beginning or at the end, only one comma can be used.

1   Now discuss where commas should be put in these sentences:

e   Some rioters their pockets stuffed with fruits and vegetables jeered at the vendors.
f   Cyclists and motorists did not stop of course as they went through Cross Roads.
g   The boys recognising the men realised what was happening.
h   Obeying his order they set off up Half Way Tree Road.
i   The boys lost sight of the rioters being too high above them.

2   When you have discussed sentences e to i, and understand clearly what to do, write these sentences with commas in the right places:

j   Her voice although low-pitched and precise quavered slightly.
k   Without waiting to hear anything else he ran round the side yard and locked the gate.
l   Most of the residents with terrified screams and cries ran around in confusion.
m   They stood and looked at the damage not understanding the cause of anything.

Writing What You Know

Information in a letter

Someone from a foreign country has written to you asking these questions, as well as others:

What is the population of your country?
In what ways do the people earn money?
What is grown on a large scale?
Is it mountainous or flat?
Are there forests and rivers?
Do you have many manufacturing industries?
What kind of climate do you have?
What is its size?
Which products are exported?
Does it have mineral deposits?
How is it governed?
Do you have your own forms of music and dance?
What creative activities do the people engage in?
Where exactly is it located?

Get into teams of about five or six and, first, arrange the questions in the order in which you think they should be answered. Then discuss the answers to be given to them, sharing your knowledge with one another. Share your ideas too on how you can find out the answers to the ones you cannot answer as yet.

Then, in class or at home, sit down to write the letter. Put your address and the day's date in the top right-hand corner, as usual. On the next line, on the left side, write *Dear …*, and below the *ea* begin to write the first sentence you have in mind to answer the first question on your list.

Answer question after question with one or more sentences each, but begin a new paragraph when the questions move to a different sort of matter.

When the letter has been written get back into your group and read all the letters written, suggesting ways of improving them to one another.

Drama for Fun

A mini mini play

Here is a mini mini play to use for fun pretending to be the characters. Read it through quickly and silently first, then choose players to read it aloud, using suitable tones of voice.

When you are quite familiar with it begin to act it with the book in your hand reading your parts, moving from one place to another at the right time, and putting in pauses to make it sound real.

Good news

An ordinary living room, but small. Mr Foster in a chair on the right, reading a newspaper. Mrs Foster is at a small table, mending a shirt. There are two more chairs and a small table in the room. There is a door on the left and a window at the back.

ELSA: (*off-stage*) Mum! Dad! Where are you? Dad!

MUM: In here, Elsa. What's the matter?

ELSA: (*rushing in*) Guess what!
(MUM *and* DAD *stop what they are doing.*)

DAD: Well, it must be something very important to have you so excited.

ELSA: I did it! I did it!

MUM: Did what, dear?

DAD: You mean …?

ELSA: Yes! I won the scholarship! (*Throwing her hands up and doing a little skip.*)

MUM: Oh, thank heaven. (*Clasping her hands together.*) Oh, merciful heaven. It's a miracle. (*Getting up.*)

DAD: My dear child. I am so happy, so happy for you. (*Rising and going to* ELSA *as he speaks. He holds both her hands in his.*)

ELSA: And we don't have to worry about anything. I will get enough money to pay for everything.

MUM: (*Going to the other side of* ELSA.) It's the answer to all my prayers. Now you will be able to become somebody.

ELSA: No, Mum. Now I'll be able to get the qualifications for a good job to have enough money to take care of you and Dad.

DAD: Elsa, your future is yours. You must make the most of your life. We'll be all right. I have a lot of good working years left in me still.

ELSA: Oh Dad! Oh Mum!
(*The three of them are almost overcome with emotion. Tears are about to roll down* MUM'S *face.* ELSA *holds* MUM *and* DAD *on both sides of her and squeezes them to her.*)

18 The Sound Of The Bell

Everyday Life

Wisdom in proverbs

In some moments of spare time see if your friends know the meanings of these proverbs:

Absence makes the heart grow fonder.
Charity begins at home.

Every cloud has a silver lining.
Necessity is the mother of invention.
No cross, no crown.
No news is good news.
Still waters run deep.
Where there's a will there's a way.

Reading to Enjoy a Poem

Getting ready

Quite often people get pleasure from the way something is said even when what is said is sad. Life has sadnesses in it and poets often use them to stir our feelings.

The words of the poem below have a beat or rhythm that puts you in the mood the poet wants you to share with him. See if you can feel it.

to yield (l. 3) = to give in
Trades (l. 16) = winds that blow over the Caribbean islands
tassels (l. 18) = bunches of threads or cords
mortals (l. 27) = human beings, who must all die

My Mother

Reg wished me to go with him to the field.
I paused because I did not want to go;
But in her quiet way she made me yield,
Reluctantly, for she was breathing low.
5 Her hand she slowly lifted from her lap
And, smiling sadly in the old sweet way,
She pointed to the nail where hung my cap.
Her eyes said: I shall last another day.
But scarcely had we reached the distant place,
10 When over the hills we heard a faint bell ringing.
A boy came running up with frightened face–
We knew the fatal news that he was bringing.
I heard him listlessly, without a moan,
Although the only one I loved was gone.

II
15 The dawn departs, the morning is begun,
The Trades come whispering from off the seas,
The fields of corn are golden in the sun,
The dark-brown tassels fluttering in the breeze;
The bell is sounding and children pass,
20 Frog-leaping, skipping, shouting, laughing shrill,
Down the red road, over the pasture-grass,
Up to the schoolhouse crumbling on the hill.
The older folk are at their peaceful toil,
Some pulling up the weeds, some plucking corn,
25 And others breaking up the sun-baked soil.
Float, faintly-scented breeze, at early morn
Over the earth where mortals sow and reap–
Beneath its breast my mother lies asleep.

Claude McKay, JAMAICA

Discussion for developing comprehension skills

A Understanding explicit statements:

1 Who made the narrator, the 'I' telling the story, go with Reg?
2 What do you understand by 'she was breathing low' (l. 4)?
3 What was hanging on a nail?
4 Where did he and Reg go?
5 What did they hear?
6 Who came to them?
7 At what time of day is the narrator now telling us the story?
8 How are the children behaving while he is thinking about it?
9 What are the older folk doing?
10 Who or what is told to 'float' (l. 26)?

B Using context clues:

1 How is the clause 'she made me yield' (l. 3) connected with the meaning of the word 'reluctantly' (l. 4)?
2 Knowing what the 'news' (l. 12) was, how can a reader guess the meaning of 'fatal' (l. 12)?
3 In what way is the phrase 'without a moan' (l. 13) related to the meaning of 'listlessly' (l. 13)?

C Seeing implied connections:

1 'She pointed to the nail' (l. 7). Why?
2 What does the narrator mean by 'Her eyes said' (l. 8)?
3 How do you know the narrator's mother had been ill for some time?
4 Why was a 'bell' (l. 10) heard ringing? Why was it 'faint'?
5 Where is the narrator now as he tells the story?
6 'Beneath its breast my mother lies asleep' (l. 28). Explain that line.
7 'The bell is sounding' (l. 19). What bell do you think that is?
8 Why are the fields of corn 'golden in the sun' (l. 17)?

9 What comparison is made in using each of these words? 'whispering' (l. 16) 'golden' (l. 17) 'tassels' (l. 18) 'breast' (l. 28) 'asleep' (l. 28)
10 What would you say is the main difference between what the narrator tells us about in lines 1–14 and what he tells us about in lines 15–28?
11 Can you suggest any reason why there is a bell in both parts of the poem?

To Enrich Your Word Bank

Using words you read
Put each of these words into the sentence below where it belongs:

moan   toil   yield   fatal   shrill
plucking   crumbling   fluttering
reluctantly   listlessly

1 We caught them _____ the guavas from a low branch.
2 She answered me _____, as if she didn't want to.
3 We all have to _____ to earn a living.
4 The walls of the old building were _____ into gravel.
5 You are trying to force me to _____ to what you want.
6 She was moving _____ as though she had no strength or energy.
7 The pain in his tooth made him _____ all night.
8 Three people died in that _____ accident.
9 Do you hear the _____ voices in the playground?
10 There are some flags _____ on their poles.

Words related in meaning
Discuss which word related in form and meaning to the one in brackets after each

sentence best fits into the blank space in the sentence.

1 We had travelled a great _____ before the car stalled. (*distant*)
2 There was some _____ in his voice. (*shrill*)
3 The _____ time for my plane was postponed. (*depart*)
4 There was only one _____ in that crash. (*fatal*)
5 She did me the favour, but she showed her _____. (*reluctantly*)
6 I was feeling so _____ I could hardly run after the ball. (*listlessly*)
7 The children were too young to like the _____ of such a quiet place. (*peaceful*)
8 The _____ rate for infants was high but now most babies live. (*mortals*)

Choosing the right word

Discuss which of the four words given with each sentence best fits into the blank space in the sentence.

1 They refused to _____ to the threats he made.
   affirm   bargain   yield   toil

2 If the weather is good this year the farmers will _____ good crops.
   trade   reap   derive   plough

3 We heard some _____ voices but we were too far away to know who they were.
   distant   audible   oral   mortal

4 The flags of all the nations were _____ in the breeze.
   blowing   weaving   sowing   fluttering

5 If you drink poison it could be _____.
   indigestible   mortal   sickly   fatal

6 A _____ cry came from the wounded animal.
   listless   moan   shrill   sheer

7 It is hard work to _____ the seeds of a new crop.
   reap   mulch   sow   pollinate

8 Every morning a plane _____ with a full load of passengers.
   departs   removes   altitudes   revolves

9 I didn't want to eat so I took the sandwich _____.
   reluctantly   deliciously   greedily   fully

10 The day was so hot that all the players moved _____.
    reluctantly   passionately   listlessly   robustly

GRAMMAR

Grammatical Sentence Patterns

Reported speech sentences

Look at this sentence:

a *Reg asked, 'Where is my cap?'*

In the sentence the actual words that Reg said are put in, enclosed by quotation marks.

But the same thing can be said like this:

b *Reg asked where his cap was.*

What are the seven differences between sentence a and sentence b?

The differences are that in sentence b:

i   *is* is changed to *was*
ii   *my* is changed to *his*
iii the order of the words is changed
iv   the comma is left out
v   the question mark is not used
vi   *where* begins with a small letter
vii the quotation marks are not used.

Very often, however, errors are made with

such sentences. For instance, someone might say or write *Reg asked where is my cap* or *Reg asked 'where is his cap?'* or *Reg asked 'where was his cap?'* or make some other errors.

To help yourself to avoid such errors use the sentences below to play a game of 'battling' between two teams. (See Unit 10 to remind yourselves how to battle.)

These sentences are written as direct speech, with the actual words said enclosed between quotation marks. Say each one as if you were reporting it to someone else, like sentence b above.

a   The girl asked, 'Why should I have to sit here?'
b   Mother told Jim, 'You won't go until you have tidied your room.'
c   'Do you think it's a good idea, Dad?' Betty asked.
d   'I may come with you,' Fred said.
e   Savi asked Abdul, 'Are you going to the show?'
f   'Will you please assist me, Victor?' his wife asked.
g   'I have a toothache. I think I will go to the dentist,' moaned Nellie.
h   'The weather is getting worse,' observed Mr Green.
i   'Come inside, Cynthia,' Mum said, 'and have a drink.'
j   'Do you know how to play chess?' Dave asked his friend, Kenny.

Some Idioms We Use

Matching meanings

People often say someone *has an axe to grind*, meaning that the person has something to gain by taking one side or the other of an argument.

Take these similar idiomatic expressions

and see if you can fit each with its meaning below:

a   to make a clean breast
b   to bury the hatchet
c   to mind your p's and q's
d   to take the bull by the horns
e   to flog a dead horse
f   to play second fiddle
g   to feather your nest
h   to blow your own trumpet
i   to smell a rat
j   to give someone the cold shoulder
k   to make a mountain out of a molehill
l   to pay through the nose

i   to let someone else go in front for the praise or admiration
ii   to suspect something bad
iii   to put an end to your quarrel
iv   to deal with your troubles in a bold way
v   to pay too high a price
vi   to confess all about doing something wrong
vii   to boast about yourself
viii to increase what you have in a greedy way
ix   to try to change something that is already well set
x   to make a little difficulty seem quite huge

Writing a Story

From words of a poem

Here is a chance to give your imagination some freedom to make up a story, just as you did in Unit 1.

Form groups of about five or six and choose an excerpt below that makes you think about something that could happen. Then just let your thoughts come out and tell one another things you imagine could happen.

Later on, in class or at home, write a brief story that you yourself made up. But try not to tell it as a summary (see Unit 15). As you go along tell the details of what was seen, heard, felt and so on.

1   I remember the night my mother
    was stung by a scorpion. Ten hours
    of steady rain had driven him
    to crawl beneath a sack of rice.

    From *The Night of the Scorpion* By Nissim Ezekiel, INDIA

2   Over the paved yard
    small boys were still chasing
    each other with yells,
    filing up the old stair-
    cases after the bell.

    From *School Building* By Cecil Gray, TRINIDAD

3   All week it seems they live for this
    – the football match, the tedious bus-trip –
    and love it, live it, when it comes.

    From *To The Match* By Mervyn Morris, JAMAICA

4   His pants are torn; he does not have a shirt;
    his face, a mask of sunflaked grease and dirt,
    too young to understand his day's events
    dreams mountainslide of magic dollars and cents.

    From *Jamaica Journal, 1969* By Cecil Gray, TRINIDAD

5   This wind brings all dead things to life;
    Branches that lash the air like whips
    And dead leaves rolling in a hurry.

    From *Windy Day* By Andrew Young, SCOTLAND

6 I was angry with my friend;
   I told my wrath, my wrath did end.
   I was angry with my foe;
   I told it not, my wrath did grow.

   From *Poison Tree* By William Blake, ENGLAND

Words in Literature

Metaphor

People often say things like *His aunt is asleep in her grave* or *Your words lifted my spirit* or *The sun peeped out*.

In these examples the words *asleep, lifted, spirits* and *peeped* are used to compare one thing with another. The aunt is not literally or really asleep. The sun does not literally peep. Comparisons are made by using the words *asleep* and *peep*. Such a comparison is called a metaphor.

Look for the metaphors in these instances.

a Listen to the sweet violin strings of the rain.

   From *The Rain and The Rainbow* By Leo Fredericks, INDIA

b Here was the tea of freedom brewed.

   From *Freedom Tree* By H. M. Telemaque, TOBAGO

c one day upon a hill
   where random plants and trees
   grow as they will
   some tall cathedral towers
   some mere umbrellas still

   From *Song Upon A Hill* By Cecil Gray, TRINIDAD

d This older tree, this well-grown shade,
   This solid rooted sentinel
   Knows all about the tale I tell

   From *Freedom Tree* By H. M. Telemaque, TOBAGO

e They have planted sharp lines of barbed wire

   From *Letter 2* By Martin Carter, GUYANA

f There runs a dream of perished Dutch plantations
   In these Guyana rivers to the sea.

   From *There Runs a Dream* By A. J. Seymour, GUYANA

g No error mars the white page
   Of her mind. No asterisks. No stars.

   From *The Stenographer* By Barbara Ferland, JAMAICA

19 Riot In The Market

Everyday Life

Private reading

In your spare time consider what the words *rocks*, *unarmed* and *stinging* stand for in this poem. To prime a gun is to get it ready to fire.

The Quarrel

Put down those words,
rocks picked hastily from the beach of mind
for your defence. There is no need
for such an action
to be taken.

Unprime your anger. Cannons
never stopped a war but brought
more cannons in to bear. I
am unarmed. See, my hands
are empty.

If you must fight
then let it be with gestures. Once
stinging sentence tears my flesh
words cannot be
withdrawn.

Gestures can be bent
though, broken, turned from anger into love
by slightest twist of wrist.
Here is my hand:
please take it.

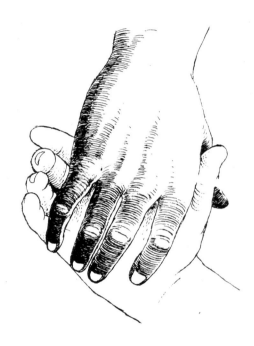

Mark Young, NEW ZEALAND

Reading to Enjoy a Story

Getting ready

Three boys, Gerald, Shifty Shanks and Fu Manchu were friends in Kingston, Jamaica. During a strike by workers in the city a riot broke out. Curious to see some of what was going on, the boys climbed a tree. They saw a lot.

What do you think they saw? Compare the action you expect with the action the excerpt describes.

ledgers (l. 17) = books with figures showing monies received and paid
apprehensive (l. 25) = expecting danger

At that very moment, an Ice Company wagon, packed with rioters, drove into Cross Roads and stopped outside the market.

Gerald, Shifty and Fu were watching excitedly from their tree-
5 top 'look-out'.

The men were very quiet. They leapt from the driver's cabin and from the open storage-carriage at the back, and slipped through the main gate; they were almost on tiptoe. They ran past the market women and the stall attendants and headed
10 straight for the superintendent's office in the centre of the market shed.

As the men burst through the door, Gerald, Shifty and Fu lost sight of them.

The men roughed up the superintendent and flung him
15 outside, and then they started to demolish his small office. It took them about a minute to reduce it to a tangle of splintered wood and ripped ledgers and broken furniture and overturned ashtrays and waste paper.

The last man out turned quickly and broke the panes in the
20 three small windows at the back of the office.

'There they are again,' Fu said. 'Like mad red ants!'

'Fantastic!' Shifty said.

'They mean business all right,' Gerald said, rubbing his hands
expectantly.

25 And yet they were all three apprehensive.

The noise had thrown the whole market into panic. The floor-
vendors and stallholders were stampeding out of the market
gates at the side and front entrances. They had all abandoned
their wares and their personal belongings and were screaming
30 and shouting their way out to Cross Roads. Following close
behind them, the rioters kicked over the displays and stands
and showbaskets wherever they ran into them. A few men
scooped up handfuls of fruits and vegetables and stuffed them
into their pockets and into the front of their shirts, and others
35 pelted the retreating market-people with eggs and mangoes
and yams and lengths of sugar-cane.

Cross Roads rang out with terrified screams and angry protests
of the vendors and the market-officers, and with the vicious
jeers and threats of the rioters. The pandemonium soon spread
40 around the vicinity, and shop-keepers started closing their
shutters and pedestrians began scampering off the streets and
running for shelter into the remaining open doors in the
shopping centre; and, of course, passing cyclists and motorists
sped through the riot-area without stopping.

45 A second wagon of rioters drew up outside the market, but the
men did not get out.

Gerald, Shifty and Fu strained forward to see if they could
recognise them.

'Some of them were in the park,' Fu said, tapping his forehead
50 and narrowing his eyes thoughtfully.

'They could've been, I suppose,' Shifty said.

'They were,' Gerald declared. 'They're some of the Broome
marchers. Most of them are.'

'What makes you so sure, Gerry?' Shifty asked.

55 'The hats they're wearing,' Gerald said confidently. 'Most of the
Broome men were wearing old Jippa Jappa straws.'

The driver shouted something to the other set of rioters. His
order was promptly obeyed, and both wagons set off up Half

Way Tree Road, towards the residential sections and garden
60 suburbs of Upper Saint Andrew. The second wagon was filled
with large mounds of rubble and stones and short sticks and
lengths of iron piping.

From *Riot* By Andrew Salkey, JAMAICA

Discussion for developing comprehension skills

A Understanding explicit statements:

1 '*The men were very quiet*' (l. 6).
Which men?
2 Which '*main gate*' (l. 8) was slipped
through?
3 Where did the men go straightaway?
4 You met the word '*demolish*' (l. 15) in
Unit 12. What did they do to the office
of the superintendent?
5 What do you think '*reduce it*' (l. 16)
means?
6 Say what this makes you imagine: '*a
tangle of splintered wood and ripped
ledgers and broken furniture*'
(ll. 16–17).
7 What sounds did the boys hear?
8 '*The noise had thrown the whole
market into a panic*' (l. 26). Tell
things that happened in the panic.
9 How did shopkeepers '*around the
vicinity*' (l. 40) act?
10 What did pedestrians do?
11 Where did the wagons head for?
12 What was in the second wagon?

B Using context clues:

1 If you did not know what '*panes*'
(l. 19) are, the phrase '*in the three
small windows*' (ll. 19–20) helps you
to know. What phrase helps someone
to know the meaning of '*stampeding*'
(l. 27)?

2 Say what connection you see between
'*showbaskets*' (l. 32) and '*displays*'
(l. 31).

3 The sellers were '*stampeding*' (l. 27)
out of the gates. How does that tell
someone the meaning of '*retreating*'
(l. 35)?

4 Can you find anything that suggests
what each of these words means?

'*abandoned*' (l. 28)   '*wares*' (l. 29)
'*scooped*' (l. 33)   '*vicious*' (l. 38)
'*residential*' (l. 59)   '*suburbs*' (l. 60)
'*mounds*' (l. 61)

C Seeing implied connections:

1 Why do you suppose the men who
came on the first wagon were '*quiet*'
(l. 6) and '*almost on tiptoe*' (l. 8)?

2 Most of the action is described
through the eyes of the boys. Where is
it seen through someone else's eyes?

3 Why do you think Gerald was
'*rubbing his hands expectantly*'
(ll. 23–24)?

4 What do you suppose '*they were all
three apprehensive*' (l. 25) about?

5 What little bit of detective observation
about the rioters did Gerry do?

6 The rioters upset the stalls of the
sellers in the market. Who else did
they set out to attack when they left
the market?

7 Why did the second wagon have
'*mounds of rubble and stones and
short sticks and lengths of iron
piping*' (ll. 61–62)?

8 How did the writer of the story get
you to imagine the panic and
pandemonium?

Riot In The Market 141

To Enrich Your Word Bank

Using words you read
Find the place for each of these words in the sentences below.

*stall wares panes displays suburbs
scooped splintered tangle
attendants promptly confidently
residential*

1 The _____ of glass in the window were smashed.
2 When the fire broke out the brigade arrived _____ .
3 The ambulance _____ gave first aid to those injured.
4 I found the cricket bat had _____ into pieces.
5 At the fair my class had a _____ with cakes on sale.
6 There are neat gardens in the _____ part of the town.
7 Put the _____ that you have to sell on the stall.
8 She _____ up a lot of ice cream for herself.
9 Look into the showcases and see the _____ .
10 The _____ are on the outskirts of town.
11 How did you get the ribbon into such a _____ ?
12 When you are questioned you must answer _____ .

Words of similar meaning
Three words in each line have similar meanings. Find the one that does not.

a vicinity display neighbourhood district
b fearful anxious apprehensive hostile
c excited spiteful violent vicious
d rush scramble stampede amble
e leave abandon crouch forsake
f fear fright panic evil
g detect withdraw retreat retire
h pandemonium exhaustion disorder confusion
i warning threat menace comfort
j objection protest complaint response

Words about a riot
Here are some words that might be used in telling about an event like a riot. See how many of them you can use in sentences of your own:

rioters screams pelted angry
scamper safety shouts sticks fear

retreat   violence   march   destruction
jeers   panic   demolish   terrified
protests   apprehensive   smashed
stampede   threats   rushed   overturned
abandoned

Grammatical Sentence Patterns

Reported speech sentences

In Unit 18 you looked at the difference between two sentences like these:

a *'I am talking to Shifty,' Gerald said.*
   (direct speech)
b *Gerald said he was talking to Shifty.*
   (reported speech)

To try to make sure you can say and write reported speech sentences correctly, get some more practice by saying the sentences below as reported speech sentences. Take turns around the class three or four times saying your sentences loudly and clearly.

1 'There they are again,' Fu said.
2 'They mean business all right,' Gerald said.
3 'What makes you so sure, Gerry?' Shifty asked.
4 'Sonia, what did you say?' her mother wanted to know.
5 Saphira said, 'I'm sorry, Mas Zeke. I didn't mean anything.'
6 Miss Fanny said, 'Come on, Miss May. Let us cook the food.'
7 'I want a whole apple,' Septimus shouted in protest.
8 'You can't have a whole one,' Mama told Septimus.
9 Mrs Belmont said to me, 'What's your name?'
10 'Now, you,' she said to the driver, 'get out of my way.'

Punctuation Signals

Quotation marks

Look at the underlined parts in these sentences. What is underlined in each case?

a <u>I want a whole apple</u>, Septimus shouted in protest.
b <u>You can't have a whole one</u>, Mama said, <u>and that's that.</u>
c He blurted out between his sobs: <u>I want a whole apple and Mama says No</u>!

Following the same principle, discuss what parts you would underline in these sentences:

d What's wrong? Aunt Bless asked.
e Bless you, children, he said. Bless you, children.
f Concerned that her darling boy was not happy, Aunt Bless asked, What's wrong Septimus? Tomorrow is Christmas!

Instead of underlining, what is done when someone is writing down the actual words somebody said? What is done in the excerpt?

In the excerpt about the riot you did not see underlinings. When someone said something his words were put between speech marks or quotation marks, like this:

'There they are again,' Fu said. 'Like mad red ants.'
'Fantastic!' Shifty said.

Now the sentences d, e and f above do not have the usual marks to bracket off the words actually spoken by the speaker. Where must such marks be put?

Write the sentences with them in the correct places.

Apostrophes

In the excerpt about the riot these words are written with apostrophes ('): *could've* (l. 51); *They're* (l. 52). They mean *could have* and *They are*.

Can you tell where apostrophes must be put in these words?

couldnt   whats   whos   thats   theres
its   Ive   shes   Im   hes

Writing What You Imagine

Answers in an interview

Suppose you were Gerald or Shifty or Fu, and, later that day, after the incident you witnessed, a reporter from a newspaper came around trying to get an account of what happened.

Write the answers you would give to his questions, trying to give as much information as you can, but answering only one question at a time.

Reporter: Where were you when the men got here?
You: ....
Reporter: Where did they go?
You: ....
Reporter: Who was there then?
You: ....
Reporter: What did the men do then?
You: ....
Reporter: Was the superintendent hurt?
You: ....
Reporter: Did the sellers in the market do anything about it?
You: ....
Reporter: What did the rioters do then?
You: ....
Reporter: What was happening in the general neighbourhood at that time?

You: ....
Reporter: Did the number of men increase at any time?
You: ....
Reporter: Who were they?
You: ....
Reporter: How do you know that?
You: ....
Reporter: What did those other men do?
You: ....
Reporter: Why did they obey him?
You: ....
Reporter: Where did they go then?
You: ....
Reporter: What do you think they were going to do?
You: ....
Reporter: Why do you say that?
You: ....
Reporter: Thank you very much. You've been very helpful.
You: ....

About the Language

Singulars and plurals to remember

Nearly all nouns have *singular* forms (for one person or thing) and *plural* forms (for more than one person or thing). But several fit into their own group and need your special attention.

A   Note the spelling of these:

donkey   donkeys
factory   factories
piano   pianos
potato   potatoes
dwarf   dwarfs/dwarves

valley   valleys
photo   photos
solo   solos
calf   calves
wharf   wharfs/wharves

B   Some make other changes, like these:

goose   geese   mouse   mice
ox   oxen   tooth   teeth

C   Some words do not end with an *s* but are plural, e.g.

cattle, people, police, youth

D   Some keep the same form:

sheep   sheep   dozen   dozen
innings   innings   aircraft   aircraft
score (meaning 20)   score

In some sentences *dozens* and *scores* are used.

E   Some look plural but are used with singular verbs, i.e. verbs ending with an *s*:

news   series   draughts   measles
West Indies   United States   billiards

F   Some have no singular form and are used with plural verbs, i.e. verbs without the *s* ending:

thanks   scissors   pliers   shears
trousers   tidings   pants

G   Some are compound words:

son-in-law   sons-in-law
maid-of-honour   maids-of-honour
spoonful   spoonfuls

mousetrap   mousetraps
passer-by   passers-by
cupful   cupfuls

H   Some that have come from other languages have special plurals:

medium (a means or way)   media
stadium   stadia
criterion (a quality)   criteria

fungus   fungi
formula   formulas/formulae
phenomenon   phenomena

I   Some have two plural forms with different meanings:

brother   brothers and brethren
cloth   cloths and clothes
fish   fishes and fish
penny   pennies and pence

20 Belonging Together

Everyday Life

Matters to chat about

Use some of your spare time in class or outside to chat with your friends about these matters.

Why do people get very excited when the West Indies' cricket team is playing against another team?

Why do you think people feel what they call love for their country?

Sometimes countries have quarrels. Would you say that whatever your own country does is always right? What do you think of people in other countries that say their country is always right?

Should a parent say his or her child is always right?

Should people stick to other people just because they have the same colour of skin, or are of the same race? Should they say people like themselves are always right?

Should people of different races join together or fight one another?

Reading to Learn Things

Getting ready

Can you think of some things that you share or have in common with other people around you? They show that you belong to a community. What puts and keeps you in a community?

See whether the excerpt answers that question or any others that might interest you.

urban (l. 5) = belonging to a town or city
legal (l. 29) = having to do with the law
ethnic (l. 31) = related to a way of living, a culture
conflict (l. 34) = disagreement
lifestyle (l. 43) = the way of living

Location

People who live in a village belong to a rural or village community. Towns and cities are often too large to give that same overall sense of belonging, but families may find this in
5 their local, urban neighbourhood community. This may be the street they live on or it may be an apartment complex or housing estate.

Religion

People who follow a religion such as Christianity or Islam feel
10 themselves to be part of a worldwide religious community. A Muslim in Trinidad and a Muslim in Pakistan live very different daily lives. But through belonging to the Muslim community they hold the same beliefs: they read the same holy book, the Koran, and follow the teachings of Mohammed, the
15 Prophet of Allah.

Ethnicity

Almost all Caribbean people came originally from other parts of the world. For some groups in society, especially if they are small in number, this link with their country of origin is still
20 very important. Examples of such groups are the Chinese community and the Syrian and Lebanese community.

Work

There are other kinds of community associated with the work people do. There are certain jobs or livelihoods which give a

25 very strong sense of belonging. It may be work which involves danger in some way, such as fishing or mining. It may be a *profession* or job which involves many years of training, such as medicine or law. People often talk about the fishing community or the legal community.

30 In a community we can find people of similar *or* different ethnic groups, religions or political views. Members may have different ways of behaving. Often this doesn't matter, because the sense of belonging is more important. Sometimes, however, this may cause conflict within the community. Frequently
35 people belong to several communities. For example, their religious community, where they follow the same faith, and the local youth club, where all ethnic groups and religions may be represented.

People often talk about 'community spirit' and say that in the
40 past people cared more for each other. Certainly, many communities have changed with the times and there is not the same degree of closeness among members. But people's lifestyles and interests have changed, so communities have changed.

From *The Caribbean: Our Land And People* By M. Braithwaite *et al.*

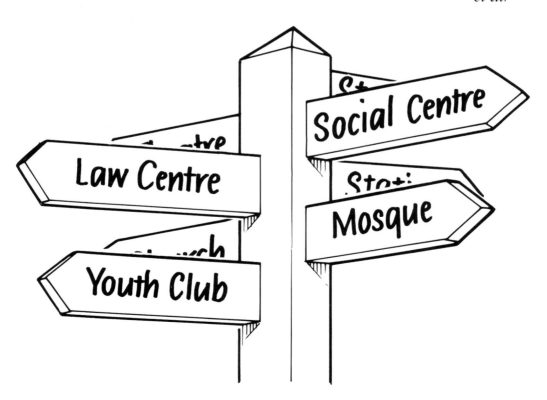

Discussion for developing comprehension skills

A Understanding explicit statements:

1 '… *families may find this* …' (l. 4). Find what?
   a a rural community
   b housing estates
   c a sense of belonging.

2 What does the excerpt say villages have but towns and cities do not?
   a families that are local
   b feeling you are part of a place
   c the smallness of a housing estate.

3 A '*worldwide religious community*' (l. 10) is one
   a that prays for the whole world
   b that travels through the world
   c found in several countries.

4 Muslims all over the world
   a may live different lives
   b read only parts of the Koran
   c are not Mohammedans.

5 Nearly all groups in Caribbean society
   a have come from the same place
   b have connections with other places
   c have never belonged to the Caribbean.

6 Sometimes doing the same job
   a makes people feel close to one another
   b causes one to be better than another
   c involves people in danger.

7 A '*profession*' (l. 27) is a job that
   a pays a high salary
   b takes years to train for
   c is for professors only.

8 In a community people with different beliefs
   a cannot feel they belong together
   b have to change their beliefs
   c still feel they are together.

9 A person
   a may belong to several communities
   b cannot belong to two communities
   c must belong to more than one community.

10 '*community spirit*' (l. 39) means
   a a ghost in the community
   b a spirit a community believes in
   c the feeling to help others in a community.

B Seeing implied connections:

1 Say what you think '*society*' (l. 18) means.
2 How can people in a town feel they are in a village?
3 Where does a community end?
4 Why does conflict or disagreement arise in a society?
5 What is suggested in the phrase '*their country*' (l. 19)?
6 Why would changes in lifestyles and interests change a community?

To Enrich Your Word Bank

Using words you read

Help one another to find the place for each of these words in the sentences below.

local   urban   society   originally origin   associated   involves   legal ethnic   conflict

1 The teacher was the judge in the _____ between the two girls.
2 Some people like everything foreign and nothing _____.
3 The idea I passed on came from my friend _____.
4 A lawyer had to be involved in that _____ matter.

5 The kind of _____ in which you live depends on you as well as everyone else.

6 Being skilled in anything _____ abundant practice.

7 In most places the colour red is _____ with danger.

8 He left the village and went to town to live in an _____ community.

9 I tried to trace the _____ of the rumour that went about in the school.

10 Every _____ group has its own customs.

Completing a series

Put your heads together in small groups and think of a word to complete each of these sets:

1 people	_____	popular
2 faith	_____	faithfulness
3 sense	sensible	_____
4 life	livelihood	_____
5 danger	_____	endanger
6 local	_____	localise
7 commune	community	_____
8 society	_____	sociable
9 origin	originally	_____
10 represent	_____	representative

The prefix pro-

The prefix (syllable) *pro-* in a word could have one of these meanings:

i   favouring or supporting
ii acting in place of
iii forwards or onwards or downwards
iv in front of

Find words in this list that you know and see which of those meanings is in each:

profession   prophet   progress
promote   protect   proceed   procession
provide   propose   prospect   propagate
proverb   prologue   programme
provoke   project   prodigy   protege
propel   pronoun

Grammatical Sentence Patterns

Reported speech sentences

Take turns changing these sentences to reported speech sentences, saying them as clearly and quickly as you can. Then go around the class doing this again and again. The time you spend doing it will be well worth it.

1 One of the girls asked me, 'Where is the phone?'

2 Putting down the chalk, the teacher said, 'Paula you are trying my patience.'

3 'When will we get there?' Dennis asked Sandra.

4 'Leave those sweets alone, Dorothy,' Esmé said.

5 Dupatee told her mother, 'I'll do the washing up now.'

6 'I think I'll have to change the colour,' the painter said.

7 Daddy told Andrew, 'We can play chess tonight.'

8 Eldridge said, 'Would you like to walk to school with me, Tanya?'

9 Maggie complained, 'I do not want to go to church.'

10 'Gerry,' Cindy said, 'I wish you would clean the car.'

11 'Sally, may I borrow your book?' Joseph asked.

12 Parry declared, 'I will give you the magazine, Arthur!'

Spotting singular and plural errors

Find the word that is wrong in each sentence and *say* the sentence correctly.

1 At the airport two aircrafts landed a while ago.

2 On the radio this morning the news were bad.

3 You can see the police is standing at the corner.

4 Every day the cattle wanders across the savannah.

5 The actress was given two dozens of red roses.

6 We scored 396 in the first inning.

7 His trousers was torn by a nail.

8 The pliers has to be used to twist the wire.

9 A series of names were pulled from a hat.

10 The youth of today does as well as can be expected.

Spelling

Spotting misspelled words

Find the 10 words misspelled in this list and say what is wrong in each case.

special ordinary transparant reservoir responsable mischief difficult residence believe seperate instead continue pencil earnest

amoung mirror approach lawyer develop quarel wrestle begger bargain waist beware fortunate cellar posess truly acident speech naked labor basin idea height jeweller parcel chaple vein

Writing What You Know

Order in an announcement

Here is an announcement someone made over the radio. See whether the sentences are in the right order and, if not, discuss together the order they should have been in.

Anyone seeing this missing child should get in touch with the police immediately. At about 9.00 a.m. today a small boy was on Avery Street near Parker's School. We are interrupting this programme to bring you an urgent message. When last seen the child was wearing a blue shirt, a pair of khaki pants and canvas shoes. A reward is offered for any information that would help in finding the missing child. He has not been seen since. Witnesses say he might have entered a brown Honda with a damaged right fender.

When you have corrected that announcement, write one of your own about a missing dog.

Drama for Fun

A short scene of a play

Here is a short scene of a play. Get into groups and prepare to act the play for the rest of the class along the lines suggested in Units 12 and 17.

There is dense bush all around. Ian, Lenny, Krishna, Mary and Zaida are trying to get through, pushing the branches and shrubbery out of the way. They are quite tired and Mary has twisted her ankle.

IAN: Come on. We have to get down to the river. Then we just follow it down to the village.

MARY: I can't go on. Just leave me here. It's all right.

LENNY: Don't talk nonsense. How we goin' to leave you here?

ZAIDA: You don't have to talk to her like that. Is not your ankle that sprain you know.

KRISHNA: Listen. I can hear the river. We not far from it. Let us rest a little bit and then make a last effort.
(*The girls try to sit, but there is only a little space for* MARY. LENNY *squats near to her and looks at the ankle.*)

IAN: Next time you suggest anything, Krishna, I doing just the opposite.

KRISHNA: So yuh goin' to blame me now?

MARY: Nobody blaming anybody. Krishna suggest taking a short cut back home and all of us agree.

LENNY: Is not Krishna's fault, man. All of us wanted to try cutting through the bush.

IAN: Yes, but when I say let us turn back nobody agree with me.

ZAIDA: We had gone too far by then. It didn't make sense turning back then.

KRISHNA: Let's stop arguing. The important thing is to get to the river.

MARY: I think the longer we rest here the more my ankle will hurt. I think we better make a move before it gets dark.

IAN: Krishna, use your super ears again and tell us in what direction the river is.
(KRISHNA *listens and then points.*)

LENNY: Off we go then. (*He helps* MARY *up and puts her arm around his shoulders to support her. They start to push their way again through the bush.*)

21 Walking To School

Everyday Life

Giving instructions

In a spare moment get a chuckle from this cartoon and remind yourself of an important rule to follow.

Reading to Enjoy a Story

Getting ready

Do you notice people and places you see as you walk or ride to school every day? Do you notice what you hear and smell? Spend about two minutes telling one another about things you see, hear and smell.

Then, when you read the excerpt below compare what the boy tells of his walk to school with what you can tell about.

enchantment (l. 18) = a feeling of pleasure and enjoyment
emerged (l. 18) = came out

loin-cloths (ll. 38–39) = garments, clothes
sweetmeats (l. 18) = delicious things to eat, delicacies

One morning I was much too early for school. I passed street sweepers at work on the Promenade and when I came to the High Street only one or two shop doors were open. I walked slowly, absorbing the quietness and noticing some of the alleys
5 that ran away to the backs of fences and walls and distant streets. I looked at the names of these alleys. Some were very funny. And I walked on anxiously so I could look a little longer at the dark funny street.

As I walked it struck me that I did not know the name of that
10 street. I laughed at myself. Always I had stood there looking along it and I did not know the name of it. As I drew near I kept my eyes on the wall of the corner shop. There was no sign on the wall. On getting there I looked at the other wall. There

was a sign-plate upon it but the dust had gathered thick there
and whatever the sign said was hidden behind the dust.

I was disappointed. I looked along the alley which was only
now beginning to get alive, and as the shop doors opened the
enchantment of spice and onions and sweetmeats emerged. I
looked at the wall again but there was nothing there to say
what the street was called. Straining my eyes at the sign-plate
I could make out a C and an A, but farther along the dust had
made one smooth surface of the plate and the wall.

'Stupes,' I said in disgust. I heard mild laughter, and as I
looked before me I saw the man rolling out his rugs. There
were two women beside him and they were talking together
and they were laughing and I could see the women were
pretending not to look at me. They were setting up a stall of
sweetmeats and the man put down his rugs and took out
something from a tray and put it into his mouth, looking back
at me. Then they talked again in the strange tongue and
laughed.

I stood there a while. I knew they were talking about me. I was
not afraid. I wanted to show them that I was not timid and
that I wouldn't run away. I moved a step or two nearer the
wall. The smell rose up stronger now and they seemed to give
the feelings of things splendoured and far away. I pretended I

was looking at the wall but I stole glances at the merchants from the corner of my eyes. I watched the men in their loin-cloths and the garments of the women were full and many

40 coloured and very exciting. The women stole glances at me and smiled to each other and ate of the sweetmeats they sold. The rug merchant spread out his rugs on the pavement and he looked at the beauty of their colours and seemed very proud. He too looked slyly at me.

45 I drew a little nearer because I was not timid of them. There were many more stalls now under the stores. Some of the people turned off the High Street and came to this little alley and they bought little things off the merchants. The merchants held up the bales of cloth and matched them on to the people's

50 clothes, and I could see they were saying it was very nice. I smiled at this, and the man with the rugs saw me and smiled.

That made me brave. I thought of the word I knew in the strange tongue and when I remembered it I drew nearer.

'Salaam,' I said.

55 The rug merchant laughed aloud and the two women laughed aloud and I laughed too. Then the merchant bowed low to me and replied, 'Salaam!'

This was very amusing for the two women. They talked together so I couldn't understand and then the fat one spoke,

60 'Wot wrang wid de warl?'

I was puzzled for a moment and then I said, 'O, is the street sign. Dust cover it.'

'Street sign?' one said, and they covered their laughter with their veils.

65 'I can't read what street it is,' I said. 'What street is this?'

The rug merchant spoke to the two women in the strange tongue and the three of them giggled and one of the women said: 'Every marning you stand up dey and you don' know what they carl here?'

70 'First time I come down here,' I said.

'Yes,' said the fat woman. Her face was big and friendly and she sat squat on the pavement. 'First time you wark down here but every marning you stop dey and watch we.'

I laughed.

75 'You see 'e laughing?' said the other. The rug merchant did not say anything but he was very much amused.

'What you call this street?' I said. I felt very brave because I knew they were friendly to me, and I looked at the stalls, and the smell of the sweetmeats was delicious. There was *barah*
80   too, and chutney and dry *channa*, and in a square tin there was the wet yellow *channa*, still hot, the steam curling up from it.

The man took time to put down his rugs and then he spoke to me. 'This,' he said, talking slowly and making actions with his arms, 'from up dey to up dey is Calcutta Street.' He was very
85   pleased with his explanation. He had pointed from the High Street end of the alley to the other end that ran darkly into the distance. The whole street was very long and dusty, and in the concrete drain there was no water and the brown peel of onions blew about when there was a little wind. Sometimes there was
90   the smell of cloves in the air and sometimes the smell of oil-cloths, but where I stood the smell of the sweetmeats was strongest and most delicious.

From a short story *Enchanted Alley* By Michael Anthony, TRINIDAD

Discussion for developing comprehension skills

A Understanding explicit statements:

1   '*I laughed at myself*' (l. 10). Why did he?
2   What had happened to the sign-plate?
3   When the shop doors opened, what enchanted the narrator (story-teller)?
4   '*I heard mild laughter*' (l. 23). What did he see the man and the woman doing?
5   What do you understand by '*strange tongue*' (l. 30)?
6   '*The smell rose up stronger now*' (l. 35). What smell?
7   How are the phrases '*stole glances*' (l. 37 and 40) and '*looked slyly*' (l. 44) related?
8   What did some people leave the High Street to do?
9   What caused the man, the women and the narrator to laugh?
10   What did the man say was Calcutta Street?
11   Who wrote the story the excerpt comes from?

B Seeing implied connections:

1   Who is the narrator in the story?
2   Why do you suppose '*only one or two shop doors were open*' (l. 3)?
3   What would you say '*absorbing*' (l. 4) means?
4   '*Always I had stood there*' (l. 10). Where?
5   '*I was disappointed*' (l. 16). What about?
6   Why do you suppose the women were '*pretending not to look*' (l. 27)?
7   Why did the fat woman ask '*Wot wrang wid de warl?*' (l. 60)?
8   Why do you think '*the three of them giggled*' (l. 67)?
9   What did the narrator feel brave enough to do?
10   '*I knew they were friendly to me*' (ll. 77–78). How did he know that?
11   Why do you think the man was '*very pleased with his explanation*' (ll. 84–85)?
12   How does the writer of the story show he is a good writer?

To Enrich Your Word Bank

Analogies

Think together and see if you can come up with the correct word for each blank space:

1 *tasty* is to *delicious* as *strange* is to _____

2 *strain* is to *force* as *giggle* is to _____

3 _____ is to *sly* as *exciting* is to *boring*

4 *surface* is to *skin* as *squat* is to _____

5 _____ is to *gathered* as *alive* is to *dead*

6 *matched* is to *paired* as _____ is to *glance*

7 _____ is to *hostile* as *ashamed* is to *proud*

8 *reason* is to *explanation* as _____ is to *pretend*

Some nouns often used

The word *wooden* is an adjective or describing word related to the noun or name *wood*.

What name or noun can you think of related to each of these words:

enchant   distant   anxiously   pretend
proud   brave   amused   pleased
friend   steal   timid   know   active
annoy   protect   scientific

Some story-telling words

Here are some verbs (doing words) that people might use in relating something that happened. Which ones would you choose as being especially useful for telling about coming to school?

admired   thronged   converged
confused   noticed   controlled
stretched   provoked   surveyed   strolled
observed   spread   flowed   annoyed
enquired   sauntered   scrutinized
charmed   perceived   teased
recognised   distinguished   attended
guided   obstructed   explored
delighted   resided   regulated   assisted
pursued   discerned   watched
discovered   traversed   retreated

Grammatical Sentence Patterns

Must have

Quite often people pick up the habit of saying and writing *must of* for *must have*. Perhaps you already have that habit. If so, to get the right habit you need to practise saying the right phrase quite a lot.

Make as many oral sentences as you can, using *must have* in each one and putting together any parts from these boxes to make sense:

1	2	3	4
He She The driver Some of the people	must have	beaten up eaten up taken up spoken to gone with	nine out of every ten boys. all the eggs in the saucepan. some of the schoolboys.

Punctuation Signals

Quotation marks, etc.

Where do quotation marks have to be put in these sentences?

1 You ever seen anything like this before? one woman said to Mr Watson.
2 What seems to be the trouble? he asked.
3 What seems to be the trouble? repeated Mr Watson, throwing up his huge arms.
4 Hmm, said the constable. They're not committing a breach!
5 Anybody else want to go? asked Josh.
6 Yes, sir! Ridley agreed and went hurrying.
7 I want to go home, Martin Duncan said.
8 Then go home, Martin, Josh said.

Now, study the use of punctuation marks in this sentence. Is there anything about how they are used that you did not know about before?

'I can't read what street it is,' I said.
'What street is this?'

How many capital letters are used? Why is each one used?

Where is a question mark put? Why?

Where is a full stop used? Why?

Which word has an apostrophe? Why?

In which places, exactly, are quotation marks put? Why?

If you understand the reasons for using those punctuation marks make sure that you do use them yourself when you are writing a letter or a story. Practise by putting the correct punctuation marks in the correct places in these unpunctuated sentences.

1 First time I come down here I said
2 What do you call this street I said
3 This he said is Calcutta Street
4 I have to go she replied It is getting late
5 Where are you going Mona asked at this hour
6 You can go this way Take the short cut Roy advised
7 Take this Dora urged and hurry

Writing a Story

In a letter to a friend

You might have thought that you had nothing you could write to tell what happens on your way to school. But the writer of the excerpt you read has shown you that whatever you see, hear, smell or do on your way to school is interesting to others, as long as when you write it you are yourself, you tell the truth and you do not pretend to tell about things belonging somewhere else.

Take some time to share with one another all the things you see, hear, do and so on, coming to school on mornings. Be frank and honest.

Then suppose you had a friend like the writer of the story and he or she wanted to know about something that happened one morning.

Sit down and write your friend a letter relating a small incident that happened, or could have happened, when you were coming to school one morning.

Try to be simple, truthful and clear, following the example of Michael Anthony.

Stories to Read

What is the most important thing you must be doing every day? Reading a book, of course.

Here are some stories to read over the next six weeks. If they are not in your class library, ask for them in your school library or a public library. If you cannot find them ask the librarian to give you another list of stories you can borrow.

◆ *The Devil Birds*
Peter and Tyra Bacon, TRINIDAD

◆ *Caldong* Peter Bacon, TRINIDAD and TOBAGO

◆ *The Cloud with the Silver Lining*
C. Everard Palmer, JAMAICA

◆ *Big Doc Bitteroot,*
C. Everard Palmer JAMAICA

◆ *Drought* Andrew Salkey, JAMAICA

◆ *A Hundred Million Francs*
Paul Berna

◆ *The Mule on the Motorway*
Paul Berna

◆ *A Truckload of Rice* Paul Berna

◆ *The Golden Fish* Paul Berna

◆ *Lemon Kelly and the Home-Made Boy*
E. W. Hildrick

◆ *The Questers and the Whispering Spy*
E. W. Hildrick

◆ *The Horse and His Boy* C. S. Lewis

◆ *Emil and the Three Twins*
Erich Kastner

◆ *The Flying Classroom* Erich Kastner

◆ *Lottie and Lisa* Erich Kastner

◆ *The Secret Journey* Harry Kullman

◆ *The Cave Twins* Lucy Perkin

22 A Dangerous Swim

Everyday Life

Wisdom in proverbs

In some moments of spare time join a friend in matching the proverbs in **A** with their meanings in **B**.

A
1. A new broom sweeps clean.
2. Familiarity breeds contempt.
3. Necessity is the mother of invention.
4. Time and tide wait for no man.

B
a. In times of need we always find new ways to do things.
b. Opportunities go away unless people take them right away.
c. Someone who is not kept back by customs will make the most changes in a place.
d. If people get too close to you they lose respect for you.

Reading to Enjoy a Story

Getting ready

Have you ever faced danger because you were afraid of something else?

In the story that the excerpt comes from Peter is afraid because someone said something and made him think he might lose Bella to someone else. So he risks his life in the waters of a raging river to get back to her and make sure.

Does he beat the river? Does he get to Bella in time? The excerpt tells what happened.

bronze (l. 2) = dark-brownish colour
latent (l. 3) = not yet used
diagonally (l. 5) = in a slanting direction
unconsciously (l. 15) = without knowing
rapids (l. 20) = places where a river speeds down in a slope, usually over rocks
marrow (l. 63) = a substance inside your bones
pass (l. 64) = a way through mountains

He stood beside the muddy water in its mad race downstream, stood stripped to the waist, muscled like a bronze god, and rippling with latent strength.

Plunge in, and swim with the current, but cutting across it
5   diagonally all the time, until you were out of it, on the other side. That was it. As easy as that. But always mind she don't pull you under.

The water took him in the first moment of impact and rolled him over and over like a log. Half of the time his head was

10 under. But always he was fighting, fighting to keep coming up.
Something sucked at his legs almost turning him straight
across to the full force of the current, but he kicked free – and
went under. Rolled over, and went under. There was a roaring
noise inside his head. His lungs felt as though they were
15 bursting. But always, even unconsciously, he was fighting,
fighting to keep coming up.

He had forgotten about the old man silently watching the
unequal struggle from the bank. Forgotten about Bella.
Something about something somebody said …

20 The roar of the rapids. The thunder of death in his ears. He
would be broken to ribbons on the rapids. The rocks. His skull
smashed in. His limbs all but torn from his body. He was
fighting like a hundred demons, fighting blind with the roar of
the rapids in his ears, and above him a million tons of water
25 like blood weighing him down.

And then he was out of the current, and across … Something
about something someone had said about a river, and what
would happen if it sucked you under … He couldn't tell if he
lived to be a thousand years how it happened. He had just
30 managed, was all he knew. He hadn't done it himself, either. It
just happened as though he had been shot out of a gun. And
there he was kicking free and near dead. But on the other side.
Out of the current. He had got across.

He pulled himself weakly up on to the bank with the aid of
35 some tree roots. And then his strength left him and he just lay
in the grass and breathed with painful gasps.

He may have lain there for hours. It was getting dark.
Someone was shouting from across the river. He suddenly
remembered the old man. They were like father and son.

40 He pulled himself up at last to a sitting posture, leaning his
back against a stone. He wanted to shout back, across the
gathering darkness. To make him know he had got across; that
he was safe. But first he must catch his breath. He still felt
strangely weak.

45 One thing, though, he would never boast about being able to
best the old river, never again. She had had him licked. She
had all but done for him back there. A miracle had saved him
alive and brought him to the other side.

He stood up now and waved his arms and shouted. Shouted to
50 the man who was as his father, standing anxiously on the other
side. A strange delirium seemed to take possession of him at
once. He was across and alive. A miracle had happened. He
shouted and waved his arms. Wanting the old man to know he
was safe, on the other side, and not somewhere inside the belly
55 of the river.

He wanted to hug the old man to him, and lift him up in his
arms, and prance with him all over the grass, he was so happy
to have come across, and to be alive and whole, and not dead
without the meaning of life, somewhere in the belly of the river.

60 Presently the shouting died down from the opposite bank. And
now there only remained the steady, tremendous roar of the
demon river. And darkness came down and found him standing
there alone, and chill to the marrow.

He turned and went slowly up the narrow pass – to home, the
65 warmth of a fire, and the woman he loved, preferring death to
the thought that he might share her with another.

From the short story *Flood Water* By Roger Mais, JAMAICA

Discussion for developing comprehension skills

A Understanding explicit statements:

1 Why would it be false to say Peters had
a weak-looking body?

2 How did he think he should get across
the river?

3 What happened to him just as he
plunged in?

4 '*... he kicked free*' (l. 12). Free of
what?

5 How did his head and chest feel?

6 Why did he think of the rapids as the
'*thunder of death*' (l. 20)?

7 '*He couldn't tell ... how it happened*'
(ll. 28–29). How what happened?

8 How did he get on to the other bank of the river?

9 What did he think he would not boast about any more?

10 Why did he wave and shout?

11 After the shouting died down what was there left to hear?

B Using context clues:

You should be getting better at recognising clues to meanings of words as you read.

See if you can spot a word or phrase or idea that is connected with the meaning of each of these words:

'impact' (l. 8)   'gasps' (l. 36)   'aid' (l. 34)
'posture' (l. 40)   'prance' (l. 57)

C Seeing implied connections:

1 You met the word 'delirious' in Unit 10. What do you now deduce 'delirium' (l. 51) means?

2 What do you understand by 'the first moment of impact' (l. 8)?

3 'Something sucked at his legs' (l. 11). What do you think it was?

4 Why was the swim called 'the unequal struggle' (ll. 17–18)?

5 Why, do you suppose, had he 'forgotten about the old man' (l. 17) and 'about Bella' (l. 18)?

6 What made him breathe 'with painful gasps' (l. 36)?

7 Who was shouting from across the river?

8 Why didn't Peters shout back right away?

9 Why did he think a miracle had saved him?

10 What was the 'strange delirium' (l. 51) that took possession of him?

To Enrich Your Word Bank

Using words you read
Find the places in the sentences below where these words fit:

bronze   latent   diagonally   impact unconsciously   aid   gasps   posture delirium   prance

1 After diving for a long time he comes up and _____ for breath.

2 Proceed _____ across the Square from north-east to south-west.

3 The food was collected and sent as _____ to victims of the hurricane.

4 While listening to me, he _____ kept pulling his ear lobe.

5 Do not let the children _____ through the room like tribal dancers.

6 They cleaned up the _____ statue until it shone.

7 A slouching _____ of your body makes you look lazy.

8 The cars made a loud _____ when they collided.

9 I think he has a lot of _____ talent he has not put to use yet.

10 She was talking wildly in the _____ the fever had put her into.

Some words ending with -ic
Work in groups and fit each of these words with a meaning below. Then use a dictionary to check how many you had right.

panic   ethnic   automaiic   frolic   logic optic   toxic   graphic   chronic

lethargic   intrinsic   specific   relic
fanatic   basic

a   to play about happily
b   having to do with your eye
c   working by itself
d   very sharp and clear to see
e   sudden uncontrolled fright
f   lasting a long time without a cure
g   having to do with a people's culture
h   at the bottom, supporting other things
i   belonging to and part of the nature of
    something
j   having a poisonous substance
k   something left from a long time ago
l   what makes ideas have good reasons
m   a person who has too much devotion
    to something or someone
n   particularly related to something, with
    no other connection
o   feeling slow to move

Use any spare time you get to check any of
these that are unfamiliar to you:

tunic   arsenic   tonic   frantic   heroic
cubic   mimic   magnetic   antic   tactic
hectic   dramatic   sporadic   epic
laconic

Words of similar meaning
Two words in each line have similar
meanings to the first one. Which one does
not?

1   broken   decreased   smashed
    fractured
2   aid   help   errand   assistance
3   pain   agony   anguish   agility
4   weak   nimble   feeble   infirm
5   anxious   eager   nervous   eloquent
6   prance   saunter   jump   dance
7   tremendous   huge   elegant
    enormous
8   fight   contest   indulge   struggle
9   danger   risk   peril   control
10 escape   elude   entreat   evade

GRAMMAR

Grammatical Sentence Patterns

Using 'amount' and 'number'
Nowadays many people, especially
Americans, find it easier to use the word
amount for the word *number*. But that is
not yet universally acceptable in English.

Take note of how they are used in these
sentences:

a   The *number* of runs he scored was a
    record.
b   The *amount* of money he received was
    very little.

In a, *number* is used with *runs*, and *runs*
can be counted as one run, two runs and
so on. The word *number* is used with all
countable nouns (names).

In b, *amount* is used with *money*, and
money cannot be counted as one money,
two monies and so on. The word *amount*
is used with *uncountable nouns*.

Now, for practice, *say* these sentences,
putting in *amount* or *number* in the blank
spaces:

1   A large _____ of people attended
    the cricket match.
2   The wicket-keeper held a greater
    _____ of catches than anyone
    before.
3   There was a certain _____ of
    satisfaction in seeing the game.
4   In the first innings we made a small
    _____ of runs.
5   We saw a great _____ of places
    where damage was done.
6   An expensive _____ of equipment
    was lost.
7   He denied a _____ of charges made
    against him.

8 Were you able to do the _____ of questions in the text?

Using many and much

Sometimes, too, *much* is used incorrectly, when *many* should be used.

Much is to be used in the same way as *amount* is to be used: with *uncountable nouns*.

Many is to be used in the same way as *number* is to be used: with *countable nouns*.

For practice in using them correctly *say* these sentences, putting in *much* or *many* in the blank spaces:

1 Throughout his career _____ of his scores were high.
2 We did not think he could tell so _____ lies.
3 The cricketer carried _____ of his gear with him.
4 The room had too _____ furniture.
5 I didn't know they had so _____ books in the library.
6 There are _____ scenes to be enjoyed on the island.
7 _____ of the scenery is dull and drab.
8 Why do you wear so _____ clothes?

Learn this rule by heart:

uncountable nouns take *amount* and *much*;
countable nouns take *number* and *many*.

Some Idioms We Use

Matching meanings

A part of each sentence below is underlined. It is an idiomatic phrase.

Choose the meaning below that matches the underlined part of the sentence.

1 By telling a lie she put herself <u>in my bad books</u>.
2 The two of them are always <u>at loggerheads</u> over trifles.
3 Since her employer refused Sue decided <u>to take French leave</u> and go to the races.
4 I will not go to all that trouble because <u>the game is not worth the candle</u>.
5 Myra always <u>falls on her feet</u> whenever she gets into difficulties.
6 It was really <u>child's play</u> solving that puzzle.
7 What did he do to earn his <u>bread and butter</u>?
8 They ran off and <u>left me in the lurch</u> when the teacher came.
9 I am not a magician who can <u>make bricks without straw</u>.
10 Lenny <u>gave me the cold shoulder</u> when I went to speak to him.

a   disagreeing
b   means of livelihood
c   out of favour
d   it will not repay the effort
e   go without permission
f   very easy to do
g   did not respond
h   recovers from trouble
i   deserted
j   do something without the means to do it

Writing Your Opinions

Giving reasons

Name some things you like a lot and some you dislike. Then say sentences expressing your opinions on some of them. For example, say a sentence like *Opera singing is the most boring singing there is.*

People express opinions in sentences like that all the time. But it is sometimes necessary to explain why you have a certain opinion about something, giving reasons why you have that opinion.

Study this paragraph and see how it gives the reasons why the person thinks boxing is a cruel form of sport.

Boxing is a cruel form of sport. In it two men are put into a ring to batter each other, as if giving each other pain is an enjoyable activity. They show no consideration for each other's feelings. The whole aim and purpose a boxer has is to hit his opponent as hard as possible and knock him to the floor. Men have been badly injured fighting each other in that uncivilised manner. Some have suffered serious brain damage (as if their brains had not been damaged enough before) and have ended up with loss of memory, or have lost control of their limbs, or have fallen into a coma, unconscious as a vegetable for the rest of their lives. Such cruelty is what the so-called sport of boxing calls for.

Notice that the opinion given in the first sentence is explained with reasons. Notice how each sentence helps to explain and support the one that comes before.

Now give yourself a little practice explaining the reasons that might be given by someone for an opinion he or she has. Write one of the sentences given below, or a sentence expressing an opinion of your own, and then write other sentences to follow it to make a paragraph with reasons and evidence.

a   Boxing is a harmless and enjoyable sport.
b   My school is a very good school.
c   Adults are too hard on children.

d   A poor person has a hard life.
e   Horror films are very exciting.

f   Dogs are the most devoted pets to have.
g   It is important to learn English well.

Words in Literature

Metaphor

In Book 1 and in Unit 18 of this book you gave some attention to examples of metaphor because almost all the time people use metaphors in speaking and writing. When you do not realise someone is using a metaphor you completely misunderstand what he or she is saying.

Look for metaphors in these small parts of poems and give your opinion on whether the comparison made is a good one or not. Ask yourself how much it helps a reader to imagine what the writer means.

i   Fighters can't pack pity with their gear.

Vernon Scannell, ENGLAND

ii   Floorboards, windows, doors,
Tossing, tumbling, flying
From the wind's murderous claws,
The thundering hooves of the rain

Barnabas J. Ramon-Fortune,
TRINIDAD

iii   a lightbeam
spotted clothing
on the ground

Mervyn Morris, JAMAICA

iv   At every first communion, the moon
would lend her lace to a barefooted
town

Derek Walcott, ST LUCIA

v   canefields to south and east
combed by the wind

Cecil Gray, TRINIDAD

vi   There, man! Look, look at him, the
writing man
Muscles of Jamaica's hills carved in his
face.

Ian McDonald, TRINIDAD

vii   The wrinkled sea beneath him crawls

Alfred Tennyson, ENGLAND

viii   For when his heart,
driven before a gale
a loneliness,
sought in our hearts
a harbour and a home,
no sign we gave
to anchor our compassion
in his soul

Judy Miles, TRINIDAD

23 Communication

Everyday Life

Matters to discuss

Get together with some friends in your spare time and discuss these questions:

When do local radio stations broadcast news?

What newspapers are published in your country?

What is printed in newspapers?

Which big businesses do you know operating in your country or abroad?

Do the poor people in your country get help to live?

Do you remember what was said when some workers went on strike in your community?

Reading to Learn Things

Getting ready

As long as you live you will use words. Why? Have any of the thoughts in your head come from someone else? How do people in a community get their beliefs? What does it mean to communicate?

Those are questions you should bear in mind as you read the article below.

symbol (l. 8) = something that stands for or represents something else, as a flag represents your country
accurate (l. 37) = having no error

People talk to one another to communicate; that is, to share their ideas by getting others to see and understand certain thoughts they are putting into words.

Communication is done in various ways. It can be done
5 through gestures or movements of the hands and eyes. It can be done with dancing and music, or with pictures and photographs. But it is done mostly by using words, or signs and symbols that represent words. A word is a sound that is taken to have a certain meaning, and we use the letters of the
10 alphabet to put that sound down on paper.

When we read we hear sounds in our heads and those sounds tell us what we must think about, what ideas or thoughts to picture in our minds. So books, magazines, newspapers and so on are used by people to pass on ideas or thoughts to other
15 people. Sometimes the ideas can be tested to see whether they are true or not, whether they are facts. But very often they cannot be tested because they are only what a person believes the truth is. They are merely opinions.

People frequently state their opinions as if they are stating
20 facts, and other people often mistake opinions for facts. As you might know, people usually take what they read in newspapers, or hear on the radio, or see on television as if it has been proven to be true. But reporters and broadcasters use most of the time to communicate opinions. For instance, a
25 reporter or journalist might write 'Grenadians had been waiting tensely since the appeal was turned down' as if he or she was stating a proven fact. However, that sentence merely gives someone's opinion of what was happening.

Sometimes the same opinion or view of things is believed by
30 many people and that makes it seem to be proven truth. Nevertheless, an idea is not necessarily true because a lot of

people believe it to be true. If the idea depends on belief and cannot be tested to see if it is a fact, then it is merely an opinion, no matter how many people believe it. For example,
35 this statement cannot be tested: *Blue is a pleasant colour.* But this one can be tested: *The house is painted blue.* So, a person who is interested in being accurate would say: *I believe blue is a pleasant colour* or *To me blue is a pleasant colour.*

To a large extent, the people in charge of newspapers,
40 magazines, radio stations and television channels control which ideas might enter your mind. They decide on what they want to tell you and how to tell it to you. Even when they all give the same news of the day, each one fixes it up or edits it in his or her own way for you to get a certain view or opinion of it.

45 For instance, many of them might want you to think it is not wrong for big businesses to make big profits even when people suffer for it. They would give you news and views in such a way that you would join them in saying that workers should not cause businesses to lose profits. They would probably also want
50 you to believe that a Government should not collect taxes from big businesses to spend the money on the needs of poor people.

It is not too early for you to be thinking about these things.

Discussion for developing comprehension skills

A Understanding explicit statements:

1 What does the writer say '*to communicate*' (l. 1) means?
2 Name four ways of communicating.
3 According to the article, what is a word?
4 What does the article say happens when we read words?
5 Why, according to the writer, are books, magazines and newspapers printed?
6 '*But very often they cannot be tested*' (ll. 16–17). Tested for what?
7 What did the writer say is the mistake people make when they hear or read opinions?
8 Which people are said to use control over the thoughts you have?
9 What does the article say '*edits it*' (l. 43) means?

B Seeing implied connections:

1 What, would you say, is an opinion?
2 Describe the work of reporters, journalists and broadcasters.
3 Why are words so important to pay attention to?
4 What, do you suppose, makes some people believe whatever is in a newspaper or on the radio or television?
5 Some people doubt popular opinions. What do you expect other people to tell them when they do that?
6 Why is this statement an opinion? *Popular music is the best thing to listen to.*
7 Why is this statement a factual statement? *That piece of music is very popular.*

8 How does the article show you that a newspaper has an axe to grind?

To Enrich Your Word Bank

Using words you read

Help one another to fit each of these words into the sentence where it belongs.

communicate various gestures symbol represent proven appeal view accurate control

1 Do you agree with my _____ of the boy's behaviour?
2 Simple words are best when you wish to _____ your thoughts to others.
3 When walking your dog _____ it by keeping it on a leash.
4 She seems to be making frantic _____ with her arms, warning us to stay away.
5 The man sentenced for the crime made an _____ for mercy.
6 There are _____ makes of car on the roads.
7 We checked to see if the list of missing items was _____.
8 We picked a good team to _____ us in the competition.
9 The statement was _____ to be true when we tested it.
10 A flag is a _____ of a nation's independence.

Some misused opinion words

All around you you hear people use words like *fantastic, superb, wonderful* or *incredible* when something is merely interesting or enjoyable. When that is done the words they use lose their meanings, and when something comes along that is really superb or fantastic they have no word to use to show that it is better than something else.

To help yourself to avoid such harmful exaggeration you must pay attention to how words have shades of meaning.

Take these sets of words and discuss how to arrange each set so that the word with the least force is first and the one with the greatest force is last. For example: *unpleasant → ugly → offensive → hideous*

a hate disgust dislike disapproval
b love adore admire like
c crowd mob throng group
d attack criticise insult abuse
e breeze gale whirlwind hurricane
f agony discomfort pain anguish
g prevent check obstruct impede
h valuable useful precious good
i shock stun surprise amaze
j stupid dull unintelligent idiotic

Grammatical Sentence Patterns

Negatives

Can you see what makes this sentence ungrammatical?

The reporter wasn't hardly listening.

It is like saying *The reporter was not never listening*, because the word *hardly* has a meaning like *not, never, no, nothing* and others like that – a negative meaning.

When you put two such negatives together one cancels out the other and destroys the meaning of your sentence. So instead of using *hardly* with *wasn't* (was not) you would use the positive word *even*, and say

The reporter wasn't even listening.

With that in mind, fill in the blanks in these sentences with a suitable word from the two in the brackets.

1 Mr Tate didn't _____ go to see Mrs Belmont. (*ever/never*)
2 Daphne didn't see _____ of them near the tree. (*either/neither*)
3 Beppo did not say _____ against Roy. (*nothing/anything*)
4 Beppo did not get _____ of the mangoes. (*none/any*)
5 Neither Roy _____ Beppo knew what to say. (*or/nor*)

Now make some oral sentences of your own with a negative (like *not, never, nothing* or *none*) and a positive (like *ever, anything, any* or *something*).

Neither … nor; either … or

There is a time when two negatives are used together. They are *neither* and *nor*. We say sentences like *She chose neither you nor me*. The words *neither* and *nor* are called correlatives. But there must be no other negative related to them in the sentence.

The same applies to *either* and *or*. We say *You must choose either one or the other*. But there must be no other positive related to them in the sentence.

Now say these sentences, fitting one of these – *neither, nor, either, or* – correctly into the spaces.

a At the door I saw _____ a man nor a woman.
b Iris would like to play _____ tennis or netball.
c Neither the red blouse _____ the blue one pleases me.
d The blame should be put on neither the boys _____ the girls.
e I think neither the army _____ the police should be brought in.
f He is certain _____ Grace or Harry knows about it.
g It is _____ the tall man or the fat woman who has taken the box.
h Neither the cat _____ the dog wants to eat.
i The letter was written either by James _____ by Michael.
j In my opinion neither the newspaper _____ the television tells the whole truth.

Punctuation Practice

Quotation marks

What are the missing punctuation marks in this passage?

Who you talkin to he asked
You Milton said walking towards him
That pot is not yours You are a thief
You callin me a thief
Yes Milton said You are a sneak thief

Write the passage putting in all the punctuation marks in the right places.

Three sentences of a story

There are 12 errors in punctuation in this short passage. Write out the passage correctly punctuated.

he caught me looking at him are you margo he asked staring at me i turned away in confusion feeling very embarrassed

Writing What You Know

Facts in a letter

It is not too early for you to think about writing letters to newspapers. What you have to remember is that the editor of the newspaper is not your personal friend, your playmate or your pal. You are strangers and you have to speak in a formal, respectful way, as you would speak to anyone you are not on familiar terms with.

Then you have to remember two things about setting out the letter. Look at this format:

Carlton Comprehensive School
8 Chiltern Avenue
St. Mark's
28 October 19..

The Editor
The Clarion Express
96 High Street
St. Mark's

Dear Sir,

Carlton Comprehensive School will be organising a drive ....

        I am, etc.

        James Beeston

Note the following important points:

1 what is put above *Dear Sir*
2 you end with *I am, etc.* and your full name. (Not *I remain, Yours truly* or *I remain, Your true friend* or *I remain, Your sincere friend* or anything like that.)

Nowadays it is more usual, too, to put your ending (I am, etc.) on the left side of the page, under Dear Sir.

Now imagine that your school is organising a drive to collect used clothing to give to needy people who have lost all their belongings in a hurricane.

Write a letter to the editor of a local newspaper giving the facts about the drive.

Give answers to the questions below and to any others you think of, arranging them in the order in which they should be answered.

i   What should be done by donors to make sure the clothing is clean enough to be handled?
ii   How will people know the students sent to collect the clothing?
iii Where will the clothing be taken to?
iv   When is the drive to take place?

v   Who will be collecting?
vi What should the used clothing be put into?

vii Where?
viii Are there any particular items most needed?

Words in Literature

Associations and connotations

If a reporter writes *The speaker lectured to his audience*, the word *lectured* tells that the person spoke, but it also suggests, or gives you the feeling, that the speaker was not very exicting to listen to.

If a person says *Let us go home* the word *home* denotes the place where he lives, but it also brings to mind a feeling that comes with ideas of family, rest, safety and love.

Many words carry extra meanings and feelings with them, in addition to the basic meanings they have in a dictionary. They suggest certain extra meanings which are called *connotations*.

For example, *childish* and *childlike* both mean *of a child*, but *childish* suggests *babyish*, while *childlike* suggests *innocence*.

The extra feelings and ideas that a word might bring to mind come from what the word has been associated with for a long time – its associations.

To bring us the full meaning of what they write, poets and other writers depend a lot on the associations and connotations that words have. That is something you have to be sensitive about to understand and enjoy fully what you read.

See if you can detect what feelings and associations are meant to be brought to mind with the words underlined:

a   But I have <u>promises</u> to keep
    And <u>miles</u> to go before I <u>sleep</u>

    Robert Frost, USA

b   'Is there anybody there?' said the Traveller
    Knocking on the <u>moonlit</u> door;
    And his horse in the <u>silence</u> champed the grasses
    Of the <u>forest's</u> ferny floor:

    Walter de la Mare, ENGLAND

c   Today we have naming of <u>parts</u>. Yesterday,
    We had daily <u>cleaning</u>. And tomorrow morning,
    We shall have what to do after <u>firing</u>. But today,
    Today we have naming of parts. Japonica
    <u>Glistens</u> like <u>coral</u> in all of the neighbouring <u>gardens</u>,
    And today we have naming of parts.

    Henry Reed, ENGLAND

What connotations do you sense are associated with each of these words?

*wreath   art   pirate   fox   naked
church   gentleman   screams*

24 In Search Of A Play

Everyday Life

Speech sounds to make

Give some attention to this in your spare time and give yourself some practice you might need.

The word *conduct* is said in two different ways, according to how it is used. In one case the stress is on the first syllable, *con*, and in the other case it is on the second syllable, *duct*.

Using it as a noun or name we say *CONduct*, as in this sentence:

His cónduct was appalling.

Using it as a verb or doing word we say *conDUCT*, as in this sentence:

You must condúct yourself properly.

Some other words like that are:

ally   contest   suspect   produce
conflict   process   content   addict

Use a dictionary to check on the exact meanings of any words you are not very familiar with and use each in two sentences *orally*: (a) as a noun and (b) as a verb.

(Take note, however, that Americans now are not aware of this difference made in speaking English.)

Reading to Enjoy a Play

Getting ready

If you have been doing drama for fun you would have improvised, or made up on the spot, dialogue and action for a scene of a play.

The actors and actresses in the play excerpt below were asked to improvise a play. They are on the stage in front of an audience trying to think of what to make up. Would you like to be in that situation?

Choose four readers to be Lora, Winifred, Ernest and Tony and one to read the directions in the brackets. Change the five readers after a while.

Winifred means the stage manager when she says '*God Almighty*' (l. 9).
ingénues (l. 13) = young persons without any knowledge of the world
humiliating (l. 46) = making you ashamed
caricature (l. 85) = an exaggeration, an overdone picture of someone's faults
governess (l. 87) = a home teacher and nurse
sticky (l. 13) = over-emotional
theatre is spelt *theater* (l. 8) because the play is American

In Search Of A Play   175

LORA:	I should think a mother would be a nice change for you.
WINIFRED:	Me!
ERNEST:	What do you want to do?
WINIFRED:	*(looking from one to the other, wondering if she ought to say it)*: Well, I'm sticking my neck out, but once – just once, mind you – I would like to play the sweet young thing everybody falls in love with. Don't laugh! Don't laugh any of you or I'll leave the theater this minute – I don't care what God Almighty out there says. I'm serious.
ERNEST:	But that's Lora's part.
WINIFRED:	It's always Lora's part. I want to do it once.
LORA:	I'm sure I don't know why. Ingénues are such sticky, spineless things.
WINIFRED:	I want to be sticky!
LORA:	But there's so much more to a good character role.
WINIFRED:	Then you play the mother!
LORA:	*(Really wishing she could)* I'd like to, but I don't think Ernest would let me. *(She looks at ERNEST hopefully.)*
ERNEST:	I certainly wouldn't. That's Winifred's part.
WINIFRED:	All right. I just thought I'd have my say.
ERNEST:	And Tony will play your son.
WINIFRED:	Is that the best I could do?
TONY:	Don't worry, Winifred; I don't like it any more than you do.
ERNEST:	And what's the matter with you?

Line numbers: 5, 10, 15, 20, 25

TONY:	Me play her son? I wouldn't know the first thing to do.
WINIFRED:	Try hopping up and down on one foot.
TONY:	Another joke! Good for you, Winifred!
WINIFRED:	Stop feeling sorry for yourself. 30
TONY:	The reason I can't play the part is because I've never been a son. Oh, I had parents – wonderful parents – so wonderful that when I was six they told me I'd been a mistake, they hadn't wanted me, and would I please not get in their way. I was keeping them from having a good 35 time. They wanted to laugh. That was what they did best. They laughed at anything – especially things they didn't want to understand. The way Winifred does. (*There is a pause.*)
WINIFRED:	(*Quietly, but with bite*) They were probably very cruel. 40 Am I?
TONY:	If I say yes, you'll think I'm feeling sorry for myself. If I say no, I won't be telling the truth.
WINIFRED:	I never intend to be cruel. I feel very kindly about most things. But I'm ashamed of it, so it doesn't come out 45 that way. There's something humiliating about letting yourself go. (*Directly, sincerely.*) I think you can play my son, Tony.
TONY:	All right. I will.
ERNEST:	And Lora will be your sweetheart. You've just become 50 engaged and you've brought her home to meet your mother.
LORA:	What will you play, Ernest?
ERNEST:	I'm a friend of the family. Wealthy, handsome, dashing, influential, wise. The backbone of the play. The one 55 who resolves the conflict in the end.
LORA:	(*Rather alarmed*) Does there have to be a conflict?
ERNEST:	Of course. Whoever heard of a play without a conflict?
LORA:	What will it be? Am I in it?
ERNEST:	Yes. Winifred doesn't like you because you're stealing 60 her son. And she's a fighter. She's determined to break up the engagement. But it so happens you're a fighter, too. Neither of you will give in. Conflict.
WINIFRED:	How do you propose to resolve that?
ERNEST:	(*To* WINIFRED) You're only jealous of Lora because you're 65 lonely and you have no one but Tony to love. So I'll marry you and that will settle everything.
WINIFRED:	Won't Tony's father object?
ERNEST:	(*After a moment's thought*) He's dead.
WINIFRED:	That's the part I want to play. 70
LORA:	And Tony and I get married?
ERNEST:	Yes.
LORA:	I'm so glad it has a happy ending. That's perfect, Ernest.

	I don't know how you thought it up. Go ahead and say the first line.	75
ERNEST:	Give me a minute. (*He puts his hand to his brow and moves slowly around the stage. He ends up by* TONY, *removes his hand from his brow, and speaks very dramatically.*) My boy. This is a very serious step you are about to take. Marriage is the most important event in a man's life. (*Turning majestically to* LORA.) In a woman's, too. (*Spreading his arms to include them both.*) Be sure, my children, be terribly sure that you love each other. (*Long pause.*) Enough.	80
WINIFRED:	(*Drawing herself up into a caricature of an old, grand lady*) Of course she loves my son. Women have always been attracted to him. When he was three, his governess cut her throat for unrequited love.	85
LORA:	(*With stars in her eyes*) Oh, I do love him! I do, I do, I do! Just the sight of him – the sound of his voice, the touch of his hands – the way his eyes crinkle up at the corners when he smiles!	90
WINIFRED:	How sticky can you get?	
LORA:	Wasn't that line all right? It's a sentimental comedy.	
WINIFRED:	It's a farce.	95
ERNEST:	You're both wrong. It's a drama.	
TONY:	What difference does it make? The important thing is that you don't mean what you're saying – it doesn't make sense.	
ERNEST:	(*Icily*) You don't like it.	100
TONY:	It's not a question of liking.	
ERNEST:	Now, listen, Tony, I have been in the theater a great deal longer than you have, and I'm tired of your telling me how to do things.	
TONY:	But it's pointless if we don't believe in ourselves. Isn't it? (*He looks imploringly at the three of them.* WINIFRED *has been listening to what he said.* ERNEST *turns away impatiently.*)	105

From the one-act play *Impromptu* By Tad Mosel, USA

Discussion for developing comprehension skills

A Understanding explicit statements:

1 What does Lora mean by '*a mother would be a nice change for you*' (l. 1)?

2 '*I'm sticking my neck out*' (l. 5). Say that in your own words.

3 What kind of part did Winifred want to play?

4 Who usually played the part of '*the sweet young thing*' (ll. 6–7)?

5 What did Lora wish to be in the play?

6 What did Tony's parents tell him when he was six?

7 '*... with bite*' (l. 40). What do you take that to mean?

8   What did Winifred say that she was ashamed of?

9   '... *resolves the conflict*' (l. 56). Try to explain what that means.

10 How did Ernest think the conflict in the play they were making could be solved?

11 What do you imagine from '*speaks very dramatically*' (ll. 78–79)?

12 Describe what Ernest should do when he gets to '*Turning majestically to Lora*' (l. 81).

13 '... *unrequited love*' (l. 88). What do you think that is?

14 How did Lora and Winifred disagree about the kind of play they were making up?

15 What did Tony not like about what they were making up?

Seeing implied connections:

1   Why do you suppose Winifred had to say '*Don't laugh*' (l. 7)?

2   What do you think is a '*character role*' (l. 16)?

3   How did Tony let out something inside himself?

4   What kind of parents would you say Tony had?

5   Why did Winifred ask if she was cruel?

6   What did she always want to hide?

7   According to Ernest, between whom was the conflict of the play to be?

8   Why did Ernest wait for '*a moment's thought*' (l. 69) to say '*He's dead*' (l. 69)?

9   '*That's perfect, Ernest*' (l. 73). What does Lora show of herself there?

10 '*Oh, I do love him!*' (l. 89). Love whom?

11 What does Ernest mean by '*I have been in the theater a great deal longer than you*' (ll. 102–103)?

12 How should the actress playing Winifred say '*Is that the best I could do?*' (l. 23)?

13 When Winifred says '*Try hopping up and down on one foot*' (l. 28) she is making a joke at someone's expense. Where else does she make a teasing or humorous remark?

To Enrich Your Word Bank

Words about plays
In small groups put your ideas together in trying to fit each of these words with a meaning given below.

comedy   tragedy   melodrama   farce sentimental   character   theatre conflict   role   improvisation

a   a place where plays are staged
b   a play, film, or book that ends happily
c   making up on the spot the action and dialogue for a play or a scene
d   a person of a play that an actor or actress must pretend to be
e   a play, film or story that has a sad ending
f   the reason why persons of a play have the disagreement
g   showing a lot of emotion or feeling for something that is not worth so much feeling
h   an actor's part in a play
i   a kind of drama with exaggerated, sensational events and characters, usually with violence
j   a type of drama that amuses people because a lot of unlikely things happen

Words you read
In which sentence would you use each of these words?

propose   implore   humiliate   crinkle caricature   unrequited

1   Make sure the paper remains smooth and doesn't _____.

2 He went on his knees to _____ her to marry him.

3 When she refused he realised his love was _____.

4 I _____ that we make an anthology with our stories.

5 The cartoonist took his pen and drew a _____ of the rock star.

6 Sandy tried to insult and _____ Vern by shutting the door in his face.

Odd one out

In small groups of three or four examine each set of words to find the one in each set that is quite different in meaning from the others.

a theatre stadium auditorium museum

b innocent wonderful marvellous admirable

c mistake judgement error fault

d understand comprehend create perceive

e portable incredible likely expected

f influential powerful sober persuasive

g improvise conflict clash differ

h originate end settle resolve

i useless belligerent pointless futile

A crossword puzzle

10 Someone who limps is this
11 South-east (abbreviation)
13 North-west (abbreviation)
16 A caterpillar changes … a butterfly
17 A young goose
18 To finish
20 This soft stuff is used to make pots
21 Spheres or globes

Down

1 Dropping
2 Elizabeth II is Queen … England
3 Smallest pieces of matter
4 It grows on your head
5 Six … eight make fourteen
8 Between you and …
9 Sixty of these make a minute
12 A strong feeling of annoyance
14 What many sheep are reared for
15 All work and no … makes Jack a dull boy
16 Opposite of *out*
19 Make a careful note (abbreviation)

Across

1 A young horse
4 To expect and desire
6 Stern part of a ship. Shorter than *after*
7 The driver of this machine stops to pick up passengers

Grammatical Sentence Patterns

Combined sentences

Read these three sentences:

a   I can't play the part.
b   I've never been a son.
c   I can't play the part because I've never been a son.

You will notice that c is a combination or joining together of a and b.

Can you tell which two sentences were combined to make this one:

d   Different characters are played by actors who act in plays.

Now think about how each set of sentences below can be combined into one sentence without using *and* or *but* to join them.

When you have formed the combined sentence correctly say it loudly and clearly at least twice.

1   I would like to play the sweet young thing. Everybody falls in love with the sweet young thing.
2   Leon cannot be the leader. He likes to lead. He does not know where to lead us.
3   I am embarrassed by it. I make a joke of it. Nobody knows how I feel.
4   Another actor of the cast has left. He was in the new play. It is due to start soon.
5   A bird has wings. They enable it to fly.
6   We want to pass the examination. What do we need to practise?
7   The owner does not live here. The cat belongs to her.
8   They laughed at everything. They laughed at things they didn't understand.
9   They do not do anything about the noise. The noise will deafen us.
10   There is the bin. We put litter in it.
11   I have brought him home. I want him to meet my mother. My mother always wants to know my friends.
12   People are dying of starvation. We do not seem to care. We can do something to help.
13   The music is too soft. It is difficult to hear it.
14   My father doesn't like him. My father thinks he is no good. My father is very suspicious.
15   You're jealous of Lydia. You're lonely. She is very popular.

Judging What You Hear and Read

Opinions and factual statements

A factual statement may be found to be false when we test it to see if it is true. But an opinion cannot be tested to see if it is true or false, except to find whether other people have the same opinion.

See if you can sort out the statements below into those which are factual statements because they can be tested, and those which are merely opinions and cannot be tested.

a   Seven hundred students attend this school.
b   It is the best school in the country.
c   My brother is 6 feet tall.
d   The play we saw at the theatre was well acted.
e   There are some insects in the water.

f   Some people try to spoil this beautiful country.

g   Our souls live on after we die.

h   You can get on a plane at the airport.

i   Communism is a bad system.

j   My friend, Marass, has a new radio.

k   Barbados is smaller than Antigua.

l   The people of the Caribbean are friendly.

m   The red car is the faster of the two.

n   There was happiness on his face when he left.

o   The young people of today are more independent.

p   Dawson is handsome and charming.

Writing What You Imagine

A Conversation in a story

If the author of the play *Impromptu* had written a story instead, he would have written sentences like this:

Ernest said, 'But that is Lora's part.'
'It's always Lora's part,' Winifred replied. 'I want to do it once.'

Some other words used instead of *said* and *replied* are:

remarked   whispered   shouted
muttered   stated   declared   exclaimed
sighed   stammered   drawled   stuttered
asserted   cried   mumbled   murmured
commented   disclosed   affirmed
revealed   observed   recalled   explained
answered   spoke

Now imagine a conversation between four of your classmates about something that happened in class, or something somebody suggested, or something they have been asked to do.

Let the conversation go in your head for a bit, then sit and write as much of it as you can using quotation marks properly and using various words for *said*.

Drama for Fun

Story into play scenes

Read this newspaper report. Then get into groups and make up the dialogue and movements for a scene that you can practise, just as you did before.

After seven years with a kindly kidnapper, schoolboy Steven Stayner returned home to the parents he had almost forgotten.

His mother, Kay Stayner, sobbed quietly as she hugged the strapping 14-year-old lad she had not seen since the day he vanished – just before Christmas 1972.

'This is a miracle', she said, 'I always knew one day our prayers would be answered, but now I cannot believe the nightmare is over.' Then, after more hugs and kisses from the rest of the Stayner family, Steven told for the first time the story of the most incredible kidnappings ever known …

The little boy, only seven years old, was walking home from school, excited by thinking of Christmas only a couple of days away. He was 100 yards from the Stayner's neat bungalow when a stranger drew up in a car.

'He told me that my parents didn't want me any more and from now on he was going to look after me,' said Steven.

Then they drove away and Steven's strange new life began in a one-roomed log cabin several hundred miles away. The kidnapper, according to the police, was Kenneth Parnell, a 48-year-old hotel clerk.

'At first I was frightened and I was very sad and lonely,' said Steven, 'I missed everyone.'

'But he didn't treat me bad and he got me a dog', – a little terrier called Queenie who is still with him. After a time Parnell 'adopted' the boy, changing his name to Dennis Parnell.

Steven called him 'Daddy' and he even went to a local school, believing he really had been given a new parent. He was never abused or molested.

But Steven was growing up. He could remember the name of the town he came from and he started searching for it on maps.

The final break came a couple of weeks ago when the astonishing 'Daddy' Parnell arrived home with another youngster, five-year-old Timothy White. He had just kidnapped Timothy too.

When Steven saw Timothy's tears he secretly vowed the two of them must make their escape. Then Parnell left for work on the night shift at the Palace Hotel. Steven took Timothy by the hand and they hitch-hiked to the police station 40 miles away.

As Steven's brother and two sisters joined in the cutting of a 'Welcome Home' cake, his father Delbert Stayner said of the abductor: 'I don't think he should get the book thrown at him. I guess he just wanted a son of his own.'

25 Minute By Minute

Everyday Life

Private reading
Read this poem a few times in your spare
time, by yourself or with a friend.

Spanish Town Road

Because he was more reck-
less than the rest
his wristwatch ticked quick-
er than theirs

he had more places to go
faster. Speed-
ometer needle
at happy-go-lucky seventy-

five was his true
centre; there he could settle
there he would feed.
It was no

accident, then,
that he burst
into someone equally
urgent, some-

one equally dragged by speed.
But it was dust.
They died
equally.

Edward Brathwaite, BARBADOS

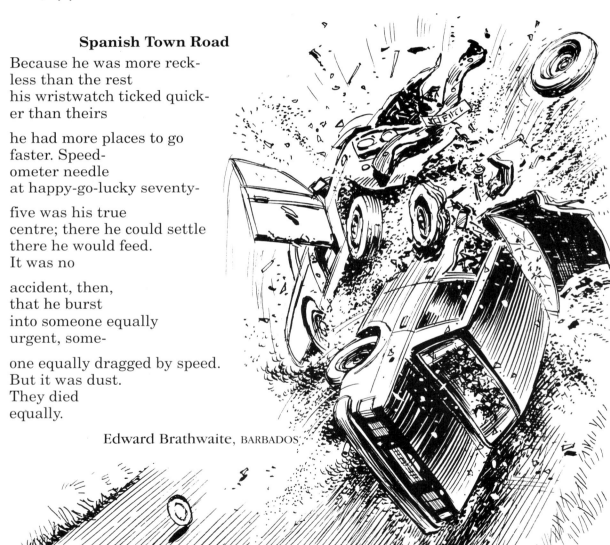

Reading to Learn Things

Getting ready

Your body is an amazing machine. How much do you know about it and how it works? Do you know why we cannot live in the sea like fish? Do you know that rhythm begins with your body?

See whether the article tells you anything you did not know before.

Man must breathe to live. You could live for three weeks without any food, but you could not live for more than three minutes if you could not breathe.

You know that you breathe air, but what do you breathe with?
5 The air enters the nose, and from there it travels down the back of the throat to your voice-box (or *larynx*) 1. You can feel the larynx in your neck as a lump which moves up and down as you swallow. It also vibrates as you talk or sing.

From there the air goes along the windpipe (or *trachea*) 2. The
10 trachea divides into two branches. One branch goes to each of the two lungs in your chest. These air passages (or *bronchi*) 3, divide again and again until they end up in tiny little air-sacs (or *alveoli*) 4. The alveoli are like little balloons which are blown up when you take a deep breath, and collapse again
15 when the air goes out as you breathe out.

But *how* do you breathe? Each one of us breathes twenty or more times a minute, but usually so easily that we do not know we are doing it.

The lungs are enclosed in a bony cage called the *thorax*. If you
20 put your hand on your side, above the waist, like the man in the picture, you will feel your ribs which form this cage. Now

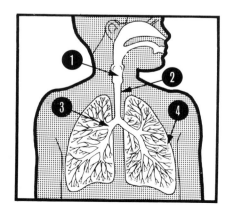

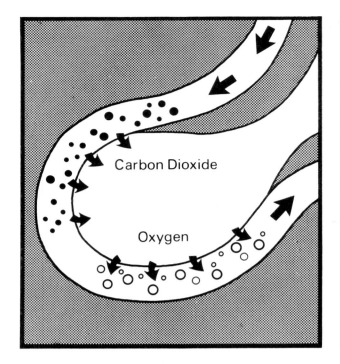 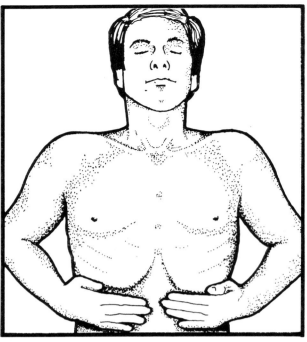

take a deep breath. You will feel your ribs rising up and
becoming further apart. This makes the space inside the bony
cage bigger. Air is drawn into the lungs and fills up all the little
25   air-sacs, just as a balloon fills up if you blow air into it. Now,
with your hand on your ribs, breathe out. You will feel your
ribs go down and become closer together, squeezing the air out
of your lungs.

Now we know how we breathe, and what we breathe with, but
30   the most important question is *why* we breathe. We breathe to
get *oxygen* out of the air. Oxygen is a gas in the air which
provides fuel for the body, just as petrol provides fuel for a
motor engine, or wood provides fuel for a fire.

When we breathe we draw oxygen or fuel into our bodies. But
35   we also get rid of *carbon dioxide*, which is another gas. Carbon
dioxide is the waste product of our fuel system, just as smoke
and ashes are the waste products of a fire.

The oxygen has to be picked up by the blood to be used by the
body. The blood is carried in very fine tubes (called *capillaries*)
40   around the walls of the air-sacs in the lungs.

You can see from the small drawing that the air and the blood
are now close together. The oxygen can pass from the air-sacs
to the blood, and the carbon dioxide can pass from the blood to
the air-sacs.

45 The oxygen travels in the blood to all parts of the body, and it gives the blood its bright red colour. When all the oxygen is used up, the blood returns to the lungs to give up its carbon dioxide, and to take on a new store of oxygen.

50 Just as a fire needs more fuel if it burns brighter and hotter, so we need more oxygen if we work or play harder. You will notice that when you run about you breathe more deeply and faster. You draw more air into your lungs to give you extra fuel for the extra effort you are making.

From *Finding Out, No. 2*

Discussion for developing comprehension skills

A Understanding explicit statements:

1 For how long could a man hold his breath and still live?
2 Name two gases that are in the air.
3 Where is your '*larynx*' (l. 6)?
4 Of what use is the '*trachea*' (say trakkia) (l. 9) to you?
5 Explain the difference between '*bronchi*' (say bronkey) (l. 11) and '*alveoli*' (l. 13).
6 What will you find in '*capillaries*' (l. 39)?
7 Where is your '*thorax*' (l. 19)?
8 How is the gas called '*oxygen*' (l. 31) of use to your body?
9 Say what '*carbon dioxide*' (l. 35) is.
10 Why is your blood red?

B Seeing implied connections:

1 What does a woman who is running need more of than a woman who is lying down?
2 What do you think is meant by the circulation of the blood?
3 Why do people with lung diseases have trouble breathing?
4 Another word for breathing is *respiration*. Why do life guards have to know how to give *artificial respiration*?
5 Of what importance to you is the kind of air you breathe in?

6 What do you think smoking cigarettes does to a person's lungs?
7 Vehicles and factories give off poisonous gases. Is there any reason for you to care about such pollution?

To Enrich Your Word Bank

Words about your body

Here are some words used to talk about your body and your health. If there are any you cannot now use find out what they mean and use them in sentences of your own.

respiration   digestion   nutrition
immune   diet   vitamins   tonic   toxic
remedy   dental   medicine   disease
ailment   virus   surgery   inoculation
laxative   bacteria   microbe   pharmacist
chronic   antiseptic   obese   spasm
malady   environment   epidemic   dose

Words related in meaning

The word that is missing in each sentence is related in meaning to the word in brackets. Discuss which word you think fits best.

1 A great amount of _____ takes place when the toothpaste tubes are left half-squeezed. (*waste*)

2 Where is the _____ who maintains the factory? (*engine*)
3 We walked into a very _____ dining room with about 40 tables. (*space*)
4 Petroleum is used to _____ petrol for cars. (*product*)
5 You can feel the _____ of the bridge when the heavy trucks pass. (*vibrates*)
6 In its _____ state water is called vapour. (*gas*)
7 The horse that came first went into the winner's _____ . (*enclosed*)
8 Despite its size the umbrella is still _____ . (*collapse*)
9 He lifted the heavy bike as _____ as if he was lifting a child. (*effort*)
10 If we search in a _____ way we are sure to find the lost ear-ring. (*system*)

Grammatical Sentence Patterns

Dialects and English

Here are some sentences in local Caribbean dialects. Say each one in the dialect and then say it as a sentence in English.

Practice this first together as a class and then individually, taking turns around and around.

Jamaican

a I mashed a lady on her toe who got ignorant and started to trace me, you see?
b It nice. You do good, man.
c Yes, sar. I did help get her up here. Is my country she come from. I did tell you bout it. Seven years now.
d Is him alone have foot big so!
e Drax no get shoes but him tell we him driving car in Montego Bay.
f Look how him treat him family like they have leper.
g Him not so bad looking though him have a mouth so big when him smile him lip curl up.
h None of us could lie so good, so nobody take it serious.
i A whole heap of new thing start disappear from the store.
j Him send off to call police while him close the door and tell all of we to go sit on the steps.
k You and me gwine have to be detective and search fe clue.
l Mas Ran, is no me do it, sah.
m She look vex can' done with me, so is wha' fe me do?
n The army need able-body young men but them is taking them own sweet time to answer me application.
o Louise, weh yuh a go? Mine yuh fall down hurt yuhself.

Eastern Caribbean

a There was a magistrate live in we village name Dorcas.
b The onliest thing I had was to do was pelt dong de road too.
c De man hol' up de two hats an say we go have a raffle.
d Where de fete holding this year? I going and make sure I go to it.
e It turn out that she come home and see de note she leave fuh him.
f I goin' start learnin' a trade soon.
g Maisie come rong de corner an before I could escape she take she han' and give me one slap.
h If you take my advice we best not make joke wid he.
i Couple nights later they was talking to some fellars in de club.
j You tink is true that it have fellars does go rong by he?
k Tell she I had was to find which part Jack hide de money.

l Boy, it have traffic fuh so speeding true dis place.
m Well, even if is 10 dollars to go in we still goin'.

n Yuh goin to wait till she dead before yuh ask to married she?
o The money will done if dey go on tiefing so.

Spelling

Health words you need

As you know, to learn to spell a word you have to try to fix a picture of it in your mind.

Look at each of these words, paying special attention to any part that you think you might mix up, and try to 'see' it in your mind:

hygiene protein fever ague patient dose prescription medicine physician physique fatigue exhaustion eczema asthma headaches capsule disinfectant vaccine muscles contagious communicable cereal ointment antibiotic

Punctuation Practice

Checking up

A There are 24 punctuation omissions in this short passage, including capital letters. Write the passage correctly punctuated – full stops, commas, question marks, quotation marks – and with capital letters in the right places.

the rain had fallen the man arose he passed by the bed and out of the door are you going the woman asked to come back soon he did not answer she called again taking a step into the road when are you coming back bill

B Write each of these sentences correctly punctuated:

1 did you go to the show
2 my brother having lost his money had to walk home
3 come in he said and make yourself at home

C Write out the following short passage properly punctuated:

norman ken dawn and helen were walking up the steps ken having the longest legs got to me first we want to talk to you he said and what i said does that have to do with me don't be a stubborn fool norman blurted out listen to some good advice but i didnt want to hear anything i turned and walked away

Check your version and see if you have 14 capital letters, 7 commas, 1 question mark, 10 quotation marks, 7 full stops, 2 apostrophes and whether you began on a fresh line three times after the beginning.

Writing What You Know

Answering a letter

Suppose you have received a letter from a friend who now lives abroad explaining to you that she has to tell the students in her new school about the health services of the country she used to live in (your country).

She needs up-to-date information about the health services that provide care for people who are going to have babies, give protection for babies and young children against diseases, provide proper nutrition for schoolchildren, and care for ill people and the elderly.

Talk together, exchanging whatever you know about your country's health services – clinics, doctors and nurses, school meals, hospitals, medicines, ambulances, etc.

Then write your own letter of two or three paragraphs giving your friend all the information you have.

Words in Literature

Imagery

When we wish to communicate things we see and hear in our minds, we try to use words that would help a person hearing us or reading what we wrote to see in his or her mind the same pictures. When we do that we are using what is called *imagery* to communicate with.

Quite often, too, we might try to make the picture we describe give the other person a certain feeling by saying what we have to say in a metaphor or comparison.

Here is an example where the writer is trying to give you a picture of a sunset. Do the words *drain, bruised, colours* and *shriek* help to make a picture for you? If they do not, say no.

> Dusk begins to drain
> the day's bright light
> and where the sky
> is bruised
> colours shriek their pain.
>
> Cecil Gray, TRINIDAD

What do you think of this as a picture of an old man?

> An aged man is but a paltry thing,
> A tattered coat upon a stick ...
>
> W. B. Yeats, IRELAND

Consider each of these others and come to your own opinion about whether they present imagery or not, and whether the imagery is helpful and suitable.

> i Yes I have seen them perched on paling posts
> Brooding with evil eyes upon the road,
> Their black wings hooded ...
>
> A. J. Seymour, GUYANA

> ii But I have seen them emperors of the sky,
> Balancing gracefully in the wind's drive
> With their broad sails just shifting ...
>
> A. J. Seymour, GUYANA

> iii The grey sea and the long black land;
> And the yellow half-moon large and low;
> And the startled little waves that leap
> In fiery ringlets from their sleep.
>
> Robert Browning, ENGLAND

> iv From beginning my world has been a place
> Of pot-holed streets where thick, sluggish gutters race
> In slow time, away from garbage heaps and sewers.
>
> Dennis Craig, GUYANA

26 A Memory Of Childhood

Everyday Life

Person to person

In moments of spare time think about these matters.

1 You have been standing at a corner waiting for a bus for a very long time and it is getting dark. A car stops at the red light. How would you ask the driver for a lift?

2 You are somewhere you are not familiar with and you are looking for a nursing home to visit a relative. How would you ask someone for directions to find the place?

3 You go into a record shop to get a record which is very popular at the time. How would you ask the sales clerk about it?

4 You are standing having a chat in the school yard when a stranger comes in and asks for the teachers' staff room. How would you reply?

5 You are a sales clerk in a large department store. A customer comes in and begins looking around. What would you do?

6 You are walking along and a stranger in the district asks you where a certain place is. You do not know. What would you say in reply?

7 How would you say to a clerk that you have been waiting a long time for attention and that another person who came in after you is getting attention before you?

8 How would you say to a friend or a teacher that you think he or she is wrong about something?

Reading to Enjoy a Poem

Getting ready

Have you ever watched your mother, father or someone else doing some daily task at home? Did you feel like doing it too? Do your parents want you to have the same kind of life they have when you grow up? Why, or why not?

As you read the poem below ask yourself three questions: What did the narrator do as a small girl when her mother baked bread? What did her mother not want to happen? What does the narrator now think of her mother's life?

damper (l. 6) = a cover to control a fire
crater (l. 9) = a shape like your mouth opened a little with your lips pushed out a little
pantaloons (l. 14) = wide baggy trousers
rite (l. 20) = something done regularly like a sacred practice
chafes (l. 37) = rubs against and causes soreness
cultivated (l. 37) = educated
untutored (l. 39) = unschooled, untaught

Baking Day

Thursday was baking day in our house.
The spicy smell of new baked bread would meet
My nostrils when I came home from school and there would be
Fresh buns for tea, but better still were the holidays.

5 Then I could stay and watch the baking of the bread.
My mother would build up the fire and pull out the damper
Until the flames were flaring under the oven; while it was heating
She would get out her earthenware bowl and baking board.

Into the crater of flour in the bowl she would pour sugar
10 And yeast in hot water; to make sure the yeast was fresh
I had often been sent to fetch it from the grocer that morning,
And it smelt of the earth after rain as it dissolved in the sweet water.

Then her small stubby hands would knead and pummel
The dough until they became two clowns in baggy pantaloons,
15 And the right one, whose three fingers and blue stump
Told of the accident which followed my birth, became whole.

As the hands worked a creamy elastic ball
Took shape and covered by a white cloth was set
On a wooden chair by the fire slowly to rise:
20 To me the most mysterious rite of all.

From time to time I would peep at the living dough
To make sure it was not creeping out of the bowl.
Sometimes I imagined it possessed, filling the whole room,
And we helpless, unable to control its power to grow.

25 But as it heaved above the rim of the bowl mother
Was there, taking it and moulding it into plaited loaves
And buns and giving me a bit to make into a bread man,
With currant eyes, and I, too, was a baker.

My man was baked with the loaves and I would eat him for tea.
30 On Friday night, when the plaited loaves were placed
Under a white napkin on the dining table,
Beside two lighted candles, they became holy.

No bread will ever be so full of the sun as the pieces
We were given to eat after prayers and the cutting of this bread.
35 My mother, who thought her life had been narrow, did not want
Her daughters to be bakers of bread. I think she was wise.

Yet sometimes, when my cultivated brain chafes at kitchen
Tasks, I remember her, patiently kneading dough
And rolling pastry, her untutored intelligence
40 All bent towards nourishing her children.

Rosemary Joseph, ENGLAND

Discussion for developing comprehension skills

A Understanding explicit statements:

1 When did the person called 'I' in the poem get a chance to watch the baking?

2 Why was she sent to the grocer that morning?

3 'They became two clowns' (l. 14). What became two clowns?

4 How was 'the right one' (l. 15) different from the left one?

5 '... a creamy elastic ball' (l. 17). Where did that come from?

6 What did the 'I' think was 'the most mysterious rite' (l. 20)?

7 'I imagined it possessed' (l. 23). With what meaning is the word 'possessed' used?

8 'My man' (l. 29). Which man?

9 Where was the bread before the prayers were said?

10 What do you take 'narrow' (l. 35) to mean?

11 What 'chafes' (l. 37) the cultivated brain of the 'I'?

12 'I remember her' (l. 38). Doing what?

B Using context clues:

Each of these words has a word or phrase not far from it that tells someone what it means. Can you find the word or phrase that is the clue?

'pummel' (l. 13)   'heaved' (l. 25)
'moulding' (l. 26)

C Seeing implied connections:

1 Say what is the imagery in 'the crater of flour in the bowl' (l. 9). (See Unit 25.)

2 What is the metaphor or comparison in line 12?

3 Describe the metaphor or comparison in 'they became two clowns in baggy pantaloons' (l. 14).

4 What had happened to 'the right one' (l. 15)?

5 Why, do you suppose, does the poet use the word 'rite' (l. 20)?

6 What made the 'I' 'peep at the living dough' (l. 21)?

7 How did her imagination scare her?

8 'They became holy' (l. 32). What does the 'I' really mean?

9 Why did she think 'No bread will ever be so full of the sun' (l. 33)?

10 'I think she was wise' (l. 36). Why?

11 Why do you suppose her 'cultivated brain chafes at kitchen tasks' (ll. 37–38)?

12 '… nourishing her children' (l. 40). What would you say is the feeling the 'I' has about her mother's life?

To Enrich Your Word Bank

Words about poems

In small groups of four or five see if you can fit each of these words with its meaning in the list below. You met them in Book 1 and in Units 3, 6, 7, 10, 11, 18, 22, 23 and 25 of this book.

*verse   rhyme   stanza   simile   accent
alliteration   metaphor   imagery*

a   a sameness of vowel sounds between words or the endings of words

b   the same consonantal letter or sound at the beginning of nearby words

c   the use of words giving a regular or repeated beat

d   where the stress or emphasis is put on a word to give words their rhythm

e   a comparison made between two things, beginning with the word *as* or *like*, or a word meaning *as* or *like*

f   a comparison made by saying something *is* something else that it resembles in some way

g   a set of lines or verses in a poem arranged according to some plan or design

h   the use of words to bring pictures or images of things, people, places and so on to a listener or reader

Choosing the right word

Discuss which one of the four words given with each sentence best fits into the blank space in the sentence.

1   The bread had fallen into the saucer of milk and was quite _____.

*devoured   subdued   soggy
purified*

2 The plane was _____ about to land, because its wheels were down.

similarly partially maturely apparently

3 All of the dogs were properly _____ to prevent them from roaming around.

fetched ruffled branded leashed

3 She was in a great _____ because her child was lost.

frenzy fate labour uptight

5 The area was _____ covered with grass and shrubbery.

partially lengthily harshly cheaply

6 Those hypocrites always _____ angelic behaviour when a teacher is nearby.

obey imitate imagine express

7 The knife he threw was almost completely _____ in the wood.

branded flown lodged carved

8 They suffered a great deal in the _____ they went through as prisoners.

display chronic coma ordeal

Verbs ending in -ify

The verb *certify* is related to the word *certain*; the verb *vilify* is related to the word *vile*; the verb *personify* is related to the word *person*.

Work in teams to write the verbs related to these words:

verse class simple pure horror mystery fort beauty sign quality clear ample peace just grateful specific quantity solid dignity glory

Grammatical Sentence Patterns

A game with verbs

Suppose this is part of a list of what the mother in the poem *Baking Day* does:

5.30	gets up
5.45	bathes and dresses
6.00	prepares breakfast
6.30	serves breakfast to children
7.00	sees children off to school

Monday mornings: washes the clothes
Monday afternoons: cleans the bedrooms
Monday evenings: sewing and darning
Tuesday mornings: cleans the rest of the house
Tuesday afternoons: irons the clothes
Wednesday mornings: polishes the cutlery
Thursday afternoons: bakes bread

One of you must begin by asking your classmate on your right a question like *'What does she do at 6 o'clock in the morning?'* or *'What did she do this morning, Tuesday?'* The person to whom the question is addressed will answer according to what is on the list, and then ask the person on his or her right a question too, and so on.

Change the list. Make a list of some of your class activities and write it on the chalkboard and proceed as before. The first person asks *'What do we do …?'* or *'What did we do …?'*, the person on the right answers, and so on.

Change the list again. Make a short one of your own personal activities and write it on the board (three or four lists at a time). Let a member of the class ask '*What do you do …?*' or '*What did you do …?*' Answer the question and then ask him or her '*What do I do …?*' or '*What did I do …?*' When he or she answers, do the same with somebody else.

Judging What You Hear and Read

Spotting opinions

Consider each of these statements and discuss whether it is an opinion, or a factual statement that can be tested to see if it is true.

a   Thursday was baking day in our house.
b   Better still were the holidays.
c   It smelt of the earth after rain.
d   It dissolved in sweet water.
e   The grocer sells yeast.
f   Her hands became two clowns in baggy pantaloons.
g   My mother thought her life had been narrow.
h   The most mysterious rite was covering it on a chair by the fire.
i   Plaited loaves are under the white napkin.
j   The poem was written by Rosemary Joseph.

Writing Up a Point of View

About transistor radios

In real life you may find yourself having to report the reasons that someone gave for his or her point of view about a matter.

You will probably have to do it in your school-leaving examination too.

Here is a discussion that took place between Kathy and Frank who took different sides on the question of transistor radios.

KATHY: You know, people carrying around transistor radios do not care at all where they go blaring out their noise.

FRANK: What do you mean by noise? Music is not noise. We all need music in our lives, don't you agree?

KATHY: What we need in our lives is choice. People want to be able to choose when they wish to hear music, and not have their eardrums damaged by some selfish, insensitive goat with a radio.

FRANK: What is so selfish about sharing what you have with other people? It is unselfish guys who share their pleasure with others by carrying around a big, heavy radio.

KATHY: Looking like loaded donkeys! They should be put in prison for being public nuisances.

FRANK: So you want to take people's freedom away now? That is your idea of choice. You will probably order prison for anybody who does something you don't like.

KATHY: It is not a matter of what I like or do not like. Some things are criminal. These toters of poison should be punished just as a person who comes and pours hot oil in your ear.

FRANK: What you call poison is pleasure and entertainment for most people. The guy who walks with his radio is doing people a service, supplying them with food for the soul, not poison.

KATHY: But don't you think it should be a crime to interfere with someone's peace of mind? And then, if you ever make the mistake of asking the moron to cut out the noise all you get is a lot of abuse and insults.

FRANK: In my experience anybody who is playing a radio, say on a bus or on the beach, would turn it off right away if someone objects to it. They are usually quite considerate of others.

KATHY: You must be joking! Only devils go around with that instrument of Satan, a transistor radio.

FRANK: On the contrary. It is angels who carry around heaven's gift to poor and worried people to help them to forget their troubles for a little while.

Now, suppose you needed to put together what Kathy said in a paragraph of your own. You might write a paragraph like this:

Kathy said that people who go around with transistor radios blaring are selfish and insensitive. She thought that, just as a person would be imprisoned for pouring hot oil into another person's ear, people who send the noise from their radios into your ear should be sent to jail. They are nuisances who interfere with one's freedom to enjoy peace and quiet, she argued. She added that, to make matters worse, those who tote around what she called Satan's instrument are always full of insults to direct at anybody who does not like it.

Study carefully how that paragraph sums up Kathy's argument. Then consider what Frank said and *in your own words* write a paragraph putting together his side of the question.

You may state his claims in any order you think best.

27 Tricks Of A Trade

Everyday Life

Wisdom in proverbs

A

Here are some proverbs. In your spare time see if you can find out what each means. Ask anybody who might know, or use a book which might help.

A poor workman blames his tools.
Blood is thicker than water.
Truth is stranger than fiction.
Still waters run deep.
Easy come, easy go.
Absence makes the heart grow fonder.
Out of sight, out of mind.
Walls have ears.
He who pays the piper calls the tune.
Do not look a gift horse in the mouth.

B

Put together the part of a proverb on the right with its other part on the left, and discuss what you think the proverb means.

Two heads — while the sun shines.
The early bird — no crown.
No cross — who laughs last.
Penny wise — tastes sweetest.
One man's meat — catches the worm.
Make hay — pound foolish.
Forbidden fruit — are better than one.
He laughs best — is another man's poison.

Reading to Learn Things

Getting ready

In times past people all over the world knew less about how things happen than they do now, and many communities believed in spirits and magic.

When you read the article be careful to remember that the writer is talking about tribes in Africa more than 60 years ago, when the priest or witchdoctor still had power.

Read it to see what power he had and why.

apt (l. 3) = likely
acute (l. 10) = sharp and strong
perception (l. 10) = intelligence
genuine (l. 12) = true and real
regions (l. 37) = lands
python (l. 38) = a snake
hypnotise (l. 41) = to put into a kind of sleep
apprenticeship (l. 47) = a time of training and learning a job
utterly (l. 65) = totally, completely

The witchdoctor may also be called a shaman, wizard, sorcerer, or medicine man. He is generally the most important person in the tribe, often more important than the chief. He is apt to be

one of the most intelligent members of the tribe. He is able to predict weather because he has probably watched nature with great care. He knows the habits of animals, and knows a good deal about human beings, and can often spot the man who is lying, or has stolen cattle, or has killed a fellow-tribesman. His senses of smell and hearing are often very keenly developed. His acute perception may help him in treating an illness he is asked to cure.

Medicine

Often the witchdoctor uses herbs and plants of genuine value in curing illness. These include garlic, cyclamen, squill, wormwood and the castor-oil plant. Barks such as cinchona, and resins like camphor and sweetgum, are also often used to help a patient.

Many of these plants are used in making our commercial medicines.

Some tribes believe in the magical qualities of water, and a witchdoctor may bathe a patient to cure him of infection. Whether or not this is very effective, it is certainly not a harmful practice.

One of the most important functions of the witchdoctor is to bring rain during a drought, or stop rainfall during a long wet spell.

A great many methods are used to try to bring on rain.

Some witchdoctors sprinkle a magic stone with water. Others build fires, using green wood so that the black smoke will look like rain clouds. Some imitate frogs. Other witchdoctors threaten to kill a frog, or a particular bird which is favoured by the rain spirits; then it is supposed the rains will come to save the life of the creature.

The witchdoctor must also work hard at impressing his own people. He does this by all kinds of magical songs, prayers, and special dances. He dresses in bright colours and wears masks or paints his face. In some regions the witchdoctor wears a headdress of python skins which spread out for 18 feet or more as he dances. Signs such as little chains of blue and white beads in the hair enable witchdoctors to tell each other. A witchdoctor may actually hypnotise people to make them believe that he is responsible for their good luck.

Very often, as the people grow a little more curious and knowledgeable, the witchdoctors will form a brotherhood and trade information amongst themselves. The newcomer who wishes to become a witchdoctor has to serve a long apprenticeship, learning all the rituals and skills.

Black Magic

One special part of the witchdoctor's art is black magic. Those who have studied primitive groups believe that the witchdoctor turns to black magic when he thinks he is losing authority among his people. He uses black magic to frighten the people with his power and to make them follow his wishes. With black magic, for example, a witchdoctor might choose to bring a curse on a man. He may do things to make his crops fail, to make his children ill, or to make the man die. There are a number of methods used to try to cause a man's death. The witchdoctor may make a small figure of the man and stick pins in it, or wind rope around it. Or he may get some of the man's hair or his fingernail cuttings. The witchdoctor buries these so that, as they decay, the man will die a slow death. Some people believe in this so completely that they will go to great lengths to conceal their hair and nail cuttings from an enemy.

Black magic is based not on scientific knowledge but on superstition. However, when people are utterly convinced that some evil happening is going to occur, they make no effort to oppose it, and without realising it they may even do things that help bring it on. This is one reason why witchdoctors can often use black magic so effectively.

From *Knowledge, Vol. 3, No. 30*

Discussion for developing comprehension skills

A Understanding explicit statements:

1 In a tribe the witchdoctor
   a was never as important as the chief
   b was probably very intelligent
   c lacked any real experience.

2 A witchdoctor
   a used his knowledge of how people behave
   b just seemed to care about nature
   c kept animals to study their habits.

3 A witchdoctor might have cured an illness
   a by using his knowledge of science
   b if he was very keen to do it
   c because he had developed his senses of smell and hearing.

4 'Of genuine value' (l. 12) means
   a having very little use
   b really able to cure someone
   c valuable to the witchdoctor only.

5 A witchdoctor might have had knowledge of
   a commercial medicines
   b the magical qualities of water
   c useful, medicinal herbs and plants.

6 To be able to predict weather, a witchdoctor
   a relied on a weatherman
   b must have observed weather changes
   c carried out some experiments.

7 A witchdoctor might have made black smoke
   a to make the tribe think they saw rain clouds
   b to cause rain to fall for the tribe
   c to carry out a function successfully.

8 A witchdoctor used magical songs and prayers
   a because that would please the spirits
   b to make them suit his particular region
   c to make people think he was powerful.

9 '... to tell each other' (l. 40) means to
   a recognise each other
   b speak to each other
   c give secrets to each other.

10 Witchdoctors formed brotherhoods
    a to protect themselves from chiefs
    b because information got scarce
    c when their people began to get knowledge.

11 A witchdoctor uses 'black magic' (l. 49)
    a to practise his different methods
    b when his people seemed to doubt his powers
    c to improve the crops of the farmers.

12 The witchdoctor's 'black magic' (l. 64) sometimes seemed to work because
    a the actions of those who believed in it often caused the bad things to happen
    b scientific knowledge did not yet know the truth of superstition
    c it was based on secrets unknown to scientists.

B Using context clues:

If you did not know the meaning of 'methods' (l. 27) before, the paragraph that follows it gives you several clues.

See whether you can find a clue – a word, a phrase, a sentence – that helps someone to guess the meaning of each of these words:

'infection' (l. 21)   'functions' (l. 24)
'primitive' (l. 50)   'decay' (l. 61)
'convinced' (l. 65)

C Seeing implied connections:

1 What knowledge made the witchdoctor valuable to his tribe?

2 Say whether it would be true, or false, to say that the writer thought witchdoctors could bring rain.

3 Why do you suppose the writer and others call certain practices 'black magic' (l. 49)?

4 Why do you think witchdoctors pretended to be able to do things which could not be done?

5 Do you think their people called them witchdoctors? Give the reason for your answer.

6 How would you explain what 'superstition' (l. 65) is?

7 Do you think that if people get knowledge and education in schools they would have faith in obeahmen? Give your reason or reasons for your answer.

To Enrich Your Word Bank

Some words you read
Thinking about how these words are used in the excerpt, work together and put each one in its place in the paragraph:

*convinced   threaten   genuine
authority   apt   oppose*

In nearly every group, society or culture some people must have the power and _____ to lead. But some people are always ready to _____ whoever is given a leadership function, and do things against them. Is it that they are _____ that the leaders are going in a dangerous direction? Or is it that they have no _____ interest in the welfare of the group, and only wish to have the power themselves? Some of us are _____ to believe those who protest against anything, especially when they _____ that they would use violence.

Opposites
In small groups of four or five match a word in list **A** with one of opposite meaning in list **B**.

A useless   ignorant   dull   remember   developed   ripen   scarcely   reveal

B decay   acute   conceal   effective   utterly   predict   primitive   knowledgeable

Words related in meaning
The words in each row are related in meaning in some way. Think together of a word to put into the space left in each.

a	magic	_____	magical
b	inform	_____	informative
c	_____	imitation	imitative
d	_____	opposition	opponent
e	author	_____	authoritative
f	intellect	_____	intelligent

g	_____	infection	infectious
h	_____	impression	impressive
i	_____	methodology	methodical
j	_____	prediction	predictable
k	perceive	perceptive	_____
l	_____	hypnotism	hypnotic

Grammatical Sentence Patterns

Dialects and English

Say these dialect sentences in English, taking turns around the class again and again.

1 You mustn't fraid me so much man.
2 All yuh move from dey.
3 Him got fe be careful.
4 Them was happy days.
5 Yuh mighta ask me tek a walk.
6 Dey woulda tell yuh what to do.
7 Mek mih pass fe get mih seat.
8 Is dat you want, don't it?
9 Since early o'clock dem bwoy dem a mek noise.
10 Leh we go to Fred house.
11 I is a Indian and I ain't have no prejudice.
12 What you so vex-up about?
13 Which part of Port of Spain allyuh really livin?
14 From him was small him was one little devil.
15 I fine he change because he so quiet quiet now.
16 Is what yuh tell she bout me?
17 She cyan feel she better because she have a black-and-white TV too.
18 You woulda fire box eena fe who face, gal?
19 A ready to dead dis morning self.
20 Talk again mek me hear you.

Some Idioms We Use

Of cats and dogs

The underlined part of each sentence contains an idiom in English. See if you can find which meaning given below fits each sentence.

1 Fran with her big mouth <u>let the cat out of the bag</u>.
2 If I lend you my book do not <u>dogear</u> the leaves.
3 She bought it <u>dog-cheap</u> in the sale.
4 Our neighbours seem to lead a <u>cat and dog</u> life.
5 You have a <u>dog-in-the-manger</u> attitude about those old shoes.
6 I will stay at home only if it <u>rains cats and dogs</u>.
7 We must not let our school <u>go to the dogs</u> because nobody seems to care.
8 You can see how his wife <u>makes a cat's paw</u> of him to get her own way.
9 You can laugh because you got the better of me now, but remember <u>every dog has his day</u>.
10 Without a job and without money he was leading <u>a dog's life</u>.

a be destroyed
b my turn will come
c fold over the corners
d for very little money
e miserable
f keeping from others what is useless to you
g told someone a secret
h quarrelling all the time
i pours with long, heavy showers
j use like a tool to do something

Writing Views and Opinions

An argument

Do you remember the exchange of ideas between Kathy and Frank in the last unit? They had a conversation in which each one gave reasons for his or her opinion about transistor radios. Read it again.

When you have read it get into groups of about six or eight and consider what two people might say about *one* of these, if one person was *for* and the other *against*:

a   Living in a country village is better than living in a town.
b   Adults know best what is good for children.
c   Parents should be strict with their children.
d   Television does harm.

After talking for about 10 minutes in your group about both sides of the topic that you chose, go back to your desks and begin to write an exchange between Phyllis and Michael, with one on one side and the other on the opposite side.

Finish writing it at home or whenever you have the time.

Words in Literature

Imagery

Study these lines taken from a poem and find all the places where the poet uses imagery to get a reader to see and feel what she wants to communicate.

Blazing tropical sunshine
On a hard, white dusty road
That curves round and round
Following the craggy coastline;
Coconut trees fringing the coast,
Thousands and thousands
Of beautiful coconut trees,
Their green and brown arms
Reaching out in all directions –
Reaching up to high heaven
And sparkling in the sunshine.
Sea coast, rocky sea coast,
Rocky palm-fringed coastline;
Brown-black rocks,
White sea-foam spraying the rocks;
Waves, sparkling waves
Dancing merrily with the breeze;
The incessant song
Of the mighty sea,
A white sail – far out
Far, far out at sea;
A tiny sailing boat –
White sails all glittering
Flirting with the bright rays
Of the soon setting sun.

From *Darlingford* By Una Marson, JAMAICA

28 End-Of-Year Progress Test

If you have been reading books from a library and getting the practice you need with the help of these books, you should be able to score more than 70 marks when you do this test, and be ready to go on to next year's work.

Section One: Comprehension
(24 marks)

Read each passage carefully at least twice and then choose answers to the questions.

Write only the number of the question and the letter of each answer you choose.

Passage A

Peeta panicked. There was nothing he could do. He was trapped. Trapped with hundreds of others. The Monster had come and was slowly, surely, dragging them from the deep. Peeta swam through the excited crowd to try the bottom. Then he tried the top again. The great
5   Monster had encircled them completely. There were millions of holes in its great hands, but none large enough. If only these holes were a little larger. Peeta tried to push himself through one of the holes again. He squeezed and squeezed. Great tails lashed around him. Not only he but the whole crowd were in desperation. He tried to ease himself through.
10 The threads pressed against his eyes. If only his head could get through. He pushed again, hard, and the pain quivered through his body. Down to his tail. He turned around. But it was no use trying it from that end. His tail was much wider than his head. There was nothing he could do. He heard the breakers roaring above now. That meant they were
15 nearing the shore. Peeta whipped his tail in fury. The Monster was closing its hands gradually. He could feel the crowd heaped against each other. He was knocked about by the giant tails. Good thing he was so small and could avoid being crushed. Around him were his friends and his dreaded enemies. The bonito was there, the killer shark was there.
20 None of them thought of him now. They were all trying to escape.

From *Cricket in the Road* By Michael Anthony, TRINIDAD and TOBAGO

1 The crowd was heaped against each other because
a giants were pushing them
b they were afraid of the breakers
c they were being pulled in.

2 When Peeta heard the breakers
a he was glad he could escape
b he knew death was near
c he used his tail to get out.

3 The phrase 'in desperation' (l. 9) means
a without caring about others
b being angry and violent
c losing all hope of escape.

4 What was the first clue to what the Monster was?
a great tails lashed around him
b encircled them completely
c pain quivered through his body.

5 What was the first clue to who or what Peeta was?
a there was nothing he could do
b dragging them from the deep
c his tail was much wider.

[10 marks]

Passage B

Slavery was a very common thing throughout the world in earlier times. Much of the wealth of the Ancient World was not only produced by slaves, but also *counted in slaves*. The enslavement of conquered peoples and prisoners of war was a common practice among nations. It was
5 done by the Egyptians of old, by the Greeks and the Romans, and in the empires of the East. After the Saxon conquest of Britain, we read that prisoners captured in the tribal wars were sold to slave dealers, and taken the long journey from Britain through Gaul (France) to the slave market in Rome, there to be sold together with Greeks, Africans and
10 people from Eastern Europe. The Mohammedans in Africa acted in much the same way. But the Portuguese were the first Europeans of modern Europe to enter into the slave trade. African chiefs, engaged in tribal wars, were often ready to sell their prisoners to the Moorish or Portuguese traders, and even to help them to obtain more captives. In
15 this way Portuguese landowners obtained labourers for their farms and gardens, and the Spaniards purchased slaves from their Portuguese neighbours for the same purpose.

The enslavement of Africans by Africans was quite common too, especially throughout West Africa. There were different degrees of
20 slavery. The domestic or household slaves, usually born of slave parents, were the most kindly treated. Others were field labourers like the serfs of Europe, while a third type were criminals reduced to slavery as a punishment. In the frequent wars between tribe and tribe, captive enemies were added to the ranks of the slaves. In one West
25 African kingdom (Dahomey) it was the custom, at the death of the king, to sacrifice a number of his slaves so that they might attend him in the next world. As a rule the more powerful tribes of West Africa made

slaves of the weaker and less warlike ones, and many of the people
taken to the West Indies from that land had already been slaves in their
30   own country.

From *History of the West Indian Peoples, Book 3*

1 When nations won wars in times long ago
   a they used slaves as sacrifices
   b they produced slaves to be counted
   c they made slaves of those who lost.

2 The riches of countries in ancient times
   a were used to do trade in slave markets
   b came very much from what slaves did
   c were used to purchase slaves for labour.

3 The word '*conquest*' (l. 6) means
   a taking as one's own
   b making a country independent
   c travelling through a country.

4 The Portuguese
   a were the first people to buy and sell slaves
   b began buying slaves in the 18th century
   c did not buy slaves from African chiefs.

5 In West Africa
   a field labourers were like serfs of Europe
   b wars were fought over degrees of slavery
   c Africans made slaves of other Africans.

6 The phrase '*degrees of slavery*' (ll. 19–20)
   means
   a differences in treatment slaves received
   b the kind or quality of slaves captured
   c the length of time people were kept as
      slaves.

7 Many who came as slaves to the West
   Indies
   a had parents who were kindly treated
   b broke away from the ranks of slaves
   c were slaves owned by a powerful tribe.

[14 marks]

Section Two: Vocabulary, Grammar, Punctuation, Spelling   *(52 marks)*

1 Pair a word from list **A** with one of
   opposite meaning in list **B**.

A	**B**
scarce	gradual
local	universal
willing	cautious
delicate	crude
probable	abundant
abrupt	unlikely
reckless	reluctant

[7 marks]

2 Choose one of the words in the brackets
   that best fits into the sentence.

   Write the letter of the sentence and the
   word you choose.

   a Bertie felt he was
      (*fascinated/humiliated/associated*) by the
      way Sarah turned her back on him.

   b The conflict between the two tribes was
      (*convinced/absorbed/resolved*) by an
      agreement between the chiefs.

   c The mistake we made proved to be
      (*fatal/apprehensive/delirious*) to all hopes
      of success.

   d From her frantic
      (*perceptions/gestures/caricatures*) I
      gathered she was in some sort of
      trouble.

   e The so-called 'psychic' claimed she could
      give (*ethnic/commercial/accurate*)
      predictions of the future.

   f The crew decided to
      (*abandon/conceal/demolish*) the ship that
      seemed to be sinking.

   g The time she spent on the beach was
      quite (*serene/endowed/adequate*) to give
      her a tan.

[7 marks]

3 Write each of the sentences as a reported speech sentence.
   a Bobby asked Rex, 'Where is the key to the door?'
   b Rex said to Bobby, 'I am coming with you.'
   c 'The weather looks bad,' Dawn remarked.
   d Eugenia answered, 'On Sundays I go to church.'
   e 'Do you work here?' the customer asked me.

   [5 marks]

4 Each of these sentences has a grammatical error. Write the word or phrase that is an error in grammar and write the correct word or phrase that should replace it.
   a She was shocked to see the amount of people in the waiting room.
   b In the first inning of the match he made a duck.
   c I never had no idea she was so pretty.
   d In the newspaper there are news of a war.
   e Stooping down to hide, he tore his pant.

   [5 marks]

5 Write each of these sentences making the change you are directed to make, and making any other changes necessary to make sure your sentence is grammatically correct.
   a She paid her debts when she received some money.
      Begin: *Having*
   b The little boy was so scared that he trembled.
      Use *because* in your sentence.
   c Tom's answer showed how bright he was.
      Use *that* in your sentence.
   d The teacher asked her where she was going.
      Begin: *She*

   e Sonny climbed the fence and looked into the yard.
      Begin: *Climbing*

   [5 marks]

6 Combine each set of sentences into one sentence without using *and* or *but* to join them.
   a The island was small. It was in the Caribbean Sea. It was used by pirates as a home.
   b I think they entered through the door. The lock was not broken. The door was probably open.
   c Sugar was an important crop. The price for it went down. The islands suffered.
   d The latest news came over the radio. It told us about the fire. The fire had destroyed the town.
   e The first photograph was taken in 1826. A Frenchman took it. Many years passed before prints could be fixed.

   [5 marks]

7 Write the following passage putting in capital letters, full stops, commas, an apostrophe, an exclamation mark, a question mark and quotation marks where necessary.

   The children heard a scream and one of them shouted lets get out of here the guide said very sternly walk in a line to the exit where is the exit said martin who was much younger as he started to cry.

   [10 marks]

8 Find the eight misspelled words in these columns and write them correctly.

measure   useable   rhythm   develop   bridge
favourite   mirror   controle   behavior
attendant   wagon   screech   vendor   straight
imediately   film   posession   giggled   cautious
appear   vicious   stomach   guava   familar
residential   decieve   whistle   determine
material   vicinity   allready   definite

   [10 marks]

Section Three: Written Expression *(24 marks)*

Here is the substance of a story summarised in 40 words.

Write the full story in about 200 words, filling in the helpful descriptive details of what was seen, heard, said, felt, done and so on.

Just after dark a boy and a girl were walking home on a lonely country road. They were

frightened by something they were sure was a spirit. It was a dry tree branch rolling down the side of the hill.

Be careful with the grammar, punctuation and spelling in your sentences. You will lose marks for such errors.

[24 marks]

Answers to Multiple Choice Questions

Unit 14: Mid-year Progress Test

Section One

Passage A

1b   2a   3c   4c   5a

Passage B

1b   2c   3a   4b   5c   6a   7b

Section Two

1   a. brotherhood   b. brotherly
    c. horrible   d. horrified   e. scientist
    f.. scientific   g. venturesome
    h. adventure   i. confidence
    j. confidential   k. intruders
    l. intrusion   m. procedure   n. process

2   a. elastic   b. glare   c. distinguish
    d. applaud   e. approve   f. veteran
    g. assemble

3   a. The plane flies at great speed high
       above us.
    b. The dogs were chasing the cat towards
       the tree.
    c. All mothers think their sons are
       innocent.
    d. Every boy has heroes he admires.
    e. The teachers busy themselves
       preparing each lesson (or the lessons)
       they have to teach.
    f. My brothers do not like school as much
       as I do.
    g. The student was sitting at his (or her)
       desk reading a book (or some books).
    h. She disagrees with the reasons that you
       give for your opinion.
    i. The men go to work in a factory that
       makes electronic equipment.
    j. One of us takes what he/she hears as the
       truth.
    k. Records have been set by the school's
       best athlete.
    l. Persons I know were questioned by the
       police about the robbery.

m. What he does in his spare time shows
   the quality of his life.
n. Noises in the yard disturb us in class.

4   a. Is the music loud? b. Do you do the
    same thing every day? c. Does the village
    have a church? d. Did his mother come
    to see him? e. Do I have nothing to do
    today? f. Are some/any streets in the city
    flooded? / Are streets in the city flooded?

5   It was a day in January. Do you know what
    happened? David asked his mother not to
    send him to school any more. Would you
    believe it? His mother, a very
    understanding mother, asked him what
    was wrong. He didn't answer. She knew
    that David was worried about going to the
    new school. he thought he wouldn't make
    any friends there.

6   separate   among   speech   develop
    favourite   grammar   label   approach

Unit 20
Understanding Explicit Statements
1c   2b   3c   4a   5b   6a   7b   8c   9a
10c

Unit 27
Understanding Explicit Statements
1b   2a   3c   4b   5c   6b   7a   8c   9a
10c   11b   12a

Unit 28
Passage A
1c   2b   3c   4b   5c

Passage B
1c   2b   3a   4b   5c   6a   7b

Section Two

1   scarce – abundant
    local – universal
    willing – reluctant
    delicate – crude
    probable – unlikely
    abrupt – gradual
    reckless – cautious

2   a. humiliated   b. resolved   c. fatal
    d. gestures   e. accurate
    f. abandon   g. adequate

3   a. Bobby asked Rex where the key to the
       door was.
    b. Rex told Bobby that he, Rex, was
       coming with him.
    c. Dawn remarked that the weather
       looked bad.
    d. Eugenia answered that on Sundays she
       went to church.
    e. The customer asked me if I worked
       there.

4   a. (amount) number   b. (inning)
    innings   c. (no) any   d. (are) is
    e. (pant) pants

5   a. Having received some money, she paid
       her debts
    b. The little boy trembled because he was
       scared.
    c. Tom's answer showed that he was
       bright.
    d. She was asked by the teacher where
       she was going./ She was asked where
       she was going by the teacher.
    e. Climbing the fence, Sonny looked into
       the yard.

6   a. it was a small island in the Caribbean
       Sea used by pirates as a home
    b. Since the lock was not broken, I think
       the door was probably open so they
       entered.
    c. Sugar was so important that when the
       price for it went down the islands
       suffered.
    d. The latest news over the radio told us
       the fire had destroyed the town.
    e. Although a Frenchman took the first

photograph in 1826 many years passed
before prints could be fixed.
(OTHER VERSIONS COULD ALSO BE
ACCEPTABLE)

7   The children heard a scream and one of
    them shouted, "Let's get out of here!"
    The guide said very sternly, "Walk in a
    line to the exit."
    "Where is the exit?" said Martin, who was
    much youger, as he started to cry.

Acknowledgements

We are grateful to the following for permission to reproduce copyright material: Andre Deutsch for extracts from *The Wooing of Beppo Tate* by C Everard Palmer, short stories *Enchanted Alley* by Michael Anthony and *Peeta of The Deep Sea* in *Cricket in The Road*; BIM The Literary Magazine of Barbados for an extract from *Septimus* by John Wickman; Chronicle Feature, San Francisco, CA. for *Bizarro* cartoon by Dan Piraro; Heinemann Publishers (Oxford) Limited for an extract from *The Caribbean: Our Land and People* by Braithwaite, *et al*; Marjorie Joseph for a poem *Baking Day* by Rosemary Joseph; Macmillan Caribbean for an extract from *Barbados, Our Island Home* by F A Hoyos; Methuen London from an extract from a one-act-play *He Who Says No* by Bertold Brecht; Oxford University Press for an extract from *Riot* by Andrew Salkey; Michael Reekord for an extract from Dog Food in the *Faber Book of Company Contemporary Caribbean Short Stories*; Scholastic Publications Ltd for extracts from *The Cloud With The Silver Lining* and *The Wooing of Beppo Tate* by C E Palmer; The Women's Press Ltd for an extracts from short stories *A Grenadian Childhood* in *Jump up and Kiss me* by Nellie Payne and Gemini by Merle Collins in *Rain Dancing*.

We are unable to trace the author or copyright holders of an extract from *Caldong* by Peter Bacon; E. Evtushenko for poem *Lies*; an article on cricket bat from *Finding Out, No 34*; an extract from short story *Millicent* by Merle Hodge; extracts from *Knowledge* Vols 1, 3, 8; an extract from *Floodwater* by Roger Mais in *Listen, The Wind*; poem *My Mother* by Claude Mckay in *Selected Poems of Claude McKay*; Comic strip Peanuts; extract on food from *Spotlight on Tomorrow's World* by Clive Riche; short story *A Drink of Water* by Samuel Selvon in *Caribbean Stories*; extract from *Photography* by Phil Sternberg; poem *Jamaican Bus Ride* by A S J Tessimond; an extract from one-act play *The Creatures* by Cicely Waite-Smith; poem The Quarrel by Mark Young, and we would appreciate any information that would enable us to do so.